Thinking Big, Building Small

Low-tech Solutions
for Food, Water, and Energy

Thinking Big, Building Small

Low-tech Solutions
for Food, Water, and Energy

Marianne Brandis

Thinking Big, Building Small
ISBN 978-0-9877663-0-4

© Marianne Brandis, 2011

Marianne Brandis
96 Water Street
Stratford, Ontario
Canada
N5A 3C2

Information about the front-cover illustration can be found on page
102, and about the back-cover illustration on page 294.

Cover design and layout
Karl Griffith Fulton
www.ancrann.com

Printed
Pandora Press,
Kitchener, Ontario

All Pandora Press printing is on FSC Approved paper.

Table of Contents

List of Illustrations

Epigraph

"It is my experience that it is rather more difficult to recapture directness and simplicity than to advance in the direction of ever more sophistication and complexity. Any third-rate engineer or researcher can increase complexity; but it takes a certain flair of real insight to make things simple again."

E. F. Schumacher, *Small is Beautiful: Economics as if People Mattered.*

Introduction

The developing world's problems form a familiar list: poverty and child mortality, malnutrition and disease, the lack or expense of education, deforestation and problems with fuel supply, soil degradation and desertification, an often crippling dependence on chemical fertilizer, a shortage of clean drinking water. Poverty is increasing: World Bank figures state that in 2008 there were 1.4 billion people living below the poverty line of $1.25 per person per day, 430 million more than previously estimated.[1]

Although there are thousands of NGOs working in the developing world, their efforts haven't always had the success they deserve. There are debates about how aid can be designed and delivered more effectively, but every year there are more hungry people.

This book tells the story of the Full Belly Project, a small NGO based in North Carolina which invents,

---

1 Bill McKibben, *Eaarth* (Toronto: Alfred A. Knopf Canada, 2010). 76. Quoted from "An Even Poorer World", *New York Times*, September 2, 2008.

promotes, and distributes low-tech food-growing and food-processing equipment. The inventor is a Canadian engineer and social entrepreneur named Jock Brandis. (Yes, I'm his sister, which gives me lots of advantages in writing this account.)

The FBP's work is directed mainly to the developing world, but the "two worlds" image of the planet, while still accurate in some ways, is becoming blurred. In an era of global trade, global climate change, global problems with food and energy and water, connections and even similarities are increasing. As though to emphasize this, in early 2009 the Full Belly Project was contacted by an NGO in North Carolina – FBP's own back yard – which was working with people who had lost their jobs when the textile industry moved to developing countries. (To see where the jobs went, check the labels on your clothes.) This factor and others are bringing third-world conditions to parts of the United States; according to Bill McKibben, climate change will contribute to the process.[2]

So technology of the kind developed for Africa is now being used by small farmers in North Carolina. "Reverse technology," Jock Brandis calls it. The Full Belly story is not just about *over there*. "Africa is the continent where Homo sapiens was born, and with its worn-out soils, fitful rain, and rising population, it could very well offer a glimpse of our species' future."[3] Even now, McKibben writes, "more and more Americans no longer live in the rich world; instead, they struggle to

2 *Eaarth*, passim.
3 Joel K. Bourne, Jr., "The End of Plenty." In *The National Geographic*, June 2009, Vol. 215, No. 6, p. 38.

get by."[4] Helping the "poor" world is becoming a way to help the whole planet.

The story of the Full Belly Project – a tale full of weird and quirky stuff, of heart-lifting successes and unaccountable failures, of difficult miracles – therefore has widespread ramifications.

* * *

One of the story's starting points is peanuts, so it's important to know a bit about them.

In most countries in the developing world, peanuts are not "just peanuts." For perhaps half a billion people, to whom meat is a rare luxury, they're an important source of protein. Millions of small farmers grow them for their own families – to be eaten as nuts, or processed to produce oil, flour, or paste (peanut butter) – or to sell in the local market, or to sell to traders who resell them to large processors.

When they come out of the ground, they're soft, so to make it possible to shell them, they're dried in the sun. If they're left out for too long, however, they become like little rocks. Sometimes the women put them in a sack and pound them in order to loosen the shells slightly. Sometimes they soak them in water; that makes them easier to shell but also spreads a fungus which produces aflatoxin. Aflatoxin suppresses the immune system, increases the risk of liver cancer, and aggravates deficiencies of certain vitamins and other

4 *Deep Economy: the wealth of community and the durable future* (New York: Henry Holt and Company, 2007) 103. The reference is to James Lardner, "What's the Problem?" in James Lardner and David A. Smith, *Inequality Matters*, (New York: 2005), p. 15.

nutrients. The industrialized world is protected from it by the ways in which peanuts grown here are stored and processed, but most people in developing countries are chronically exposed.[5]

In villages in the developing world, women and children shell the nuts by hand. It takes an hour to shell one kilogram (just over two pounds),[6] and it's delicate work: the inner brown seed coat must not be damaged because it protects the kernel from decaying and the oil in the nut from going rancid. Nuts with broken seed coats can't be used as seed.

That's why, at the village level, shelling is done by hand, and it's laborious and painful.[7] It takes a long time

5 J. H. Williams, T. D. Phillips, P. Jolly, and J. Styles, *Preventing Aflatoxicosis in Humans in Developing Countries.* © Peanut Collaborative Research Support Program: 2002. The authors state that this exposure occurs in developing countries "largely because their food systems do not allow the easy and economic management of the problem. Technologies applied in developed countries to limit exposure are capital intensive, large scale practices and are seldom applied in developing countries, probably because of predisposing factors in production, inadequate storage facilities, and system factors associated with subsistence farming and small scale, informal food industries. Because separation technologies (sorting) may [be] used to maximize quality, cheaper foods often consumed by the poorest people are most likely to be contaminated."

6 Natalie Hampton, "Full Belly article" (work in progress, sent to me on 14 October 2009).

7 Business plan written by Illac Diaz. This document – titled "Piloting an Urban and Rural Community Model of a Food-based Livelihood for the Poor" – was written in Spring 2006, though neither the author's name nor the date appear on it. It was prepared in connection with a

to do even what is needed to feed a family, but shelling enough to make peanuts a cash crop is much worse. Farmers *can* sell them in the shell, but then they're paid very little. Therefore, although poor farmers would welcome the income, many grow only enough nuts for domestic use.[8]

It would be good if peanuts were even more widely grown. Besides producing nutritious food, the plants restore nitrogen to depleted soil. The tops, if dug in, add humus which makes the soil more fertile and better able to hold moisture – a big factor as drought becomes more common and desertification, in some places, worsens.[9]

What discourages farmers from growing more peanuts has been the shelling. Now, however, there's a small, inexpensive, manually operated device, made mainly of concrete, which shells nuts fifty times faster than can be done by hand, with an average breakage rate of only

project to bring peanut shellers to the Philippines; Diaz was at that time a graduate student at MIT. I draw on it hesitantly but am guessing that the general picture it gives is reliable.

8 "The peanut is one of the world's most popular and universal crops, cultivated in more than 100 countries in all six continents. ... A substantial proportion of total production is consumed by growers, without ever being recorded." http://lanra.anthro.uga.edu/peanut/knowledgebase/worldproduction. Accessed on 2/2/2010.

9 In Mali, for instance, the southward spread of the Sahara desert is forcing people to move to the cities because the farms can no longer support them. Source is Martin Harbury, *Peanuts* [film]. Produced and directed by Martin Harbury and Catherine Swing for Bar Harbour Films, 2002. Distributed by Bullfrog Films, Oley, PA.

about 5%.[10] When properly adjusted, the machine sorts out the aflatoxin-contaminated nuts, which are smaller and softer than uncontaminated ones.

The peanut sheller and other low-tech devices, such as small water pumps invented and distributed by the FBP, are now in use in 35 countries. But this is not a story of unbroken success. While many people enthusiastically welcome the devices, others mock the idea that concrete can be used to make a precision machine. For people accustomed to high-tech equipment, the simplicity of the nut sheller – a concrete cone, barely hip-high even when raised on four thin legs – makes it almost literally invisible.

However, the issue of success or failure, while important, is not the critical element in the story. What is critical is the process of invention and dissemination, and the insight provided into conditions in developing countries and into the mixture of good and bad luck

10 Natalie Hampton, "Cultivating Efficiency: CALS [College of Agriculture and Life Sciences at NC State University] Extension and research faculty members help Ghana peanut growers with new shelling technology." http://www.cals.ncsu.edu/agcomm/magazine/winter10/efficiency.html. Accessed on 7/3/2010. The sheller, along with other sustainable improvements in production [in Ghana] means that "growers have increased their peanut acreage as they discovered they could actually make money on groundnuts [=peanuts]. 'We got lots of stories of where farmers were able to buy taxis and farmers were able to build new houses. And the acreage just keeps increasing, which tells you that they're finding groundnuts to be a profitable crop,' Brandenburg said." Dr. Rick Brandenburg led the group from N.C. State University which – along with Jock Brandis – went to Ghana in 2009. Details in a later chapter.

involved in inventing, promoting, and distributing devices of this kind.

New inventions continue to emerge from the FBP shop. Jock Brandis figures prominently in this account, not only because he is the inventor but also because, as a result of changes in the FBP staff and Board, he is now the only person who has been there from the beginning: in an e-mail he describes himself as "the guy with the institutional memory of how it all works." FBP volunteer Tom Ellsworth calls Full Belly "an organization based on one person."

This is also a story about appropriate technology (AT), a field in which Jock has been described as a leader.[11] The term refers to devices that are low-tech, small-scale, inexpensive, environmentally friendly, and easily made and repaired. They're designed to fit a village without disrupting small, delicate social structures. Instead of creating one wealthy person and turning the other villagers into employees, they are small enough to be owned by individual farmers or by a co-op of the sort that already exists in many villages. Because few of those villages have electricity, and because petroleum is expensive, much AT is hand-powered. Jock remarks that in the developing world there's a huge resource of energy in people's arms and legs, and that the FBP technology makes it possible to turn this energy into products that will compete with those manufactured

11 http://www.popularmechanics.com/blogs/technology_news. Page titled "6 Questions for Third-World Tech innovator Jock Brandis." Accessed on 14/5/2008. This article appeared in connection with Jock's winning a Popular Mechanics "Breakthrough Award" in 2006. The author was Logan Ward.

by industrial-sized machines. Because it uses resources lightly and sustainably, AT may play a role in all our futures; certainly the story of an inventor who is a leader in the field is a good way to start thinking about it.

Above all, this is a story about the basics of our lives: food, water, energy. In industrialized countries we generally take these things for granted. Water comes from the tap, food mostly from the supermarket. Fuel is dispensed at the service station or is almost invisibly piped and wired into our dwellings. But this system is under stress, and learning about places and lives in which it can't be taken for granted, and ways in which other people live without it, is a useful exercise in taking thought – and perhaps finding cause for hope.

* * *

Writing about the Full Belly Project has been an adventure. It's a moving target: the situation changes constantly, not only at the leading edge but over the entire area, because recent developments alter the significance or proportions of earlier ones. Throughout the book I mention the people – mainly the staff and volunteers of NGOs and university outreach departments – who promote and distribute the FBP machines: much of my information comes from e-mails between them and Jock, but what I get is fragmentary because e-mails are only part of the constant communication. E-mails, however, are what I have: mostly hurried ones reporting a problem, asking a question, outlining plans, expressing goals and hopes, organizing a visit from FBP staff or Board members. The writers have perhaps just come in from the fields where they've been consulting with villagers or back from a meeting about aid and development. They're driven by idealism yet also engaged in hand-to-hand combat with poverty, sickness, and desperation. They hurtle through their days. Any reflections or assessments that go beyond the immediate purpose of the e-mail are likely to change with further experience and observation, or with changing circumstances.

When I was in Malawi with an FBP team in May 2009, I watched and listened as the group collected the local aid workers' assessments and made their own observations. Over a beer at the end of a long day or a dinner of pasta or Chinese food we used our accumulating information and impressions to make plans and reach tentative conclusions. The guys talked while making and testing a concrete water pump in the Assistant Peace Corps Director's back yard, or waiting for the overdue opening of a hardware store where (it was hoped) the right size of nuts and bolts would be available. Discussion – and invention – went on constantly: "How are people going to move this water pump from place to place? Here, help me carry it and see how the handle works. This cement takes a long time to dry. What size of hose ...? Sprinkler or nozzle?"

Much of the information is never written down. The notes in Jock's head come from specific observations which, though correct for there and then, are not so for always and everywhere. This experience infuses and drives the FBP's work.

Besides the e-mails, I've had extensive talks with Jock: some of what he carries in his head has gone into this book. Except for what I found in other print sources and on the internet, this is what I had available, and – after much frustration – I've come to see its value, because what is sometimes lacking in the way of balanced pictures, carefully weighed arguments, and objective assessments is gained in immediacy. Conditions and life in developing countries, and the work of the Full Belly Project, are changing constantly; what I give in this book is an outline of how things happened, a sense of how things are. This is not a photograph but a sketch, and one on which (had there been no publishing deadline) I could be continually erasing and re-drawing. The situation I describe is as accurate as is reasonably possible at the time of going to press, though things will have changed by the time you read it.

With all this, there is the risk of contradictions, inconsistencies, and mistakes, of "facts" and opinions and experiences that are incomplete or incorrectly evaluated, or that will be (or have been) overtaken by new facts. But that's not a good reason for not writing about it. From what I've had available I've tried to select and sort, to assess and weigh, and to find the essential story amid the constantly changing detail.

Jock and Marianne in Malawi. Eddie Toll, a free-lance journalist who accompanied the team that went to Uganda in 2007, wrote about Jock: "He is a thin, alpine character who gestures incessantly when he speaks. He comes off as an aesthetic professor, at once dignified and vagabond, elegant and ruffian. He has a gentle voice with a literary air, and people are inclined to listen to him because of this commanding quietness." Eddie Toll, "Shelling Peanuts to Save the World." Unpublished article.

Photo credit: Gregor Wilson

PART I

A Billion Hungry People

ONE

The Woman in Woroni

A woman in Woroni, a village in Mali, is squatting on the ground, shelling peanuts by hand. She and a few other women and children are working their way through a large pile. The shells are tough. Her hands are bleeding. Yesterday she put the nuts in a bag, a batch at a time, and pounded the bag with a stick to break the shells up a bit, but it still takes her an hour to shell a few double handfuls. The work is slow, painful, mindless – tiring and very tiresome.

She needs some of the nuts to feed her family and will try to sell the rest at the market.

She knows that peanuts are good food and she would like to grow more. They are also good for the soil, which is getting worse every year because the cotton that she grows as a cash crop is so bad for it. But growing more nuts would mean yet more of this awful shelling.

As she works, her mind goes round and round in this well-worn groove. If only there were a better way of shelling them!

* * *

It was a woman like this who, in 2000[1], spoke to Jock Brandis when he was in Mali. It took a lot of courage for her to speak to him. With the help of the Muslim imam, who translated her words, she asked Jock whether, in America, there was such a thing as a small machine for shelling peanuts, something that wouldn't need electricity (which the villagers didn't have) or gasoline (which they couldn't afford).

Jock was in Woroni – a "tiny little mud-hut village in a remote part of southern Mali"[2] – to repair the solar pump which (when it was working) ran the village water system. Carrie Young, the Peace Corps Volunteer stationed there, was a friend from their film-making days; contemplating the broken pump, and thinking

---

1   Most of the names, dates, and details in the next few paragraphs come from Ben Steelman, "Coastal Carolina Returned Peace Corps Volunteers promote Malian Peanut Sheller," *Wilmington Star-News*, September 22, 2002, from http://peacecorpsonline.org/messages. messages.2629/1009178.html., accessed on 21/4/2008, and from http://fullbellyproject.org/history.php, accessed on 13/3/2008. The "history" which formerly appeared on the Full Belly Project website, as well as other accounts of the FBP's origins, give June 2001 as the date of Jock's first trip to Mali. Jock told me that he hadn't kept good records in those early years, and that he didn't remember the dates precisely. However, an e-mail which he wrote on 8 April 2001 to Dr. Bonny Ntare at the International Crops Research Institute for the Semi-Arid Tropics (ICRISAT) and copied to his own father reports that by then he had a working prototype of the sheller and would be going to Woroni, in Mali, in July 2001 to "make the first machine there." So in fact the first trip took place in the summer of 2000.

2   Jock, quoted in the *Wilmington Star-News* article cited above.

of Jock's interest in Africa and his cleverness at fixing things, Carrie had suggested that he might like to come for a visit.

When she told him about the increased cultivation of cotton in the area, Jock – a Dutch-Canadian living in North Carolina – was worried. People in the American South know what cotton does to the soil; George Washington Carver (1864-1943) had promoted the cultivation of peanuts to restore soil depleted by cotton.[3]

It was clear that a simple, efficient, village-sized peanut-shelling machine would permit farmers to grow more peanuts and give the women and children time for other things. With more income in the family, and fewer hours and hands needed for shelling nuts, more children might be able to go to school. Jock promised the women that he would send a sheller to them the following year, and in turn they said that they would plant more peanuts.[4]

Inventing a peanut sheller

Back home in Wilmington, N.C., Jock searched the internet for a sheller. Not finding one, he contacted former U.S. President Jimmy Carter, and also Marilyn Meares, an agricultural extension worker for the federal government in eastern North Carolina. Carter's office referred Jock to Dr. Tim Williams, director of peanut programs at the University of Georgia's College of Agriculture and Sciences, the world expert on the non-industrial production of peanuts. Dr. Williams

3 Article on Carver in http://en.wikipedia.org. Accessed on 15/8/2009.

4 Harbury, *Peanuts*.

said that no sheller of this kind existed – he called the idea of such a machine "the holy grail."[5] He said that none of the designs tried had worked well. "For information, he sent Jock a sketch of one such device from Bulgaria – a sort of cone within a cone that was supposed to roll the shells off the kernels."[6] Jock made one but it didn't work.

The goal was to invent a device that, besides shelling the nuts efficiently and with little breakage, would be inexpensive, would operate without petroleum or electricity, would be easy to construct in developing countries from locally-available materials, and would be simple to replicate: in short, a machine that could be built in any middle-sized town in the developing world. Building it themselves would give people control over that part of the food-processing operation and make them, in this respect at least, independent of technology supplied by industrialized countries. Doing the first stage of the processing themselves would allow them to keep more of the profit from their crop.

Jock persevered. Initially he envisioned making the machine of steel, but a friend, Wes Parry, suggested concrete, a material available everywhere in the world and much easier to handle.

In December 2000 Jock attended a Christmas party for the Coastal Carolina Returned Peace Corps Volunteers. He was not a RPCV but he had worked with the Canadian University Service Overseas (CUSO) and had Peace Corps friends. He talked about his project and asked whether anyone had worked with concrete.

5 *Wilmington Star-News.*
6 *Wilmington Star-News.*

One had: he was Jay Tervo who, while serving ι
Peace Corps in Gabon, had built schools. Jock's idea
caught his interest.

During that winter, Jock received some help from
friends in the film industry, where at the time he had
his paying job. One group was making a giant fiberglass
castle for a film called *Black Knight*; when Jock had
created wooden forms, the film people used leftover
materials to make fiberglass molds from them. Marilyn
Meares provided sun-dried peanuts so that the machine
could be tested. (It was then that Jock discovered just
how nasty the sun-dried nuts were to shell.)

The successful sheller consists of a vertical, conical
concrete tube (the stator) inside which is a concrete
cone (the rotor) which is turned by a handle on top. It's
mounted on legs so that a basket can be put underneath.
The space between the stator and the rotor gradually
narrows from the top down; raising or lowering the
rotor quickly adjusts the space to accommodate nuts of
different sizes. Peanuts are fed in at the top, the flow
being controlled by a metal metering plate, and as the
handle is turned they fall between the surfaces and are
rolled and squeezed until the shells separate from the
kernels. The mixture of kernels and broken shells which
drops out is then winnowed. Aflatoxin-contaminated
nuts, which are smaller and a bit doughy, can be sorted
out if the machine is initially set to allow the smallest
10% of the nuts in a batch to pass through untouched;
the operator can quickly go through those and discard
the contaminated ones, then put the rest of the unshelled

ones through the machine again – the setting can be adjusted in a few seconds.[7]

Having developed a working prototype, Jock returned to Mali in June 2001 with the molds to build the first in-the-field sheller there.

What went into the invention of the sheller

Looking back, it's obvious that Jock Brandis spent much of his earlier life becoming the kind of person who could invent a machine like this. Born in the Netherlands in 1946 and brought to Canada as a baby, he spent his first nine years living on a pioneer farm in the small town of Terrace, in northern British Columbia. His parents Wim

---

7 Based on a passage from http://www.fullybellyproject. org/faq.php, on the instructional DVD prepared by the FBP, and on personal information from Jock. See also the Wikipedia article on the sheller – "Universal Nut Sheller" – which also gives a cross-section diagram of the sheller.

Calling this simple device a machine raises questions. E. F. Schumacher, in *Small is Beautiful: Economics As If People Mattered* (Vancouver, Hartley and Marks Publishers Inc., 1999, page 39) distinguishes between a tool and a machine. A tool "enhances a man's skill and power" while a machine "turns the work of man over to a mechanical slave, leaving man in a position of having to serve a slave." According to this distinction, the peanut shellers and other forms of appropriate technology are clearly tools, but Jock explains that in developing countries they are regarded as machines, so he often uses that term.

The peanut sheller in Senegal. On the left is Ibou Fall, of Baol Environnement, a Senegalese NGO; on the right is David Campbell, the Peace Corps Volunteer who has done so much to promote the sheller in West Africa.

Photo credit: Ellen Jefferys-White.

(Bill) and Madzy came from professional-class families, but Bill had always wanted to have a farm.[8]

Life on the farm was primitive. In the very beginning we had a privy, and in the kitchen we drew water with a pump over the sink. The house was, for the first few years, heated only by a wood-stove, though later we also had a wood-burning heater; firewood came from our own woodlot. Initially there was only a horse for transportation and farm-work. The house was built largely by Bill himself, and the farm buildings entirely so.

Pioneering is one of the mothers of invention. Because of a shortage of money, and the town's isolation, we were unable to buy many things we needed and had to contrive them from what was available. Much later, one of Jock's favourite quotations was a remark by Isaac Azimov: "A real genius is someone who can solve a problem with the tools in the room." In Terrace we had only the most basic tools. Jock and Gerard made many of their toys, including wagons constructed from scraps of lumber; the wheels were the wooden discs from the ends of rolls of the tarpaper used for building. Jock, at about three years of age, discovered that when he turned his small wheelbarrow upside down it became a bulldozer, and he had a lot of fun with that.

---

8 The story is told in more detail in my book *Frontiers and Sanctuaries: A Woman's Life in Holland and Canada.* (Montreal: McGill-Queen's University Press, 2006). That book, the biography of Jock's mother, Madzy Brender à Brandis, gives glimpses of Jock's life from his birth until Madzy's death in 1984.

In what follows, I'm drawing on my personal experience: I was nearly nine when we emigrated, Gerard was five, and Jock was not quite a year old.

Gerard remembers how "free" he felt – growing up in a safe place, having the farm and woods to explore, and, most of all, having very little media interference with the growth of his imagination and creativity.[9]

In Terrace Jock began learning about the developing world. The immediate neighbours – Mr. and Mrs. Hamlin and Mr. and Mrs. Thompson – gave us some old *National Geographic* magazines, including issues dating back to the beginning of the 20th century. All of us loved them, and Jock still has some copies. He read eagerly about Africa.

In 1956 we moved to Vancouver. Bill and Madzy, given credits for their education in the Netherlands, earned Canadian degrees in two years of study at the University of British Columbia, and I did my first two years at the same time. I was a member of International House, a club for students from overseas as well as Canada; Jock hung around the clubhouse – a converted army barrack, like many UBC buildings at that time – to talk with people from Africa and the Caribbean.

From there we moved to Nova Scotia, and finally to southern Ontario. By the time we reached Burlington, Ontario, Jock was twelve. He was interested in science; when his grandfather, a chemical engineer and professor visiting from the Netherlands, saw the science kit which someone had given Jock, he shuddered at the damage which the contents could potentially cause. Madzy, in a letter of 1961, writes: "Jock spends most of his time in the garage. He made a blow-torch, and now a jet-engine. He plans to try it out today, so may the gods help us."

---

9 Personal communication. Gerard Brender à Brandis has become one of Canada's best-known wood engravers and makers of hand-made, limited-edition books.

Jock's first summer job was at a small firm in Burlington, Electronic and Microwave Laboratories, which made specialized electronic parts for aircraft radar systems. Though hired as the handyman, he also learned to do precise machine work, and he invented a demonstration kit, to be used in schools, for explaining microwaves. He doesn't think that the kit was ever completed, but the project gave him experience working in a machine shop.

In the summer of 1965 the family moved to a six-acre property just north of Burlington. That fall Jock would start studies at McMaster University in Hamilton, living at home and commuting to the campus about ten miles away. His solution to the transportation problem was to buy two elderly Jaguar automobiles, neither of them operating, and – using a shop manual – to combine them to make one Jaguar that worked.

At McMaster he first enrolled in Economics but very soon switched to Anthropology. He became a member of the University Naval Training Division and spent the next few summers receiving basic training.

Upon graduation in 1968, he joined the Canadian University Service Overseas (CUSO) and was sent to teach in a school in Trench Town, just outside Kingston, Jamaica. He told me later that Trench Town was at that time probably the worst slum in the western hemisphere. About this experience, he wrote:

> The original plan was that I was going to be teaching auto mechanics. I was pretty excited about this, largely because I wasn't naïve enough to believe that slum kids stood much of a chance in an academic track. When I arrived at the school, it was decided that, since I was

one of the few teachers with·a college degree, it would
be inappropriate for me to teach a shop class. Hence
I became the science master, teaching chemistry and
biology.

The biggest problem with Trench Town Comprehensive
High School was that it had been built, perhaps five years
earlier, in an area that had [till then] no schools. The
elementary school was built at about the same time.
What this meant was that when students arrived for the
first time in a school setting, they were put into grades
based on their age, not their skill level. And the Ministry
of Education insisted on following the Cambridge "O"
and "A" Level Syllabus. So I was supposed to be teaching
students who might learn from what I said, but whatever
exams they had to write were to be graded in England.
And many of my students were fairly illiterate so their
ability to write sufficiently well to get passing grades
was limited. Most of the time I taught penmanship and
grammar. I tried to teach skills that might get them simple
jobs outside of the Trench Town slum. (Trench Town was
basically the slum that grew on the land formed from
the centuries-old habit of dumping garbage in Kingston
Harbour.)

The biggest impediment to students' future employment
was their accent [and the local slang]. The Trench
Town accent was unmistakable and it told every other
Jamaican that their mothers were, at best, street vendors,
and, at worst, prostitutes and thieves. It was assumed
they never knew their fathers. This was generally not
the truth, but the national prejudice ran very deep. So I
tried to improve their speech to hide their backgrounds.
Sort of Pygmalion at a classroom level. The Canadian
High Commission would lend me a 16mm projector
every Friday and I would show films. In theory, I told
the Headmaster, these were educational films. The High
Commission had a large library of National Film Board
of Canada titles (fascinating to kids who had never seen
movies or TV or travelled outside the neighborhood) and
some 1930's Hollywood stuff. Their favorite film was
Don Shebib's *Satan's Choice*, about outcast bikers. My

students were amazed by the idea that white people, who they imagined were all totally privileged and had servants, could be, somewhere in the world, as "written off" as they themselves were, and with as few good prospects in life. I also showed Cary Grant and Katherine Hepburn movies and we spent a lot of time trying to talk like them. Improving their accents and removing their jargon would, we hoped, enable them to get jobs in Kingston.

And I taught them to use the telephone. None of them had ever touched a phone and they seemed totally terrified of them. I would take the kids, one or two at a time, into the teachers' lounge when no one was there, and they would get phone numbers from advertisements in *The Daily Gleaner* and ask questions about stock availability or whatever. That was also a good test of the accent.

Needless to say, this went over badly in the school. (So did my habit of not filing lesson plans for classes not taught.) Then there was a situation where one of my best students stabbed another to death in the schoolyard and the 'legal' process that followed. I was told that the next year everything I did was to be by the book. That, added to a six-week bout of dengue fever, and I gave up. I felt truly horrible about quitting but the CUSO country director was supportive and arranged for me to help prepare the next batch of volunteers, on the theory that a lot of the training was a bit too rosy and optimistic.[10]

At the end of his time there, when he was about to go home, Jock was hired as navigator on a private yacht sailing from Jamaica to Puerto Rico. (He had learned some navigation in the navy.) A hurricane forced the yacht ashore in Haiti, then under the dictatorship of

10 Later in that summer of 1969 he went to Antigonish, Nova Scotia, to help train a group of CUSO workers going to the Caribbean.

"Papa Doc" Duvalier, and the crew was imprisoned in a military garrison. When they were visited by a priest and served a suspiciously luxurious meal, Jock decided that things looked serious. Using his high-school French and what he had learned of the language from reading Simenon mysteries in the original, Jock wrote to the prison commandant. After complimenting him on how well he was doing his work, Jock wrote that he had an uncle in Canada who allocated all the scholarships for Haitian students who came to study in Canadian universities. This uncle, Jock wrote, would be upset at hearing that his favourite nephew had been executed in Haiti, and that no doubt very few scholarships would from then on be given to Haitian students. This venture into fiction – the only factual part was that indeed most Haitian medical professionals were at that time trained in Canada – succeeded in freeing the whole group, and they continued their trip to the United States. In Miami Jock picked up the motorcycle that he had shipped from Jamaica and, drenched by a hurricane moving up the coast, drove back to Ontario. He had just enough money for gas but not for bed or food. He scrounged where he could. At one point a policeman – worried about his ability to drive safely – gave him a dollar, and also a voucher for a free meal and a box lunch at a diner. Jock got the man's name and returned the money as soon as he reached home. "I was a bit of a wreck," he recalls of the whole Jamaica experience. "It was a fast way to grow up."[11]

---

11 This passage, quoted/adapted from *Frontiers and Sanctuaries*, is based on information which I obtained from Jock when doing research for that book.

* * *

So now, back from Jamaica in the fall of 1969, Jock had to decide what to do with his life. He was interested in the film industry – in high school he had done lighting for the drama club's productions – but his immediate attention was caught by the crisis in Biafra. This region of Nigeria, populated mainly by the ten million Igbo (Ibo) people, had since 1967 been fighting a war of independence against the Nigerian government and had been punished by massacres. In 1969, Nigeria began a blockade designed to starve them to death.[12]

This stirred world-wide outrage, and a group called Joint Church Aid organized an airlift which would fly relief supplies from the island of São Tomé to the beleaguered Igbo. Among the ten *ad hoc* carriers which took part was Canairelief, organized by a group including a member of Oxfam Canada.[13] Jock offered his services. In *The Ship's Cat*, an account of this experience – fictional characters, real setting – he wrote:

> My first involvement with this tragic footnote in history was as an office boy in the Canairelief office on east Eglington Street [sic] in Toronto. At the age of twenty-two, with my idealism glands working overtime, I answered phones, showed movies in church basements, and did

---

12 "Several million Eastern Nigerians, especially Igbo, are believed to have died between the pogroms and the end of the civil war" in January 1970. http://en.wikipedia. org/w/index.php?title=Igbo_people. Accessed on 4/5/2008. A figure of "over a million" is given in Robert O. Collins and James M. Burns, *A History of Sub-Saharan Africa* (Cambridge; Cambridge University Press, 2007), 364.
13 Roy Thomas, "The Birth of CANAIRELIEF". http:// www.vanguardcanada.com.CANAIRELIEFThomas. Accessed on 13/3/2008.

everything to raise money and political pressure. Most
of all I filled out and signed receipts for the hundreds of
donations mailed into our office every day. [When another
plane was added to the small Canairelief fleet and had to
be flown from Canada to São Tomé] I hopped on the 'new'
Super Connie, as any foolish twenty-two year old might.
I told my mother I was just going as far as Holland so I
could visit the relatives. Once I was in São Tomé I was put
to work fixing the shrapnel holes in the fuel tanks. I was
also 'volunteered' into working as a loadmaster on some
of the simple cargoes. Generally these were situations
where someone else did the loading and I organized the
unloading at the other end. Nothing in my life has ever
been that terrifying.[14]

It was terrifying because the planes, flying by night
to a Biafran airstrip – a two-lane highway with an extra
lane added – were regularly shot at by Nigerian aircraft,
which also bombed the airstrip, leaving craters which
were hurriedly filled by Biafrans on the ground.[15] The
unloading had, therefore, to be done as fast as possible.
The planes, after being emptied of relief supplies, carried
dozens of starving Igbo babies back to São Tomé, where
they were "processed" as tourists and then put in the
care of Austrian nuns.

One of the characters of *The Ship's Cat* explains the
title: "… it's like you are the only witness to an ocean
liner sinking in a storm. You try as hard as you can to

14 Jock Brandis, *The Ship's Cat*. (Lincoln, NE, Writers Club
Press, 2000). 303-4.
15 Of the five Super Constellations owned by Canairelief,
one crashed in August 1969 and the four Canadians
on board were killed. Another was so badly damaged
by shell fragments in October that it was no longer
operational. Another was damaged in November and
abandoned on the airstrip. http://www.vanguardcanada.
com/CANAIRELIEFThomas. Accessed on 13/3/2008.

save the thousand people or even a dozen of them, but you fail. Despite all your efforts every last one drowns. All you find alive, floating among the wreckage, is the ship's cat. And trivial though it seems, saving the cat is the only thing that keeps your sanity. We will all need one tangible thing, one tiny victory to take from this place."[16]

It is in these experiences that the peanut sheller has its roots. Twice, as Jock observed to me, he had tried to help people in poor parts of the world and had failed. Trench Town was as bad when he left as it had been when he arrived, and Biafra (after the deaths of perhaps several million people) never did gain its independence. The third time, with the peanut sheller, he has succeeded.

* * *

When he left São Tomé in December 1969, however, that success was more than thirty years in the future. He flew to the Netherlands and, without advance notice, knocked on the door of the house of a cousin of ours – Madzy Boonacker – in Bentveld, near Haarlem. The five of us had been there when we made our first trip back to the Netherlands eleven years earlier. Now he arrived on the 5th of December, which – something he had not realized – was the feast of Sinterklaas, a

16 *The Ship's Cat*, 106-7. There is a footnote to this story. When Jock was in Washington DC in 2009 to meet with the Peace Corps about the peanut sheller, he talked with the black security guard at Peace Corps headquarters. The guard had been born in Biafra during the war, and when he found out that Jock had taken part in the airlift he thanked him for what he had done.

very important holiday for the Dutch, with lots of partying and gift-giving. He had with him a duffel bag of dirty laundry, much of it covered with engine grease, which Madzy washed. Madzy describes him as being "dazed",[17] an unsurprising result of the sudden move from the equator to northern Europe in December, and even more of the transition from the indescribable awfulness of Biafra – the terror of the relief flights, and the intolerable, heart-wrenching anguish of handling hundreds of dying babies – to being dropped into a Dutch Sinterklaas celebration which was all about gifts, good cheer, family life, and especially about well-fed and excited children. The contrast between the two groups of children is part of the story of the peanut sheller.

* * *

After three or four days in the Netherlands, Jock returned to Canada and went to live in Toronto. He continued volunteering with Oxfam, making two trips to deliver medical vehicles to Belize. He worked on low-budget films as a cameraman and head of the lighting department and was also involved with sound and special effects. This too was to lead to the invention of the peanut sheller. Movie people, Jock

---

17 In the Steelman article already cited, Jock describes the Biafran experience as "kind of like post-traumatic shock in Vietnam." The main characters in *The Ship's Cat*, which Jock wrote 20 or 25 years after these events, are described as having symptoms (nightmares, etc.) which sound very much like PTSD.

says, are "very good at thinking outside the box." No matter what's required, "you say 'All right, no problem. I can do that.'"[18]

He also applied his inventiveness to the process of film-making. Early on, discovering how awkward it could be to have lights mounted on stands on the floor and surrounded by cables, he devised and built (in a machine shop that he set up) expandable aluminum beams which would be installed overhead between two walls and from which lights and cables could be hung. Furthermore, he realized that the perfect vehicle for transporting equipment to shooting locations was a soft-drink truck with its outward-facing compartments that allowed for quick loading and unloading. He developed a silent generator which could be set up much closer to the spot where the filming was taking place. Some years later, during the making of a movie (*The Legend of Zorro*) on location in Mexico, he was told that the director wanted to film sword-fighting that would take place on top of moving railway cars. The cameras had to be suspended in mid-air on a vehicle that would have to move very smoothly over rough roads and that could carry ten people and more than a ton of equipment. Using the biggest pickup truck he

18 Dorothy Rankin, "The Future in a Nutshell: The Full Belly Project." *Wrightsville Beach Magazine*, July 2007. http://www.wrightsvillebeachmagazine.com. Volume 8, issue 7. July 2007. Accessed on 3/5/2008. Jock told me that one of the special effects he designed was a beautiful snake that moved in a very lifelike manner. When the movie was over, he watched it being thrown into a dumpster. The experience helped him to realize that he wanted to invent more useful and long-lived devices.

could find, Jock added another axle and a huge platform on the back, and mounted the cameras on long arms projecting sideways.

He began his film career in Toronto and then, in 1984, he moved to Wilmington, North Carolina. The move was partly dictated by his health – a southern climate suits his asthma better – and partly because he obtained work with Dino De Laurentiis, whose studio made Wilmington, at that time, "one of the busiest centers of American film and television production."[19] He also worked as technician for the Wilmington Public Radio station WHQR[20] and as Eastern-seaboard representative for a company that rented out generators. After that, for a time, he worked for The Entertainment and Sports Network (ESPN), driving generator trucks to football games all over the United States and, once there, operating the generators.

Back to Mali

This was where Jock was when, in 2001, he returned to Mali with molds and parts to make the peanut sheller. He had no money to pay for the trip but Martin Harbury, a film-making friend from Toronto, could get funding from the Discovery Channel, the Canadian International Development Corporation (CIDA), and TVOntario, provided that he make a film. So Jock was accompanied by a film crew.

It would be fitting if I could report that Jock built the first sheller in Woroni, but he didn't. Carrie Young, the

---

19 http://en.wikipedia.org/w/index.php?title=Dino_De_ Laurentiis. Accessed on 16/5/2008.
20 Ben Steelman article.

Peace Corps Volunteer there, was uncomfortable about having a film crew intrude into the life of her village, so in fact the building took place in a village called Katele. A sheller was, however, taken to the women in Woroni.

There were problems. The box containing the molds and parts was delayed and arrived five days after Jock. In the first machine, the rotor wasn't centred; even the second machine was not perfect. Jock says now that they went to Africa too early, but the timing was dictated by Martin Harbury's deadline. Nevertheless, the machines worked; it's all recorded in the film, which is titled *Peanuts*. Dr. Tim Williams, the peanut expert, wrote that the film showcases "the many skills that people need for life – problem solving, determination and commitment, human relations, cultural understanding, engineering and manufacturing, economics, and environmental sensitivity while maintaining interest in a simple tale of two 'cities'."[21]

Inventing a non-profit, stage 1

Looking back in 2006, Jock told a reporter:

> After the film aired, I was inundated with requests from the Peace Corps [Volunteers] and [workers in] developing countries for information about the sheller. That's when I realized that the problem they are having in Mali is the problem they are having in South and Central America, Indonesia, Asia, and India. Depletion of the soil from the planting of cotton and other cash crops is the cause of [such problems as] breakdown in the family, because there simply is not enough food to sustain everyone. Peanuts are absolutely the best way to turn that around.

21 http://www.bullfrogfilms.com. Accessed on 6/2/2010.

They are an excellent protein source, have few diseases or parasites, are easy to transport to market, and are a great way to get the fields back in shape.[22]

Unfortunately Jock was, at that point, unable to follow up on these requests. He had no organization and no way of distributing either molds or completed shellers. He was, however, more determined than ever to press on. When he returned to the United States he demonstrated the sheller to Dr. Williams. That didn't lead to any immediate breakthrough, however, so to earn a living he continued working in the film industry and driving generator trucks to football games. But the peanut sheller had become his main interest. Jay Tervo and the Coastal Carolina Returned Peace Corps Volunteers were helping to build shellers and do office work and fund-raising. In November 2003, the group set up The Full Belly Project, Ltd., with Jay as the first president. The FBP aims "to support the farmer at the very primary level and help him to get as much value as possible for the crops that he is busting his ass to grow" by enabling him to do as much as possible of the processing locally.[23] Other aims and goals are linked to that central one.

Jay Tervo, writing in 2010, provides insight into those early days. "[We were] 'inventing' the organization called The Full Belly Project. We did not really have any idea how to go about getting this machine out to developing countries. We did not have any money. We

22 Linda Grattafiori, "Grinding the Husk off World Hunger." http://encorepub.com. Accessed on 14/5/2008.
23 *Popular Mechanics* website.

knew that while we might think the machine was a pretty nifty idea, what we thought really didn't matter. We knew the only measure of success that counted was whether women in a village in Africa agreed with us enough to do something about it (i.e. buy a machine, build one, borrow one, etc.)." George Wesoloski, another RPCV, who was the first treasurer and later a member of the Board, also wrote to me about the organization's beginnings: "A Board of Directors was organized and the group began to meet monthly at the Folks café. The obstacles to getting started took their toll. For several months, the monthly meetings came down to just Jay and [me] questioning how to get the project going."

Initially the shellers were built at Jock's house, but in June 2004 they moved into "a converted garage behind a supporter's house."[24] A boat builder, Pete Klingenberger, made the fiberglass molds, and on Saturday mornings a group of volunteers cut and welded metal parts, made shellers, and put together kits containing molds, metal parts, and instructions.

The FBP website, chronicling the history of the organization,[25] reports that in 2004 "various efforts to introduce the machine in other countries are attempted without success, primarily due to The Full Belly Project's lack of funding, lack of sophistication in choosing overseas partners, and as yet a not fully refined design." Because Jock was often away driving trucks, he had little time at home for FBP work. It's true that the Consultative Group on International Agricultural Research (CGIAR)

---

24 http://www.fullbellyproject.org/history.php. Accessed on 13/3/2008.

25 This material was on a former version of the website.

and the International Crops Research Institute for the Semi-Arid Tropics (ICRISAT) showed some interest at first. Eric McGaw at CGIAR informed Jock that peanuts were important in northern Nigeria, Zimbabwe, and Mozambique, and that he was sending information about the sheller to colleagues in ICRISAT. But this interest was short-lived, and other large organizations would, in the next years, also be unresponsive. Jock attributes this to the disdain that PhDs have for amateurs, and he understands it. "There are a lot of crazy people out there," he told me, "who claim to have supernatural inventions and weird solutions. I probably came on the heels of a dozen crackpots. Also the academics are accustomed to seeing breakthroughs come from big companies." There was a good deal of outright disbelief regarding the machine itself, largely because it was so simple and because it was made of concrete: no one – it was believed – makes machines out of concrete.

* * *

Concrete is actually central to the FBP operation. It's inexpensive and comparatively easy to work with and, being used to construct buildings in the developing world, is available everywhere. (Try to imagine making the shellers out of steel – the cost, the need for large and expensive machinery and for imported steel, the dangerous and tricky work with molten metal.) The surface of concrete is essential for "rolling" the shells off the nuts; it even has to be roughed up with a steel brush before the concrete is completely hard.

In fact, this use of concrete to make precision machines is revolutionary. The nature of the sun-dried peanut – with its thin outer shell fitting snugly around the nut – and the importance of not damaging the seed coat, means that the machines have to be very carefully built, with the rotor precisely centred in the stator. The machine has to be adjusted to fit each batch of nuts. There are many varieties of peanuts in the world, and many variations in size. The fact that the FBP sheller damages the seed coat in only about 5% of the nuts (the rate for industrial machinery is much higher) shows that these are indeed precision machines.

The precision is built into the molds. The work of Pete Klingenberger is of incalculable importance. Jock writes:

> Pete was my first friend in Wilmington. He lived next door when I was still renting a house on the beach. His kids tell me he takes a lot of pride in his work with Full Belly. That probably explains why he has infinite patience with all the subtle variations of design on the way to the final mold. The molds are very important, because that's where the accuracy is established. Concrete will come out in exactly the same shape every time, so machines can be accurate only if the molds are accurate. There are dozens of discarded ideas that Pete first had to turn into very accurate fiberglass. Because the number of molds now [2010] being sent out is so great, we have moved to making them out of plastic, but Pete and his son Chris are now making the [fiberglass] molds for the vaccu-form process.

* * *

In spite of early obstacles to the machines' dissemination, Jock was making contacts and broadening his scope.

On his second trip to Mali he met Ibrahim Togola, one of the leaders of the Mali-Folkecentre.[26] Togola taught him a lot about basic issues in developing countries and about the importance of simple machinery; in fact, he reminded Jock of what E. F. Schumacher had written in *Small is Beautiful*, a book which had influenced Jock when it came out in 1973. What Schumacher called "intermediate technology" is now "appropriate technology."

The Mali Folkecentre was one of the first organizations to work in the field of renewable energy, and was also concerned with environmental issues including forestry (in Mali, as in many other parts of Africa, the forests are disappearing), and they may have been the first people to make biofuel from jatropha nuts. Several years later, Jock developed a variation of the sheller to process jatropha; it was during the 2001 trip to Mali that he first rode in a vehicle converted to use this biofuel.

Haiti

In its attempt to get the sheller to people who needed it, FBP looked towards the Caribbean and Central America. In early 2003, even before the organization was incorporated, Jay contacted the Mercy Ships, a ship-based medical organization that, as well as providing health care, "helps communities become self-sufficient

---

26 "The Mali-Folkecentre … is a Malian NGO which represents the Danish Folkecentre for Renewable Energy. It was opened in 1999." http://www.malifolkecentre.org. Accessed on 1/3/2009. Ibraham Togola was, when I last checked, its Regional Director.

in food production through provision of seeds, tools and training."[27] He sent a sheller and molds to Mike Mullens, then serving on the ship *Caribbean Mercy*. Mullins passed them on to Dr. Wayne Niles in Haiti, an American Baptist missionary working in agricultural and rural development. Because the instructions were missing, Dr. Niles wrote to Jay. They discussed setting up a shop to build shellers in Haiti, but Dr. Niles was pessimistic. He was trying to persuade Haitians to use a sand water filter to help deal with water-borne diseases, but in six months of trying he had had no takers.

Through Niles, FBP contacted the Peace Corps in Haiti. Jay learned that there was to be a conference of the Peace Corps agricultural section at the end of April 2003, and he obtained an invitation for Jock to give a talk and build a sheller. An e-mail from a Peace Corps Volunteer present at the events reported that Jock was in Port-au-Prince "demonstrating the peanut shelling machine at a very large fair on the Champs de Mars with great success. In this process he along with a handful of Peace Corps Volunteers have been trying to work out the bugs in the peanut shelling process."

The following year Jock travelled to Haiti again, this time with a group of Peace Corps agricultural volunteers. In the course of training them to make the machines, he learned about local materials and resources. At first he and the Peace Corps team thought that the best way to manufacture shellers would be to have Peace Corps Volunteers make them. But when the first machines proved to be not good enough Jock arranged for a builder of Haiti's concrete-and-steel houses to make

---

27 http://www.mercyships.ca. Accessed on 28/7/2011.

machines which the Peace Corps would then distribute. However, before financing for the project had been worked out there was a brief civil war; the Peace Corps left the country, and contact with the house-builder was lost. What Jock learned about the problems of making machines in developing countries would, however, be useful in the future.

Ghana, Malawi, Uganda

Another promising beginning also came to very little. Early in 2003 a Ghanain student named Samuel Agyare came to Wilmington to learn how to make shellers. He took molds and metal parts back to Ghana, and he and his uncle made three machines. In answer to questions from Jay, he reported that the villagers were happy with the machines because of the amount of time they saved. Interestingly, he reported that the sheller was good for shelling shea nuts, the source of the shea butter which is now so popular in skin creams. (More about this in other chapters.) Eighteen months later, he reported that the three shellers were still in use in Ghana, but by then he himself was in the United Kingdom hoping either to attend school or to find a job. So nothing further came of this initiative. Jay, reflecting on it in 2010, wrote to me that this episode could be regarded not as a failure but as a chance for FBP to try something, see how it worked, and learn from it.

Also in 2003, a Presbyterian minister named Dave Carver found out about the peanut sheller. He wrote to FBP that the Presbyterian Church in Pittsburgh had a long-standing, far-reaching partnership with the Church of Central Africa: Presbyterian; he thought that the sheller would be "a real boon" to them. He also writes: "My friend Mr. Menes Makuluni runs the maize mill in Ntaja Trading Center, a dusty village high in the hills of Southeast Malawi. He is most interested in procuring a peanut sheller. If we can get one of these to him, it might be enough incentive for some of the local farmers to stop growing either tobacco or corn – both crops are really tough on the soil. It might also help to give our friends more protein in their diets – if we can make eating peanuts easier, they'll do it!" Carver had "just returned from a visit to famine-stricken Malawi …. I will head out again in about 10 days time, spending a month with some members of our partner church." Jay sent him a kit to take to Malawi, and Carver wrote that he hoped that the Projects Office of the Synod of Blantyre (of the Church of Central Africa) would build shellers and take them out to the villages, and that he himself might be able to take one to Ntaja.

The Carver family took the molds to Malawi in July, but in August Carver reported that they had not been able to see the sheller in operation because they were in Blantyre for only a short time and had to move on to other mission projects; in any case, "the Projects Office was going through some staff transitions and they didn't have anyone to dedicate to the peanut sheller at that time." Moreover, "it wasn't peanut season and there were not very many nuts to shell."

In 2009, when I contacted him to ask whether he knew of any further developments, Carver wrote to me: "I am afraid that the Peanut Sheller going to Blantyre was an example of well-meaning westerners bringing the answer to a question that the Malawians themselves hadn't asked. We brought [the kit] along, and they took it graciously, but I am not aware as to whether it was ever used."

The failure of these attempts illustrates some of the obstacles that prevented or slowed the distribution of the sheller in early years. Often the farmers welcomed the machines, but between Wilmington and the farmer's field there were innumerable potential barriers.

In September 2004, however, an important breakthrough occurred. A Ugandan named Tony Lumu, who worked with the Adonai Ministries, heard about FBP when he was travelling in North Carolina. He came to Wilmington and learned to build a sheller; when he returned to Uganda he took with him a set of molds and enough metal pieces to build three machines.[28]

In January 2005 he reported that he had built a sheller. "The machine was received in this area with excitement and a big number of women and young people have turned up to make use of the machine each day. This machine is the first machine probably in this country that is redeeming people from this huge task of removing the nuts from the covers." There is more about this in the next chapter.

Inventing a non-profit, stage 2

Jay Tervo used Tony Lumu's report to urge his fellow Returned Peace Corps Volunteers in the Wilmington area to get involved. Commenting on the report, which he attached to his e-mail, he wrote: "And this is just one guy trying to make a difference in one small part

28 http://www.fullybellyproject.org/history.php. Accessed on 13/3/2008.

of one small country where poverty is rampant and peanuts make up a big part of how locals get protein in their diet. And there are approximately 99 more countries just like Uganda, where peanuts play a major role in folks' diet. Some 500 million people ... are in the same nutritional boat as the people of Uganda." He explained that four to eight RPCVs had been working on the sheller project but that more were needed – for instance, to organize an upcoming fundraiser. People were needed to build shellers, ten of which were to go to Toronto for Canadian Feed the Children, who would send them to developing countries. Jay hoped that with enough volunteers they could in fact make twenty shellers. Although by then the kits were being sent out – as with Tony Lumu to Uganda – he wrote: "The concept is that by building the shellers here we can make sure they are built correctly. If they are well received in the countries they are sent to, we will have lots of great testimonials from the Canadian Feed the Children folks that will help us get grant funding to take this organization to the next level."

He goes on:

> If you have experience writing grants, we could use you. If you have experience working with tools, we could use you. If you have any experience writing letters or e-mailing, we could use you. If you have or know someone who has a corner of a warehouse we can use to store materials, we need a place to work out of. 600 square feet or so would be fine. If you have no skills what-so-ever, no problem, we'll teach you! ... If you have no time and still want to make a difference, send money. ... For every $10, some village in Uganda gets an indestructible peanut

shelling machine! For every $500, someone gets a mold that can build unlimited shellers.[29]

Five years later Jay looks back:

We struggled with working to create the structure of the organization (incorporated it as a non-profit, established bylaws, job responsibilities, board members, all the legal and ethical documents). We struggled with volunteers with differing levels of experience in running organizations and in overseas experience. Some of the most enthusiastic and vocal of our volunteers had the least third-world experience. We knew of no other organizations we could look [to] to model ourselves after. We struggled with trying to get initial feedback on Jock's designs, and for a while there [we] struggled with getting some necessary design modifications done because Jock was traveling so much in his [paid] work. We knew [that] in order to be effective in creating the structure where the sheller could be built in other countries, we had to have instructions "in excellence", something that was harder to accomplish than any of us imagined. Do we give the designs away, do we patent them? How much control do we want to maintain in who uses our machines? How much control can we maintain? How do we get local support? When do we add staff? When can we pay our staff, and how much? Do we have a membership-based organization? Do we set up chapters either here in this country or overseas?

* * *

What evolved in those years was a very small but highly productive NGO. In February 2007 the first staff were hired: the Executive Director was Jeff Rose, who had served with the Peace Corps in Guinea, and Jock was Director of Research and Development. The (very

---

29 The current (2011) price of the shellers and the molds is higher but (see Chapter Six) there is a sliding scale.

modest) salary enabled Jock to stop driving generator trucks and spend all his time on FBP.

The Saturday-morning work sessions became an important institution. Besides RPCVs, the group came to include high-school and university students and older people with many different backgrounds. At the time of writing, 20 to 25 people turn up each week. They are organized into teams who work on particular projects; Jock plans each Saturday morning's work with the team leaders.

The volunteers do everything from routine tasks such as packing kits to mechanical work like cutting and welding metal parts to helping with the invention and development of the machines. When he's working among them, Jock is constantly teaching, as well as supervising and guiding. To inform volunteers about where and how the devices will be used, Jock passes on what he learns during his trips to the developing world. He explains, for instance, that African women like working in groups of two or three, facing each other, and that standing at a bench or counter, shoulder to shoulder, makes them very uncomfortable. He explains that no one in Africa works alone. "Half of design is anthropology," he says. In the course of telling the volunteers about climate, crops, soil, the economy, and social habits and conditions he becomes a conduit between this small hub and the large world of people in need.

Having learned that every volunteer comes with skills and ideas, Jock encourages them to take initiative; those who have mastered certain procedures train newcomers.

An example of the volunteers' creativity – which is

admittedly sometimes accidental – comes from an incident with brazil nuts. Because the sheller rolls the nuts between two concrete surfaces, it was regarded as being useful only for round nuts. When a volunteer asked Jock whether it could shell brazil nuts – hard, triangular, and awkward – Jock said, "Never in a million years." Nonetheless, the next weekend, when Jock was away, someone put brazil nuts into the sheller. The machine jammed. While taking it apart to correct the problem, one of the group turned the adjusting handle in the wrong direction, thus raising the rotor and narrowing the space around it. With that setting, the machine shelled the nuts perfectly. Now there is a version of the sheller designed to handle irregularly shaped nuts.

Having about 80% of the work done by volunteers is an important part not only of FBP's operation but also of its ideology. The machines are presented as being "a gift from the American people to the people of the developing world," the term "gift" indicating that they are made by volunteers rather than salaried workers.

The use of the sheller was extended not only to brazil nuts but to others as well. Samuel Agyare in Ghana had reported that it was good for shea, and in the Philippines it was adapted for coffee. Further uses and adaptations – for walnuts, pecans, jatropha, neem, wild-flower seeds, and others (see future chapters) indicate that it really can handle a wide range of nuts and seeds. So FBP named the machine the Universal Nut Sheller (UNS).

* * *

As FBP evolved, so did the procedures for manufacturing and distributing the shellers. Initially they were made in Wilmington and sent out from there, but shipping concrete machines is very expensive, so almost from the beginning FBP began preparing kits, each of which contains a set of molds (initially fiberglass, now ABS plastic), enough metal parts for several shellers, and instructions. The metal parts are intended only to get the recipient started: more can be ordered from Wilmington, or they can be easily replicated at any metal shop in the world, and the molds can be used indefinitely. So a kit is actually a mini-factory – the term commonly used now – with which an unlimited number of shellers can be made. The mini-factory model, central to FBP's operation, dictates other aspects of the work, such as the need to design machines so that they can be built from kits.

However, the system has limitations. In Haiti in 2004 Jock discovered that the first few machines that a person makes don't turn out well, partly because the characteristics of the local sand and cement are unknown. Jock himself, when working in a developing country, needs to experiment.

Also the builder has to learn the procedure. Though not complicated for a person with some mechanical aptitude and some experience in working with cement, it requires care to produce a machine that works well. The concrete parts have to be taken out of the molds at the right time and, because of the variations in cement and the effect of temperature on the speed at which it hardens, this can't be determined beforehand. The first machine someone makes is, in Jock's word, "terrible." The second and third are better but probably not perfect, and the fourth is usually quite good. So the first few should be broken up in order to retrieve the metal parts. It's not good to allow these imperfect machines to be used, because they will break too many nuts and give a misleading impression of what a well-made sheller can do. Moreover, a builder might be discouraged if his first one or two machines don't turn out well.

FBP has worked out ways to try to ensure that machines are properly made. People expressing an interest in the sheller – aid workers heading for a developing country, for instance, or someone like Tony Lumu – are encouraged to come to Wilmington, if they can, to learn to make them, and then when they go overseas they can take the mini-factory in their checked baggage. Quite a number of people have done so. Moreover, the Full Belly Project works with NGOs and other organizations to set up overseas sheller-manufacturing shops. Jock usually goes to the destination to set up the shop and train the workers.

Jock declared the UNS as "open technology", which prevents anyone from patenting it. However, FBP requests partners to "... sign a licensing agreement which permits the organization to reproduce our technology, giving The Full Belly Project credit for the design of the Universal Nut Sheller to any local press. Recipients will also join our network of innovators. All our partners become part of a global idea-sharing network. Any improvements or alterations to our machinery must be reported to The Full Belly Project. We verify these adaptations and if they are viable and easily replicable, we disseminate these ideas back out to our network of innovators, thus accelerating innovation of our designs."[30] The sheller is in fact constantly being adapted to local needs and different crops, to locally available materials, and to the abilities of local builders.

The MIT connection

In August 2005, a connection was made between the Full Belly Project and MIT. Spencer Swinton, a Wilmington friend, put Jock in touch with Amy Smith, instructor at MIT's School of Engineering. Her specialty was "developing technologies that optimize limited resources and solve seemingly intractable problems in developing countries."[31] She had served with the Peace Corps in Botswana and was, in 2005, on the staff of the MIT Edgerton Center, where she headed the D-Lab (Development Lab) program. D-Lab is "a year-long series of classes and field trips that provide a curriculum to educate students about technical, social, and cultural aspects of development work in selected countries, and then provides the opportunity for field work and implementation."[32] Students learn how to analyze problems, design a solution, and then trouble-shoot in the field. After doing classroom and lab work in the fall semester, they travel to developing countries in January to put into effect what they have been working on, and upon their return they analyze the results.

---

30 http://www.fullybellyproject.org/history.php. Accessed on 13/3/2008.
31 "The MacArthur Fellows Program", attached to e-mail of 2 August 2005 from Spencer Swinton to Jock.
32 http://web.mit.edu/idi/programs.shtml#dlab. Accessed on 27/4/2008.

When Amy learned about Jock's work, she invited him to be a guest lecturer in December of that year. His talk was such a success that he now addresses the students every fall, and they regularly build FBP machines in the developing countries where they go, testing them under local conditions and sending Jock reports. Amy uses the *Peanuts* DVD as a teaching tool because it illustrates what D-Lab is all about: "it is the story of how you identify a simple problem, you experiment and create prototypes, you take them into the field, you make mistakes and things go wrong, you solve problems in the field, and eventually you find a solution."

Jock's first visit to MIT had immediate results. In January 2006 "teams from ... D-Lab travel[led] to the Philippines, Ghana, and Zambia with [mini-factories] in order to introduce these machines to local populations."[33] Allen Armstrong, the leader of the team that went to Zambia, reported to FBP:

> We returned from Mwape on Thursday, in a bit of a rush to make it across a swollen river, and had to leave the last 1% of the [peanut] sheller job undone, but we did go over it pretty thoroughly with a few of the villagers, and have to hope they can tune them up properly. Here's the story:
> We made 3 shellers at Mwape, got two of them adjusted and working at about an 85% "correct" rate. We demonstrated them to the headmen, who decided on locations for the 3. [Two of them] will be kept at the satellite health outposts in two sections, and [the third] at the chief's store. A small fee will be charged, they'll work that out. We brought the molds back with us to Lusaka, and will donate them to the Technology Development Unit at the University of Zambia tomorrow morning.

33 http://www.fullbellyproject.org/history-php. Accessed on 17/3/2008.

He suggests slight modifications to the design.

Information about the introduction of the sheller to Ghana in that same year comes from a later e-mail from Amy Smith. "In January of 2006, we brought a set of molds with us on a D-Lab trip. The first sheller we built was in Cape Coast with Dr. Kofi Sam, who runs an appropriate technology centre there. ... Then we moved up country, and worked with Pastor George Fuachie in the village of New Longoro ... and built another sheller. It was used quite a bit last harvest, I don't know the amount, but when we arrived in January 2007, PG's (as we call him) kitchen was filled with burlap bags of shelled peanuts. ... When we went back in 2007, we built another one."

* * *

The connection continues. In July 2007 Jock took part in MIT's first International Development Design Summit (IDDS), during which "students, mechanics, social workers, doctors, carpenters, farmers, and professors from 18 countries join[ed] forces to build technologies to improve the quality of life in the developing world. ... Forty IDDS participants formed 10 teams to design technologies that address[ed] problems in sectors including energy, agriculture, water, and health. Teams were coached by mentors and guest speakers."[34] During the four-week summit he took part in the practical work of developing new technologies. He had brought with him a pedal-powered version of the sheller, and one of his goals was "to come up with a series of add-ons so that it can be used year-round to process food, press oil,

---

34 http://www.iddsummit.org. Accessed on 28/4/2008.

and pump water." He writes: "I have been spending a lot of time with the guy from the Grameen Bank based in Saudi Arabia, [whose] boss is a fanatic about pedal power and has already been informed of our new pedal international standard platform." Nothing came of this Grameen connection, but the pedal-powered shellers are currently in use in Guyana.

* * *

And so the Full Belly Project's work began – with energy, inventiveness, and patience, and with a big vision that kept it pushing forward.

TWO

Africa

Most of the world's poorest countries are in sub-Saharan Africa, and appropriate technology, being village-scale and not dependent on petroleum or electricity, is badly needed. Drought, disappearing forests, spreading deserts, and deteriorating soil are serious problems. In many countries the population is still largely rural, but as rural problems increase people move to cities, swelling the already huge slums and aggravating housing shortages, unemployment, and crime. Already in 1973, in *Small is Beautiful*, E. F. Schumacher described the condition of the rural poor in Africa: "Their work opportunities [in the countryside] are so restricted that they cannot work their way out of misery. They are underemployed or totally unemployed, and when they do find occasional work their productivity is exceedingly low. Some of them have land, but often too little. Many have no land and no prospect of ever getting any. There is no hope for them in the rural areas and hence they drift into the big cities. But there is no work for them in the big cities either and, of course, no housing. All the same, they flock into the cities because the chances of finding some work appear to be greater there than in the villages, where they are nil."[1] This situation hasn't changed.

Rural and urban areas alike suffer from extreme poverty, malnutrition, diseases (including, of course, malaria and HIV/AIDS), and high childhood mortality. Improving the conditions of rural life could help to reduce that migration and also improve life in the cities: because, in Africa, city dwellers have strong connections with their rural relatives, earnings and improvements, as well as problems and shortages, flow back and forth.

Sub-Saharan Africa was Jock's first area of interest and is still a major focus.

Uganda in 2005 and 2006

The breakthrough in Uganda, already mentioned, is worth examining more closely.

When Tony Lumu returned to Uganda in Fall 2004 – having learned how to make shellers in Wilmington and taking a mini-factory back with him – he built the three machines for which he had metal parts and placed them in peanut-growing communities. One community, he writes in his report to FBP, consists mostly of women and young people because "the number of men decreased in the previous years due to wars and HIV/AIDS scourge."[2] He reports that "people are coming in a big way to see and to use this." One sheller is not enough

---

1   Page 143. McKibben, in *Eaarth* and *Deep Economy*, writes about such migration now being driven by the effects of climate change. Richard Dowden deals with it in *Africa: Altered States, Ordinary Miracles* (New York: PublicAffairs, 2009).

2 The report is undated, but it was attached to an e-mail sent by Tony Lumu to Jay Tervo on 15 January 2005.

to serve the area, which has a population of 6,000. "The machine has been received with great excitement so far and many other invitations are coming our way to make as many machines as possible in the areas where peanuts are grown. Success has been seen." He and the farmers adjusted the sheller to handle the small peanuts grown in the region.

There were some problems. After a machine has been used for a while, "the plates that control the amount of peanuts that fall into the hole to be processed become weak .... This causes [too] many peanuts to fall into the hole. This causes the machine to break the peanuts into pieces." Sometimes it was difficult to get the hardened concrete out of the mold; Jock had advised the use of some kind of grease, but Tony reports that "the right type of Vaseline" is hard to find. However, they solved the problem by lining the molds with polythene bags. (This is now FBP's standard practice.) Moreover, the type of sand available needed a lot of cement, but the best cement was expensive. The machine also needed better supporting legs.

A few other issues have nothing to do with the machine itself. To transport the molds, Tony hired a motorcycle. Not only was this costly, but the molds were awkward to manage on such a vehicle. Furthermore, Adonai, the organization he worked with, couldn't afford to make more metal parts. However, he concludes, "plans are underway to expand to other parts of the country with the peanut Sheller Machine."

This was definitely success. Not only were machines being built *in* a developing country, but the local people were taking to them and adapting them to their needs.

So important was it that, a few weeks later, Jay Tervo went to Uganda, accompanied by film-maker Rex Miller to document the project so that FBP would have a film to use in fund-raising. Family obligations prevented Jock from going, but in any case the film was really about Tony's work.

Jay and Rex took molds and metal parts and, once in Kampala, began building machines. Then they travelled around the country, making several more in regional centres. In their truck they took sand and cement, and the wheelbarrow in which the concrete should be mixed. (Local people were doing this on the bare ground – in an African village there is often nowhere else – but the inclusion of whatever happened to be lying there lowered the quality of the concrete.) Rex filmed everything and quickly edited the footage to produce a short video for use during the promotional meetings which Jay set up with the U.S. ambassador to Uganda, the Peace Corps, the U.S. Agency for International Development (USAID), Catholic Relief Services, World Vision, and Canadian Feed the Children. Jay addressed a national convention of Uganda Rotary Clubs and demonstrated the sheller, and Rex showed the video.

* * *

Upon his return to Wilmington, Jay formulated a plan whereby the Rotary Clubs of Uganda and Jay's own club would cooperate to "build and distribute Groundnut Shelling Machines to the residents of villages in Uganda." He obtained a Rotary Foundation Matching Grant: the total amount eventually available – which included donations from some individual Rotary groups – was

$46,000. Over a period of several months in early 2006, Jock and the volunteers made 33 machines and 150 sets of metal parts. These, together with 22 sets of molds, were shipped to Kampala in a container. Jock and Jay were there in September 2006 when the container arrived.

Part of the plan was that Jock would run a two-day sheller-building training session, to be attended by someone from each interested (and donating) Rotary Club. Each representative, having learned to build the sheller, would receive one of the machines made in Wilmington, and a mini-factory, to take to his home town. Also taking part in the workshop was Compatible Technologies International (CTI), an NGO based in Saint Paul, Minnesota, that makes a grinder which turns shelled peanuts into paste (peanut butter), the form in which they are frequently eaten in developing countries. CTI manufactures the grinders in Kampala, and their representative at the workshop was Kathleen Graham.

The training didn't work out as planned. The Rotary representatives did not make the machines themselves: they were businessmen, and each brought with him a friend who actually made the machines. Jock's impression was that these people would tell the villagers how to do it, which was several steps removed from the hands-on training that FBP had visualized. Moreover, the idea had been that during the training session each person would make five shellers. This would deal with the problem that the first few are likely to be defective and that, if they were not broken up, there would be a lot of mediocre machines in existence.

Unfortunately, this is probably what happened, and as a result the sheller got a bad reputation. When Jock was in Uganda again the following year, he found that many machines and parts had never been used. "Bad news travels faster than good news," he says. "A village which has 'a good thing' will keep it a secret because it gives them an advantage in local commerce." Now, reflecting on that experience, Jock says, "It's important to be really careful with quality control."

Moreover, two days was not enough to give people confidence that they would be able to make additional machines on their own. During the next trip to Uganda, Jock scheduled a week for a similar training session.

This confirmed what Jock had learned in Haiti: that it would be better to have machines made in a workshop or small factory *in* the developing country. He had hoped that one of the Rotary Club representatives would see the potential and set up a shop, but none did.[3]

* * *

The establishment of shops in developing countries became, then, one of FBP's aims, but for that they needed on-the-ground partners with local knowledge and contacts. Once such a partnership was established, Jock would go to the country to find a building, set up the shop, and train workers in making the machines as well as in basic business methods. The shop, an independent small business, would provide employment. Materials would be bought locally. Workers, making the shellers day after day, would turn out perfect machines. NGOs

---

3   In North America, many Rotary members are entrepreneurs and businessmen, but those who came to the training session in Uganda were mostly doctors and teachers.

with staff in the area would, it was hoped, distribute the machines; FBP had learned that if this was left to the local people, tribal divisions could hamper wide distribution, whereas NGOs like the Peace Corps and local aid organizations cross tribal boundaries.

The next trip to Uganda, in 2007, provided a chance to test the plan. This project was designed in cooperation with the Kenan Institute for Engineering, Technology & Science at the University of North Carolina, and with Nourish International, an organization which "works with students to solve some of the problems caused by global poverty."[4]

The team that went was a big one. It included Jock, FBP's Executive Director Jeff Rose, staff member Roey Rosenblith, and two friends of Jock's, Chunky Huse and Alan Toll, a Wilmington lawyer. Toll's son Eddie, a free-lance journalist, also went. There were fifteen students who were members of Nourish International. Filmmaker Rob Hill and a cameraman joined the group for a few days to shoot footage for a feature-length film on FBP's work. Financing – a total of $45,000 – came from Nourish International, Duke University, and FBP itself.

The American team worked with the Masagazi family. Henry Masagazi, son of Dr. Speciosa Wandira Kazibwe, a former Vice President of Uganda, would operate the factory, to be located in the town of Iganga where Masagazi's uncle owned a coffee-processing operation.

Jock spent his first three days in Kampala buying tools, and steel for the shellers' metal parts. When he couldn't

4   http://nourishinternational.org/about/index.php.
    Accessed on 23/1/2009.

get exactly what he needed he found replacements and invented modifications. Having rented a pickup truck with driver, he went to Iganga, where he was provided with "an empty space with a roof and two walls" – a typical structure for that climate, with the walls meant only to break the wind. He had electricity installed.

In his report, he described the workers he hired. "One, whom we called 'Hoss', was large and strong and said little and he proved to be an excellent welder. Dickson was a fussy, attention-to-detail guy, and he was the assembly [and] quality-control guy. Fred was best at problem-solving and he became the foreman. They were all paid ... about 25% more than the going rate but I wanted loyalty and hard work and I got it." He found a local metal worker to make metering plates using scrap from a steel mill in Iganga. Other members of the team "located a fiberglass man who made an excellent set [of molds for] less than the cost in the U.S." Jock built workbenches: the local people normally worked while squatting on the ground, but they discovered the advantage of standing at benches.

When the factory space was ready, Jock established the routine: the workers would pour cement in the morning and then keep testing it until the parts were ready to be removed from the molds. He showed them how to assemble the machines. By the end of the first week about 10 were finished; when the U.S. team left Iganga there were about 100. The shop had the capacity to produce 50 a week, 70 if there was a Sunday shift.

Of course peanuts were needed for testing and demonstrating the machines, but most of those available were old and moldy, and would break even when shelled by hand. Mold indicates that the nuts could be infected with aflatoxin. When Jock demonstrated the sheller to Dr. Kaaya, the representative of the Peanut Collaborative Research Support Program (CRSP) at Makerere University in Kampala, Dr. Kaaya insisted that all the shelled nuts be destroyed.

One purpose of FBP's field trips is to learn about local conditions so that, if necessary, the machines can be modified. In Uganda it was discovered that the shellers could suffer damage during transportation over the bumpy roads common in Africa, "so we cut up pieces of car tires and set the rubber between the concrete and the steel. Just in case, if units were shipped to Sudan or Kenya, we folded short pieces of rubber over the ends of the feet and held them there with twisted wire."

In his report, Jock provides "a very accurate calculation of [the cost of building the sheller]. The materials were [US] $25. Cement cost about the same [as in the US] and metal was about 20% more. I calculated $6 for labor."

They also worked with other crops. FBP had learned that in the Philippines the sheller was being successfully used for coffee, with a cross-section of inner tube pulled over the rotor like a condom. This provides one soft side which will hold the bean steady while the parchment is rubbed off by the concrete. A tractor-trailer inner tube fits perfectly. Now, in Iganga, "we set up a machine for coffee, but I found the results to be unimpressive. The locals, however, *were* impressed …. Several machines were [adapted] for coffee and sent out to the east [of the country] to be tested. Initial reviews were good."

In an e-mail to the FBP Board, Jock reports that they had done a demonstration of the sheller for the National

Agricultural Advisory Services (NAADS), a Ugandan aid organization. "They loved it and told us that they wanted one or two for each sub-district. Then they said that there were 19 counties with up to 80 sub-districts with permanent NAADS presence. You do the math. There followed a bit of arm wrestling to get our demo back. ... We promised to deliver two by Monday. It seems that in the Iganga district last year they threw away thousands of bags of peanuts because there was no one to shell them by hand."

The FBP team received an order from "a key UN/FAO guy" for 10 machines for the North. Jock assigned that project to the Nourish International group, who would "handle delivery, train people at FAO (the UN's Food and Agriculture Organization), and collect."

Jock did a presentation to The Hunger Project "which has a built-in microfinance system. That's the biggest issue when I talk to people."

Meanwhile, Roey Rosenblith went to Gulu, in northern Uganda, the site of big camps housing refugees from the civil war in Sudan. "That was a whole horrible part of Africa," Jock explained to me. "There were three civil wars – Sudan, Congo, and Uganda – going on at the same time. Rebel armies would move across borders to evade capture. It was a huge lawless area of revolutionaries who became bandits." Women in the refugee camps grew peanuts on the outskirts of the camps and used them as a cash crop. Roey was told by a worker with CARE International that each year hundreds of tons of food spoiled in the fields because there was no way of processing it, while at the same time people in the camps were starving.

Kenya and Sudan

Uganda was not the only country visited: Jeff Rose went to Kenya and Jock himself to Southern Sudan.[5]

Jeff, when I asked for information about his trip to Kenya, wrote:

> I visited the UN Millennium Village (Sauri) and met with the team there to introduce the UNS to them. We struck a deal with them whereby they would test the efficiency and economic impact of the UNS if we agreed to partner with them and provide new technologies for them to test out. We were hoping to ride on the Millennium Village Project's celebrity coat-tail by partnering with them and inserting ourselves as their R&D team. ... [However], after the uprising/coup occurred [in Kenya] in the fall of 2008 the agreement made by the field workers in Kenya became null and void in the eyes of the Millennium Challenge group [and] our deal fell through.

As regards Southern Sudan, FBP had, in the spring, received a request for information about the peanut sheller from Ezana Kassa, who worked for Norwegian People's Aid (NPA) and was in charge of one of the large refugee camps. Jay Tervo told him that the FBP team could bring a mini-factory with them to Uganda and asked if Ezana could send someone there to pick it up and learn how to build the machine. Ezana replied that he would, and that his group already had two blacksmith workshops making ploughs.

5 It's worth noting that, in among all the technical and promotion work he was doing, Jock was also managing the finances for "the army of people [on the team] and all their needs" – travel, food, accommodation. On the day after writing this e-mail, he was going to "set up my Sudan paperwork."

When he reached South Sudan, Jock ran a training session for Ezana and also for local women's groups processing shea, known in Africa as lulu.[6] The normal way of shelling them was to hit them with a stone; Jock saw women crouched down doing this, and often hurting their fingers in the process. Hurt fingers hamper further work. In a few moments, he adjusted the sheller to accommodate shea nuts, and it shelled them about 50 times faster than could be done by hand.

Jock had brought five shellers with him from Uganda and ran a training session for women's groups that were part of LuluWorks, an organization that creates sustainable livelihoods for women in South Sudan through the gathering of shea nuts and the production of oil.[7] I've been unable to find out where the five shellers are now, but none seem to be in use by the LuluWorks groups.

Assessment

While still in Uganda, Jock began reflecting on the trip's successes and failures. He was, he wrote to the FBP

---

6 Shea nuts, already mentioned in Chapter One, come from "a tree indigenous to Africa ... [whose] fruit consists of a thin, tart, nutritious pulp that surrounds a relatively large, oil-rich seed from which is extracted shea butter. ... historically, the shelling is done by mortar and pestle or by crushing the shell with a stone; however, the Universal Nut Sheller is an appropriate technology that reduces a significant amount of labor in shelling shea. ... In the West, shea is most often associated with cosmetics [but] throughout Africa it is used extensively for food and medicinal purposes. It is the major dietary lipid source for millions of Africans." http://en.wikipedia.org. Accessed on 14/4/2008.

7 Video "The Brilliance of Oil". http://infocusworld.org.

Board, looking forward to going to Southern Sudan. "It's our chance to pick a country for the right reasons." In Uganda, he wrote, except in the refugee camps in the north, there was no crisis and people were not starving, though the sheller provided "a major opportunity for poor people. ... I expect Sudan to be different."

Choosing an appropriate country is important. In Africa alone there are several dozen countries where FBP could, in ideal circumstances, do wonderful work; under less-than-ideal conditions they can still achieve something. One of Jock's requirements is that it must be

> a country where we have a rock-solid western-based NGO on the ground that is committed by its mission and money to make it happen. I expect Sudan to open us up to a circle of financial opportunities that will support Full Belly at home and abroad. I want to come back with new crops to process. Micro-credit was last year's buzz word. Post-harvest processing has now become the road block that everyone is bumping into. I want to get past peanuts and into the crops from just south of the Sahara where people's lives hang on the edge.
>
> I hope we can prove that we can do the tough projects, that we can live in tents, that we can build a factory [in a place] where everything isn't easy. Uganda was pretty easy.
>
> I realize that these are all topics and priorities that have to be decided on by the Board, that I'm not the person who sets these policies. But I am the "critter" that Noah sends out to find good and hospitable land.

In spite of the remark about Uganda being pretty easy, the Iganga project was beset with difficulties. The Masagazi family, already very wealthy, saw it not as a philanthropic undertaking but as a money-earner for themselves. FBP had heard from friends of Roey Rosenblith's who had travelled to Africa how wonderful the family were, and how dedicated to the welfare of Africa, and did not vet them any further. Jock said later that Jay's Rotary contacts in Uganda – or in fact any Kampala taxi driver – could have given them more reliable information. This is what lies behind Jock's remark about the need to have a partner on the ground who has the same mission and commitment as Full Belly. As a matter of fact, from Week Three onwards Jock in his e-mails to the FBP Board had been wondering whether another partner could be found and the whole operation moved somewhere else in Iganga. But they decided to try to make the existing arrangement work.

Moreover, the future of the Iganga shop was not secure. Everyone had assumed that it would be a year-round operation, but then they were told that during the coffee-processing season the space was needed for that work. "They would build us a new building within two months. A fast build in this country is two years."

The location was also not good. In Canada, Jock explained, a manufacturer of farm machinery would set up shop on the prairies rather than in Toronto. But in Uganda it should be in Kampala, where parts and materials are more easily found. Furthermore, every businessman would buy a sheller and take it to his native village. The strong connection which Ugandans have with their roots constitutes the best kind of distribution system.[8] And then there were the

_____

8 I've talked several times about these connections between people living in the cities and their rural families. The

finances: NAADS told Full Belly that the machine was fabulous, but after eight months there had still been no payment. Finally, because FBP just *gave* the shop to Henry Masagazi without asking for any commitment from him, FBP was unable do any follow-up. It has in fact completely lost touch with the operation, if there still is one. A rumour reached Wilmington that the shop had burned down, but an article published in the African magazine *New Vision*[9] seems to indicate that it was in operation in January 2008. Though we assume that communication is now global and almost instantaneous, it's sometimes surprisingly hard – or impossible – to get information.

It was, as they say, a learning experience and it led to the major success of Jock's later project, in Mali. However, on our way there we have to make a detour.

Malawi

While all this was happening, a connection was made with Malawi which would, by odd quirks and turns, lead to another FBP project. Roey Rosenblith had, in his hometown of St. Louis, heard about Dr. Mark Manary, also from St. Louis, who operated an NGO called Project Peanut Butter in Blantyre, Malawi. Project Peanut Butter makes Plumpy'nut, a Ready-to-Eat Therapeutic Food (RUTF). RUTF has

---

distribution system works very well *within* families or tribal groups, very badly across tribal boundaries.

9   Article dated 8 January 2008. http://allafrica.com/ stories/printable/200801090075.html. Accessed on 1/7/2010.

revolutionized the treatment of severe malnutrition [in children] ... It is a ready-to-use paste which does not need to be mixed with water, thereby avoiding the risk of bacterial proliferation in case of accidental contamination. The product, which is based on peanut butter mixed with dried skimmed milk and vitamins and minerals, can be consumed directly by the child and provides sufficient nutrient intake for complete recovery. It can be stored for three to four months without refrigeration, even at tropical temperatures. Local production of RUTF paste is already under way in several countries including Congo, Ethiopia, Malawi, and Niger.[10]

And, as we'll see, in Haiti.[11]

A few more details: malnourished infants get diarrhoea and become dehydrated. They lose weight and strength. Whatever is fed to them passes directly through their systems; milk products are vomited up. Malnutrition makes them vulnerable to disease. Until recently, the only hope was to hospitalize them and feed them intravenously. But in very poor countries there are too few hospital beds for all the sick children. Moreover, the mother is torn between the need to stay in the hospital to give her baby adequate care and the need to go home to look after her other children and carry on with the

---

10 http://www.who.int/child_adolescent-health/topics/prevention_care. Accessed on 2/7/2010.

11 RUTFs are relatively big business. In 2010, UNICEF distributed 1,229,640 cartons of the food to 49 countries. Jan Komrska, "Overview of UNICEF's RUTF Procurement in 2010 and Past Years." UNICEF Supply Division, Copenhagen, 18 October 2010. Accessed on 22 June 2011. In addition, there are manufacturers of RUTF who distribute the product directly, not through UNICEF.

farm work.

RUTFs are a solution. The peanut butter is so sticky that babies can't vomit it up, nor does it get flushed instantly through their system. In Malawi it produces a 95% recovery rate for severely malnourished children.[12] Mothers are given it to take home with them to feed to their babies.

Following up on Roey's contact, FBP had sent Dr. Manary a mini-factory, but it had never been used.

Then Brian Connors, the Assistant Peace Corps Country Director for Environment in Malawi, found the FBP website and "immediately saw the positive application of the sheller here." He e-mailed Jock, who put him in contact with Dr. Manary, who gave him the mini-factory. Brian also received the instruction DVD. In August 2006 he and a group of Peace Corps Volunteers "had a funny day watching a part of the video, then running outside to do what Jock told us in the video, then we'd repeat the process on the next stage. When there was a disagreement, someone would run in the house to watch the part where there was disagreement and then come out to inform the group."

That first sheller turned out well, but not all of them did. When two legs fell off a later machine, Brian invented a different kind of support. He writes: "I began making and destroying the shellers [saving the metal parts] to get a handle on them. Not every one came out well, and I had to try again. We don't really have a budget in the U.S. Peace Corps for that type of thing so I was doing it out of my pocket. Getting people interested was a

12 http://www.projectpeanutbutter.org. Accessed on 27/2/2009.

challenge too. I did a demonstration for the National Association of Small Holder Farmers [NASFAM] and they were amazed. They wanted to order as many as I could produce, but they never followed up on calls or emails to cement the deal."

The difficulty of finding parts in Malawi – for months Brian hunted in vain for a certain size of metal bar – didn't stop him from making shellers: he simply ordered parts from Wilmington, and sometimes a complete mini-factory. He knew about the facility in Iganga which – everyone assumed at the time – was manufacturing parts, but his ordering them from Wilmington indicates that he was not able to get them from Iganga.

His e-mails show him spreading the word: "I'm having an All Environment Sector gathering this weekend and we're having three [Peace Corps] Volunteers present their experiences (one of them shelled 10 tons of nuts in the past two weeks) and we'll do a demonstration with one of the shellers." He reports that at least two other NGOs would like two mini-factories each.

And he was evolving a longer-range plan.

> I need more practice putting [the sheller] together, and I don't want to be the one doing it. PCVs [Peace Corps Volunteers], together with local people who have invested in it, should be the ones. The way I imagine it is that PCVs could teach local people how to make them, work out a small-business plan, and supply the [mold] if others could provide the materials or at least pay the basic, or subsidized, cost. This way it isn't a giveaway. Ideally, we'd have people making the shellers to sell, and people shelling nuts as a service, and more happy people!

"Shelling nuts as a service" came to be one of the ways

in which a village used its sheller. Brian reported:

> One year ago [June 2007], when I was visiting the village [of Chilombo] to determine whether or not to put a PCV there, I was moved by the village's poverty [and] lack [of] opportunity and infrastructure .... The village leaders promised that as part of my placing a PCV there they would come together and officially submit a proposal for [a well to supply the village with drinking water] and Tim [Strong, the PCV] understood this when I placed him there. They all understood that there were no guarantees, but they were desperate.

An item on the Full Belly website continued the story, as Brian narrated it:

> New PCV Tim Strong was in the office one day 8 weeks ago and we were talking about the gnuts [ground nuts = peanuts] in his village. His community was looking for a way to raise match funding for a borehole [a well for clean water] .... Lots of money needed there! We were standing outside and I pointed to the sheller and told him to take it, as he had a ride to his site that day, and suggested that he introduce it and see if it'd work as a money maker. We talked over some quick strategies for using it to raise the match money.
>   Tim took the sheller and demo'ed it to the Village Development Committee (VDC) the next day, and they hashed out a plan to charge people for shelling nuts. As they were demo'ing the machine a business man from a nearby village walked by and watched. He spoke up and said that he was in the area to buy gnuts, and they told him of their plan. Well, he asked, would you like to shell the nuts I've got and I'll pay you for the work? They agreed, and the upshot of it is this: Last Friday, Tim's VDC completed their contract with the farmer after shelling 16 TONS OF GNUTS! ... They did another contract for another farmer for 7 tons, another for 3 tons, and a final

one for 4 tons. Final shelled amount was 30 tons in two months. On Monday they returned the machine to me, but they've got their match money in the bank. ... Borehole digging starts in early September – first potable water in the village. Once the new parts [for the sheller] are made, the VDC is going to make their own machine and continue their work. They have plans to press oil, make gnut butter, and want to try mixing chili with the shells to burn overnight in their farms to try to keep elephants out of their farms.[13]

Jim Nesbit, a member of the FBP Board who was in Chilombo in February 2008, learned that Tim Strong had "actually hauled the sheller from farm to farm on his bicycle, up and down hills and across rivers, to do the shelling for the farmers." Asked for follow-up information, Tim wrote to me that, when he left Malawi at the end of his tour of duty, the local farmers "were using the sheller to [shell] our gnuts before pressing them for oil [but that] unfortunately, as is wont to happen, an entrepreneurial businessman came to our trading center[14] and set up a diesel-powered gnut sheller and took most of the business."

Concerning the FBP sheller and CTI's grinder, Brian writes:

I do agree the two technologies go hand in glove – I just met with some doctors from a nearby rural hospital who talked about the severe malnutrition in their area; 40 children dead under the age of five in January due to

13 http://www.fullbellyproject.org. Accessed 8/5/2008.
14 A trading centre is a cluster of shops and small businesses on the highway, in the hinterland of which are found the villages where people live and farm. See picture on page 162.

complications stemming from malnutrition. Gnuts can fill a void that right now is killing people.

At this time I have 20 new Peace Corps Trainees … [At the end of the month] I'll be conducting a Mid-Service training for 20 first-year Volunteers. At this training we will be making shellers each day, hopefully about 15, and working out kinks.

In June 2008 he reports that a sheller had just been sent to a PCV whose "neighbours have collected 7 tons to shell, all of which will be sold to Plumpy'nut [Project Peanut Butter, Dr. Manary's organization] to pay for the [local] group's treadle pumps. … The PCV will get another sheller in two weeks because they've got about 150 tons of nuts in the area." By the following week, Brian would have 14 shellers ready for delivery, all of them destined for particular locations. He reported that there was a huge expansion of peanut cultivation in the area because of the demand from Plumpy'nut.

Jock, in his covering e-mail, underlines the important fact that "the village co-ops are using the surplus cash from the peanut shelling to buy other tools. The treadle pumps will allow people to stretch the growing season year round." The sheller is the basis for a whole system.

Because the project in Malawi developed into one of FBP's largest to date, a later chapter continues the story.

Ghana

Ghana is another peanut-growing country, but the use of the sheller there has been spotty.

In 2006, Full Belly was contacted by Alastair Knowles, a man from Winnipeg working in Accra. He had built several shellers for peanuts but had had difficulty centring the rotor (a badly centred rotor breaks too many nuts); however, with shea nuts, which are bigger than peanuts, the wobble didn't matter. "I focussed on promoting your machine for shelling shea nuts. ... Highly successful! The woman's group I was demonstrating it to spontaneously started dancing at the results. I have also been offering loans for the libraries to purchase their own local machine" to rent out as a fund-raising project.[15]

In summer 2009, Jock went to Ghana himself, in partnership with North Carolina State University. Dr. Rick Brandenburg, William Neal Reynolds Professor of Entomology in the College of Agriculture and Life Sciences at N.C. State, had called Jock. There was a bit of a crisis in Ghana: N.C. State, working with the USAID Peanut Collaborative Research Support Program (CRSP) and Ghana's Crops Research Institute (CRI) in Kumasi, had introduced new high-yielding peanut varieties into 30 villages. Farmers would have about four times their usual harvest, which sounded wonderful, but increased yields meant more nuts to shell by hand.

Jock went to Ghana mainly to teach technicians at CRI to make shellers. He was given workspace in a garage and began training the workers, but progress was slow: the men were easy to get along with but "by force of habit" (Jock's words) they worked for only three hours a day; Jock himself spent two days cutting the metal parts for the 30 machines. Although there was the capacity for making six machines daily, when Jock left Kumasi a couple of weeks later the workers were making only

15 I've tried in vain to contact Alastair for more details.

two per day, and only ten had been completed.

Rick Brandenburg and Jock, together with Dr. David Jordan, Cooperative Extension peanut specialist in crop science, demonstrated the shellers in several villages. Jock also showed that the sheller could be used for shea nuts, and he had with him the then-newly-developed portable water pump, dealt with in a later chapter.

Though Jock regarded the project as less than successful, Rick Brandenburg and his colleagues were pleased. "'The technicians now have completed the full complement of 30 shellers, and those are being distributed to five villages,' Brandenburg said. 'The feedback that I've gotten from everyone is that the shellers are the greatest thing since sliced bread! They think they're incredible.' ... Jordan has since incorporated the Full Belly Project into class lectures, helping undergraduate students understand the value of this development to Ghana's peanut growers." [16]

The problems Jock encountered, and the reasons for them, are instructive. The "garage" where the shellers were being built was CRI's vehicle-maintenance shop, and the workers were auto mechanics. They were not the least bit interested in making concrete shellers, knowing that as soon as the 30 machines were finished they would go back to repairing cars and trucks.

Jock's goals were also somewhat different than those of the people from N.C. State. He had hoped to arouse enough interest ·so that someone would continue manufacturing shellers, or even set up a small factory. What prevented this from happening might, oddly enough, have been the location of his temporary

16 Natalie Hampton, "Cultivating Efficiency."

operation. He discovered that in Kumasi there's a district that houses "the largest collection of appropriate-technology manufacturing shops and craftspeople in Africa. These are independent businesses who make some amazing machines from scrap. They all came here by osmosis. Machines are being invented and repaired all the time. If we had set up the shop in this area, it would have been an unqualified success."[17]

Biofuel

Besides peanuts and shea, the sheller is also good for shelling jatropha seeds, a potentially important source of biofuel.

From Uganda in 2007, Jock wrote to his colleagues in Wilmington: "Yesterday Full Belly got into the biofuel biz. We went to the big Royal Van Zanten greenhouses where they burn 250 gallons [11,360 litres] of fuel a day. They are planting huge areas of jatropha and buying from the locals, but there is the issue of husking. They were impressed by the demonstration of the machine and bought one. This is a great partner because they are very progressive ... and they are very inventive. And they are totally committed to biofuel. I believe this might be a bigger market than peanuts, in the long run."

Jatropha curcas is a shrubby tree "of Latin American origin which is now widespread throughout arid and semiarid tropical regions of the world, mainly Asia and Africa. It is a drought-resistant perennial, living for up to 50 years and growing on marginal soils." It's widely used on African farms as a hedge to keep animals out

---

17 The area is called the "Magasin"; I tried to find out more about it but haven't succeeded.

of cultivated fields and to reduce erosion by wind and water. The tree also improves air quality. The seedcake left after the nuts are pressed to extract oil is a good fertilizer and, being quite poisonous to grubs, locusts, and termites, is also a biopesticide. In fact, "the Jatropha system promotes four main aspects of development, which combine to help assure a sustainable way of life for village farmers and the land that supports them: renewable energy, erosion control and soil improvement, promotion of women [who are often the main harvesters and processors], and poverty reduction."[18]

"Traditionally the seeds were ... used for medical treatments and local soap production,"[19] and in Asia and Africa other parts of the plant are also eaten. The scientific literature reports that the plant is toxic – "all parts of the plant are considered toxic, but especially the seeds"[20] – but suggests that there may be two strains of jatropha.[21] Dr. Gael H. Pressoir, Executive Director and Research Director of CHIBAS, A Research Center on Biofuels and Sustainable Agriculture, told me that

---

18 Reinhard Henning, "Combating Desertification: The Jatropha Project of Mali, West Africa." http://ag.arizona. edu/OALS/ALN/aln40/jatropha.html.
19 Henning.
20 http://www.inchem.org/documents/pims/plant/jcurc. htm#PartTitle:2. Accessed on 12/3/2009.
21 Information from Jock: Jatropha is a relative of the plant that yields castor oil. When Jock was at the agroforestry headquarters in Bamako, Mali, he raised the question of whether jatropha is poisonous – with specific reference to whether handling the nuts allowed poison to penetrate the skin of the workers. The agroforestry people had no reports of long-term medical problems from people handling jatropha. (The people who empty the bags of husked cores wear masks, but that is because of the dust.)

there are definitely two strains: "I got to eat both and I can tell you there is a huge difference. One gets you sick and the other does not."

"As far back as the 1930s, the oil's potential as a fuel source was ... recognized. Currently, it can be used to substitute for the 'gazoil' mixture used in the Indian type diesel engines that drive grain mills and water pumps in rural areas of Mali."[22] As we saw, when Jock was in Mali in 2001, Dr. Ibrahim Togola of the Mali Folkecentre gave him a ride in a jatropha-powered vehicle. Jock saw people there processing the nuts by hand, which meant smashing them one by one with a rock. The process was so slow and laborious that it didn't occur to him then that jatropha could be used on an industrial scale. It occurred to no one that Jock had the technology that could achieve this.

Then, in December 2006, Jock heard from Illac Diaz, a contact of his in the Philippines, that they were using the peanut sheller to process jatropha.

* * *

The 2007 visit to Royal Van Zanten in Uganda had been planned in advance. RVZ is a Dutch company with greenhouses near Kampala that send cut flowers to Europe. An FBP staff member, having found an article about the company on the internet, wrote to RVZ in the Netherlands:

> The author [of the article] describes a facility to make biodiesel from Jatropha being built by Royal Van Zanten's Ugandan subsidiary in the Mukono District. The article caused a great deal of excitement amongst the staff

22 Henning.

of our organization, the Full Belly Project, as we are
about to build a production facility in the neighbouring
Iganga district that will be manufacturing hand-powered
machines that husk jatropha at a rate of 30 kg [66 lb]
an hour. The same machine is also capable of husking
peanuts, neem nuts, and shea nuts. The machine is unique
insofar as it is the first agricultural processing device that
uses concrete as its base material and is very easy and
cheap ($45 USD) to manufacture and has an estimated
lifespan of 20 years.[23]

He writes that a team from FBP will be in Uganda
in May-June and asks if they could meet with Bas
van Lankveld, the operations manager in Uganda.
Van Lankveld replied: "We started our project last
November and are currently dealing with local farmers,
who are collecting the [fruit] for us. We pick them up at
the various collection points. We have also established
our own plantation of 10 hectares [24 acres] and are
preparing the next 20 hectares for sowing. We hope
to harvest from our own plantation somewhere in the
middle of 2008. ... I think that your husking machine can
really contribute to our project. Currently the farmers
are removing the seeds with their hands, which is a lot
of work."[24]

At the meeting with the Full Belly team, RVZ bought
one husker, and later they bought several more from the
shop in Iganga. In August, in reply to a question from
Jock about how the husker was working, van Lankveld
replied, "We have put it into process, though our own
production is still little. Every time we get yellow [unripe]
fruits we use the husker and that is going perfect."

23 The 20 years is Jock's estimate: there are as yet no
   machines of that age.
24 The term "husking machine" or "husker" is often used to
   distinguish the jatropha sheller from the peanut sheller.

* * *

The biofuel potential of jatropha was at that time attracting interest around the world. In August 2007, the *Wall Street Journal* published an article by Patrick Barta about the cultivation of jatropha in India. "With oil trading at roughly $70 a barrel [as it then was], this lowly forest plant is suddenly an unlikely star on the world's alternative-energy stage. ... unlike other biodiesel crops, jatropha can be grown almost anywhere – including deserts, trash dumps, and rock piles. It doesn't need much water or fertilizer, and it isn't edible. That means environmentalists and policy makers don't have to worry about whether jatropha diverts resources away from crops that could be used to feed people."[25] However,

> ... it's still far from clear whether jatropha and its peers are economically viable on a large scale. By some estimates, the per-barrel cost to produce biofuel using jatropha – about $43 – is about half that of corn and roughly one-third that of rapeseed, two other leading materials for alternative energy. At those prices, jatropha biodiesel would be competitive with fuel made from crude oil without significant government subsidies. But such calculations are based on limited experience with the crop. ... Even some of jatropha's biggest advocates concede the plant's oil output is unpredictable and often lower than expected. Although it can grow without water, it tends to do much better when water is added, raising its cost of production and mitigating some of the perceived

25 Patrick Barta, "Jatropha Plant Gains Steam In Global Race for Biofuels", in *Wall Street Journal*, August 24, 2007, page A1. http://onlinewjs.com/article/SB118788662080906716.html. Accessed 29/8/ 2007.

benefits. ... Still, jatropha's allure is undeniable. Planting more palm oil, corn or other crops to make ethanol or biodiesel isn't really an option due to land shortages and other constraints.

Jatropha in Mali

A month later, *The New York Times* published an article that also dealt with jatropha[26] but focussed on Mali. Mali, the author writes, is "... one of the poorest nations on earth, [where] a number of small-scale projects aimed at solving local problems – the lack of electricity, and rural poverty – are blossoming ... to use the existing supply of jatropha to fuel specifically modified generators in villages far off the electrical grid." The author reports that a Dutch entrepreneur, Hugo Verkuijl, has started a company to produce biodiesel from jatropha seeds.[27] The company, Mali Biocarburant, is partly owned by local farmers' co-ops, and in December 2009 it was working with "more than 4,000 small *Jatropha Curcas* farmers in

---

26 "Poor farmers living on a wide band of land on both sides of the equator are planting it on millions of acres, hoping to turn their rockiest, most unproductive fields into a biofuel boom. They are spurred on by big oil companies like BP and the British Biofuel giant D1 Oils which are investing millions of dollars in jatropha cultivation." Lydia Polgren, "Mali's Farmers Discover a Weed's Potential Power", *The New York Times*, September 9, 2007. http://www.nytimes.com/2007/09/09/world/africa/09biofuel.html?. Accessed 9/4/2008.

27 Hugo Verkuijl, Ms Polgren writes, is "an economist who has worked for nonprofit groups." He "is one of a new breed of entrepreneurs who are marrying the traditional aim of aid groups working in Africa with a capitalist ethos they hope will bring longevity to their efforts."

3 regions of Mali and 2 regions of Burkina Faso."[28] It operates on the "3Ps" principle: "people, planet, profit, with equal priority." It has the financial backing of the Dutch government, the Royal Tropical Institute in the Netherlands, and the pension fund of Dutch Railways.[29] Mali Biocarburant "is ahead of other companies in the race to produce fuel from jatropha because it is not relying on new plantations to source its raw material. ... It is buying jatropha nuts already available from an estimated 20,000km [12,500 miles] of living jatropha fences that cover Mali .... The firm is also giving farmers seeds [seedlings, according to the Mali Biocarburant website] to increase crop output for the future." These are planted in areas where the soil is too poor for food crops or even grazing. "Rather than setting up large plantations, the venture is promoting jatropha as a means of diversification for farmers, encouraging its integration alongside millet, sorghum or maize. It has grown an additional 600 hectares [1,500 acres] since the start of the year [2007], with about two-thirds intercropped with local food crops."[30]

An e-mail from Jock (May 2008) picks up the story. He writes that the farmers collect the nuts in the fall, after their food crops have been harvested. To each village comes a truck from Mali Biocarburant, on which is mounted a high-efficiency oil press ..., a filtering system, and a tank. "The oil is pressed in the village and the farmers are paid by the litre. ... The waste solid material

28 http://www.malibiocarburant.com. Accessed on 9/12/2009.
29 Information from video on Mali Biocarburant website.
30 http://allafrica.com/stories/printable/200710311120. html. Accessed on 8/7/2008.

that remains after pressing ... is an excellent fertilizer, equal to dilute chicken manure. So that the farmers [who] arrive with bags of ... nuts leave with cash and sacks of fertilizer for their food crops."

There was, however, a major flaw in the system, and that was the gap where the low-tech village met the high-tech oil press. To husk the jatropha, the villagers threw the pods on the ground and flailed them with sticks. It was slow but, worse than that, when they scooped up the seeds (nuts) they also scooped up sand that damaged the oil press. Husking such quantities by hand was out of the question.

Hugo and Jock decided to see what the jatropha-adapted peanut sheller would do. In May of 2008 Jock and FBP Board member Diana Rohler went to Mali. They took two mini-factories and made several huskers, and set up a shop in which Mali Biocarburant could manufacture more.

> The ... machine husked 252 kg per hour, about 550 lbs. ... That means that one machine can process the total crop from 1 hectare (about 2 acres) in one day. The villagers all acted like they had just won the lottery, and so did Hugo. He will be setting up a small factory [to build the huskers], so we trained his workers. He will be distributing about 100 machines in time for this year's harvest, and given his expansion plans he will be introducing the machine all over West Africa. ... While we were there, delegations from all over Africa paraded through to see, first hand, how his system works. ... After we had demonstrated on jatropha, we did a fast adjust and shelled the local shea nut crop at almost the same rate. This gives the villagers one machine for two of their biggest cash crops.

Jock was also looking at the larger picture: "We saw that if there was ever a crop that could hold back the Sahara Desert, it is jatropha. That there will never be a surplus of vehicle/generator/water-pump fuel. And that a cheap, natural fertilizer that isn't petroleum-based could be a big food breakthrough. (In India, where jatropha production is more advanced, the companies make more money from the solid waste than from the oil.)"

Shortly after his return to Wilmington, Jock received word that the Mali Biocarburant shop was starting to make 50 machines. By January 2009 they had received an order from a different organization for 500. Peace Corps Volunteers would help promote jatropha cultivation, while Mali Biocarburant would provide free seeds. Kris Hoffer, who was with the Peace Corps there, wrote enthusiastically to Jock saying that she had received molds and that PCVs would be trained by the Mali Biocarburant people whom Jock had trained.

Fluctuations in the price of oil affect the desirability of jatropha, and at the time of writing interest in this biofuel is low. There are also problems with harvesting, to be discussed in Chapter Four. But jatropha should not be written off, even temporarily, especially not in countries where every bit of jatropha oil manufactured locally would decrease dependence on imported petroleum. In Malawi in August 2010, an official at Energem, an oil company with a significant interest in biodiesel, told Jock that "to make jatropha costs $90-95 per barrel, at a time when a barrel of oil in the Persian Gulf is $70. But the cost of importing and refining the oil, and driving it to Malawi, puts it well over $100." Hugo Verkuijl can manufacture jatropha oil profitably because in landlocked Mali all the petroleum has to be trucked in and the bribes to be paid at every "checkpoint" raise the price. "The beauty of jatropha biofuel is that you can produce it everywhere – wherever it is grown, on a small scale – and that it hardly has to be shipped anywhere."

Peanuts and water pumps in Senegal and Mali

In Senegal the peanut sheller has been introduced in several different projects. Robin Saidman, a photographer and social entrepreneur, found out about it and went to Wilmington to learn how to make it. Through his aid agency, Vital Edge Aid, he then introduced it to the town of N'dem in Senegal, where it is used in conjunction with a peanut-charcoal briquette system to provide fuel for the village bakery.

And there is another and much larger project as well.

David Campbell first saw the sheller when he was a senior at the University of North Carolina. He admired its simple efficiency, but it was only when he started working in Senegal in 2009 as a Peace Corps Environmental Education Volunteer that he realized its importance. "Senegal has a huge groundnut economy,"[31] he wrote to me. "When I arrived [in the village of Khossanto] people were shelling peanuts throughout my village in massive quantities. One evening I was shelling them by hand with my host mother, and after a

31 "Senegal is the world's sixth largest producer of groundnuts." *Random House World Atlas and Encyclopedia*, 2007, p. 175.

few hours and some very sore fingers, the light literally came on in my mind. I thought to myself, 'I know I've seen something that could save these women thousands of hours of time.' So the next time I was at the regional center and had internet access, I ran an internet search and came upon the Full Belly Project." He phoned the FBP office and ordered two mini-factories.

When they arrived, he got busy making and promoting shellers. (Having paid his way through college doing concrete work, making them was easy.) In April 2010 he wrote to me: "The past 10 months or so have been filled with experimentation with the [sheller], village trials and trainings, and we are set to launch into a new phase of the game." He had displayed the sheller at an all-volunteer conference in Dakar, the capital, which attracted PCVs from other West-African countries. A local NGO set up a production facility and began making machines for women's groups in "the peanut basket" of the country, and there was "a backlog of orders from individuals, women's groups, entrepreneurs, and whole villages."

At the same time he moved to the regional capital of Kedougou to focus his work on the sheller, linking the Peace Corps with "multiple other parties including the local technical high school, who will be producing the metal components," an NGO called La Lumière, which had "a sizable network of women's groups in the region," and several other NGOs.

A few months later he was travelling to other parts of Senegal and to neighbouring countries – Mali, Togo, and The Gambia – where interest had been shown. Also he hoped to find a larger manufacturer to make the metal parts – ideally to serve the whole country and perhaps the whole of West Africa – and also a plastics manufacturer to make molds. Another PCV had demonstrated the sheller to 15 women's groups in the central region of the country.

That fall (2010) David received a mini-factory for the rocker water pump (see later chapters for the background on this device). He wrote to Jock:

> First tests with the Rocker Water Pump were fantastic, and everyone that I've showed it to thus far has been very impressed. I put it on a Peace Corps car today to bring it to our All-Volunteer conference, [to be] held in a week in the capital. I've attached a document that I've been working on for the past month as a technical guide for the UNS that I will be using at the conference, so if you could look at it and give me some feedback I would really appreciate it. I had a co-volunteer with an arts background work on some of the graphics, and I think we put something really professional together.

A week or two later he reported: "I've been doing a lot of demonstrations on the Rocking Water Pump in the last couple of weeks since we got the first ones in order, and it looks as though we're going to have a fairly significant demand for it.... Everyone that has seen it thus far has been very impressed."

He was also building the newly-developed "midi" shellers (more about them in Chapter Six) and testing them on behalf of FBP; Jock told me that these tests showed the midi to be faster than the "classic."

Before leaving his post in Senegal in Spring 2011, David sent me a summary of what he had achieved: "There are currently over 40 UNS in operation in Senegal, in all the major regions including Kedougou, Velingara, Kaolack, Kolda and Tambacounda. They are owned/operated by a variety of individuals, microfinance groups, families and women's groups. There is a fully functional UNS assembly facility in Kedougou and one in development in Kaolack." And he lists some of the villages – there are 21 names in this partial list – that have one or more shellers each. "The rocker pumps are so much newer in our program that they haven't been distributed in mass yet. They are only in use in one village with a school garden. Their extent may spread soon thanks to two new volunteers who have committed to distributing them on a large scale in their respective regions."

Responding to my question about the prospects for his work being continued after he leaves, he wrote:

I have high hopes that the work we did will not fizzle out. To make the most of this hope, I held a technical training in my region two weeks ago to train volunteers from other regions how to build, assemble and distribute all of the technologies we have worked with over the last two years, including the UNS and the new rocker pump. Sustainability is a big theme in the PC, so I was trying to do my part to make our project durable. For three days we tried to transfer my field experience into their hands with the intent that they will take this knowledge back to their regions and start initiatives of their own. Now three regions are equipped with the skills and the molds for both the UNS and rocker pump, so the capacity is there.... These devices still need to be tested, and the only way to do so is to get as many out there as we can.

My local counterpart is now getting solicitations more and more regularly for both shellers and pump systems, so even if the Peace Corps network fails to adopt them, there is a local craftsman, Saliou Kante, who will hopefully continue to promote and market them to farmers and locals who could benefit from these devices.

The two volunteers interested in carrying on David Campbell's work are Marcie Todd and Garrison Harward, who both started work in Senegal in August 2010. Marcie is based in Kolda, one of the regions mentioned in David's final report as already having shellers. Garrison is in the Fatick region.

* * *

In Mali the sheller, already in use for jatropha, is being promoted for peanut-processing by Josh Litwin, a Peace Corps Environment Volunteer. His story, which he sent to me in May 2011, is worth quoting in some detail – one of those close-ups which takes us into people's life and work.

> I first heard about the Full Belly Project through my old Assistant Program Country Director (APCD) Kris Hoffer. An old volunteer had a UNS mold sent in order to try and shell shea nuts. Unfortunately I don't have any information on how that attempt went. When Peace Corps Mali moved locations the sheller mold was misplaced so Jock sent a second one with additional parts.[32] After a few false starts (taking the cement out when it was too wet, or not leveling the mold and having to re-pour the cement a second time) I was able to make two UNS shellers to test out in my village of Niagadina (pop. 5,000 located 1.5 hours drive south of Bamako along the Niger river).
>
> My homologue[33] demonstrated the shellers to the local women's association members who were very excited about its potential. One sheller is being housed and administered by the village chief's wife, Salimata Traore,

32 Josh eventually found the missing mold: see below.
33 A homologue was (Josh's own phrase) a "village coworker." Marcie Todd uses the word "counterpart" and explains: "A counterpart is a Senegalese person who helps you enter the community and work force."

and the second mold is … at the house of the president
of the women's association. Since most peanuts are kept
in the shells while they are stored, and shelled little by
little to make lunch and dinner sauces, the machines have
not been heavily used. I am told, however, that after the
peanut harvest (Sept-Nov) there will be a need to shell
larger quantities of peanuts. I think little by little women
and men alike are catching on to the usefulness of the
sheller and the time it saves. There are other metal peanut
shellers in the village, but the women have reported
that the UNS is easier to use (uses a rotating arm motion
rather than a jarring back and forth motion) and has a
lower breakage rate. The women agreed to charge a small
user fee per tin of peanuts, the proceeds of which will
be deposited into the association's account and used for
further income-generating activities or divided among the
group members.

We did try shelling shea nuts, although with less
success. I think there were several factors at play. One,
the rotor was not entirely centered so some nuts merely
dropped out and were not shelled. Also shea nuts have
a greater variation in shape and size making it harder
to shell them without first sorting them which is more
time-consuming. Also, the women's association members
shell small amounts of shea themselves using a mortar
and pestle which is also a social event for many women.
I think once the association is able to gain more of a
profit from the shea nuts and butter that they produce
and production increases, there will be more of a need to
mechanize the work. Also, some of the larger shea kernels
left oily shea residue on the sides of the stator which
decreased friction and allowed for more nuts to drop
through the machine unshelled. I am not saying that the
machine is not useful for shea, but merely saying that in
my village's case, it didn't catch on.

I was able to make a 3rd and 4th UNS for
demonstration at our training center (TubaniSo, located
in Bamako) and one for our Bureau (also located in
Bamako). While I was making the shellers at TubaniSo, I

ran across the old UNS mold that Kris Hoffer had sent which was very exciting! So now we are able to double production capacity of the sheller. Another volunteer, Lindsey Diericksen, a water and sanitation volunteer in Mopti, is going to make some UNS shellers ... to demo in the northern regions of Mali. My homologue ... and I are now looking for a metalsmith here in the capital city of Bamako who can reproduce the metal parts of the sheller. We have not yet created a production facility.

He reports that Mali Biocarburant is selling the shellers for about US$120 but that David Campbell was trying to get it down to about $50-70.

I think both the UNS and rocker pumps have great potential in Mali both for agriculture and small business development. Although everything here in Mali is still in the testing phases (there have been no big successes yet), I am working hard to transfer the technology to Malians and other Peace Corps volunteers. I plan on training other volunteers to take over the project and continue any progress made after I complete my service this August [2011].

* * *

In West Africa, therefore, there's a cluster of successes and a sense of building momentum. David Campbell's enthusiasm communicated itself to Marcie and Garrison – and, more important, to the local people who will be the best hope for the ongoing manufacture and distribution of the machines.

This is the success of the mini-factory model. David and Josh are working entirely from kits and instructions – neither was trained by Jock – and they're passing on their skills and experience to others.

And it is the success of appropriate technology – scaled to suit the family and the village, affordable, reproducible locally, and working with nature and the environment.

The village depicted is Pondala, in the Kedougou region, the far south-east corner of Senegal near the borders with Mali and Guinea. The drummer in the picture is the village griot, a story-teller who uses song to transmit the lineage of the people and recite history. This griot is blind and finds his way around the village by using the memory imprinted in his head.

I asked David Campbell about what looks like a piece of fibrous material attached to the drum. He said that it was actually a metal plate with rings attached to it that make a jangling sound as the drum is struck by the musician.

The village chief is named Diangoba Damfakha; the peanut sheller that I donated to the village will be kept at his house for the rest of the village to use.

Photo Credit: David Campbell.

THREE

Asia

The Philippines

One of the people who saw the *Peanuts* film in MIT's D-Lab course in September 2005 was Illac Diaz, a graduate student from the Philippines. He immediately wrote to Full Belly saying that he would like to introduce the machine to the northern Philippines, where peanuts are a common crop and where he thought the women could use it to earn money for educational supplies for their children. He also wanted to experiment with a lighter kind of cement. He asked for and received a mini-factory.

When Jock was at MIT that fall, he taught Illac how to make the sheller. Then Illac – as part of the D-Lab dispersal in January 2006 – went to the Philippines and made a machine there. It was a big success, and he realized that if he had more money he could do more with the sheller. So he and Jock decided to try for one of MIT's $5,000 "IDEAS" awards. "The IDEAS competition provides an opportunity for members of the MIT community to develop their creative ideas for projects that make a positive impact in the world. Participants work in teams to develop designs, plans, strategies, materials, and mechanisms that benefit communities, locally, nationally or internationally."[1] Each winning team – there are several every year – "has to demonstrate to the judges that their project [is] innovative, sustainable, and feasible."[2]

However, only a *new* machine would be eligible. So, for a team which Illac set up with fellow-students, Jock invented a new machine – the basic sheller operated by pedal power – and it won one of the awards in Spring 2006.

The business plan which Illac wrote as part of his project – already referred to in the Introduction – gives background information. The Philippines has an annual demand for peanuts of 92,000 metric tons, of which 59,000 are imported. Growing more peanuts locally would keep a lot of money in the country. "The main problem stems from the inability of small farmer groups to produce a consistent volume for the local industries because of the manual nature [hand-shelling] of their production. Despite the high demand for peanuts in the country, the industry continuously experience[s] low domestic yield resulting in importation ...."

Besides keeping money in the country, peanut agriculture would alleviate poverty and improve nutrition.

Peanuts provide a much-needed source of purchasing power to small-scale farmers, many of whom are women. Peanuts are nutritious food and versatile in use and thus

1 http://web.mit.edu/ideas/www.about.htm . Accessed on 27/4/2008.
2 http://web.mit.edu/ideas/www/pastprojects_0506winners.htm . Accessed on 27/4/2008.

promote health and family welfare and value-added industries in developing countries. As local markets exist for peanuts, they provide an essential opportunity for small-scale subsistence farmers to purchase ... fertilizers .... Peanuts are very important in a number of ways to food security at the household level. First, the peanut is a high energy, high protein food that is highly effective in satisfying hunger, thus a little peanut goes a long way in feeding a family. Secondly, peanut is a crop that is easily processed and transformed into higher-value products that are easily marketed. As such it provides women with a means of generating income to allow purchases of other foods, medicines and education for the family members.[3] Third, as a legume in the cropping system the peanut is one of the most effective of nitrogen fixers which allows it to sustain general cereal grain production at higher levels, directly and indirectly increasing household food security. High yields of cereals result in lower market prices and increase the availability of food per unit of income.

Illac expands on the nitrogen-fixing aspect of peanut agriculture when he talks about the effect of the 1991 explosion of Mt. Pinatubo: "For hundreds of kilometers, previously fertile clay lands [were] layered by sand and ash [which] drastically altered traditional planting practices. With this bike machine [the pedal-operated sheller], we intend to improve the transition to peanut farming, which would be perfectly suited for these new soil top layer[s]." The layers of sand and ash were, he writes, as deep as four metres [about 13 feet].

3 Elsewhere in the document he gives prices: in 2005, the farm price for unshelled fresh [i.e. not sun-dried] peanuts averaged Php 13.78 per kilogram; for unshelled dry nuts it was Php 16.03 per kilogram, and for shelled nuts farmers received Php 48.00 per kilogram. This shows the financial advantage to farmers of being able to sell the nuts shelled.

Traditional crops like vegetables and rice "no longer grow easily on this soil; but peanuts are [a] perfectly suitable alternative cash crop." Jock, on his trip to the Philippines a few months later (see below), saw buildings in the area near Mount Pinatubo that were half-submerged in volcanic ash. Moreover, the high rainfall typical in the area eroded the hillsides and spread the ash across the low-lying land. This ash is potentially fertile – Jared Diamond, in *Collapse*,[4] writes that volcanic ash brings nutrients to the surface – but it needs a starter crop like peanuts.

In January 2006, after his first demonstration of the peanut sheller in the Philippines, Illac wrote to Jock: "The Philippines peanut peeler is a SUCCESS. As we turned the handle ..., the shells fell like flakes and the peanuts dropped without even their skin being scratched. I had to really dig deep into the bucket to believe my eyes. ... Now the challenge is to eliminate this form of terrible manual labor for all here."

The sheller "raised the interest of the Holcim Cement Group in the La Union area where they wanted to introduce the machine. ... These [*sic*] began a series of talks which led to a seminar that brought a group of farmers to the factory to build 40 shellers." Eventually "hundreds of machines [were] built in partnership with the Holcim Cement Company and CentroMigrante, a Filipino NGO."[5] The MyShelter Foundation, of which Illac Diaz was Executive Director, found a Japanese fiberglass worker who would manufacture molds.

---

4   Jared Diamond, *Collapse: how societies choose to fail or succeed.* (New York: Viking, 2005.) 116, 380.

5   http://www.fullbellyproject.org. Accessed on 8/5/2008.

Back to Illac's earlier report: "Ten fiberglass molds were brought to the province [of Isabela] for a two-day workshop where 50 participants built shellers which were later distributed among the farmers. The governor has created a subsidy of Php 2000 which is 75% of the cost for people that would want to purchase the shellers for use on their farms. As of the moment[6], we are informed that more than 1000 shellers have been acquired in this manner. Universal Nut Shellers have been sent to Indonesia as a seed project.[7] We anticipate more growth as the desire to have the Sheller grows."[8]

This burst of activity took place in the early months of 2006 and involved the hand-operated sheller; Jock, in Wilmington, was still developing the pedal-operated one. The first version of the latter – this was the winner of the MIT prize – was simply an adaptation of the basic sheller, but Jock quickly realized that separating the nuts from the shells as they fell would be another major improvement. Accordingly, the next version included a winnowing fan, turned by the same pedaling motion that operated the rotor. The pedal-powered, fan-equipped machine shells the nuts only slightly faster

---

6 The precise date is not available: this comes from Illac's undated report. The chronology is obscure: what we do know is that the sheller was first made in the Philippines in January 2006, and it's not clear how "more than 1000 shellers" were made in the 2-3 following months. Illac is difficult to reach and by now (2010) he has moved on to other projects.

7 According to Illac Diaz's business plan, Indonesia was the source of 45% of the peanuts that the Philippines imported.

8 http://www.fullbellyproject.org/philippines.php. Accessed on 8/5/2008.

than the manually-operated one but, because it saves the extra step of winnowing, it greatly increases the efficiency. And, because legs are stronger than arms, it does so with much less labour. It is also easily motorized (as was to happen in Haiti – see next chapter).

Jock in the Philippines

This is, however, getting ahead of the story. In June 2006 Jock went to the Philippines to build one of the pedal-powered sheller-with-fan machines and test it at a peanut farm; he would also demonstrate the hand-operated version to the press. Moreover, he hoped to set up "a Full Belly connection with Holcim [Cement] outside the Philippines."

In his luggage he had packed "all the little time-consuming parts for the pedal-with-fan project," but that bag had gone missing. Therefore, immediately after his arrival – without taking time to overcome jet lag – he began to make these parts. What he was building was the base for the pedal machine – it was only the second one he had ever made – to which he would attach one of the manual shellers that Illac had already constructed.

In an e-mail he refers to welding in "the sauna", an allusion to the tropical heat. He writes: "It's 95 and humid. ... My shop here makes Francine's garage[9] look like MIT .... Thank God I'm an old fart and still know how to weld with a stick welder 'cause that's what we got." "The kitchen staff [of Illac's family, with whom he was staying] keeps plying me with ice water and

9 This was the supporter's garage which served as the FBP shop in Wilmington at that time.

commenting that white people don't normally get this dirty. And they CERTAINLY don't weld."

A few days after Jock's arrival, while he was still constructing the pedal machine, the hand-operated sheller was officially unveiled in an event attended by "9 big newspapers from every part of the country." Jock writes: "Big success. Lots of press. When I cranked the handle and the nuts flowed out, there was an audible 'AHHHHHH' from the reporters and photographers. ... This was supposed to be just for the press but five TV crews showed up. The Holcim people are totally on board and excited. ... Next week we go up north to their big plant where we will start mass production. They were totally amazed that you can make something else than roads, bridges, and buildings out of cement."

The connection with Holcim Philippines Inc. looked promising. The company operated three schools where masonry work was taught and which therefore had suitable facilities. Experience in building shellers would be a marketable skill for the students, and the instructors would do quality control. The country's ten agricultural schools would distribute the shellers. If this trial project succeeded, Holcim would support Full Belly world-wide.

For reasons which I've been unable to discover, this plan seems never to have worked in every detail, or not for very long. Nor did anything come of a seminar which Jock gave at the University of the Philippines' engineering school, whose students would also be trained to build the sheller. The often-inexplicable failures of some of FBP's projects will be dealt with in Chapter Seven.

* * *

When Jock took the pedal machine to a farm for its first real test, he learned that none of the existing shelling systems could cope with batches of peanuts of different sizes. The Full Belly sheller, however, sorts the nuts by size as well as shelling them: the first time a batch of nuts is put through the machine, it is set to shell the larger nuts, and the small ones emerge untouched. Then the machine's setting is adjusted, which takes only a moment, and the smaller nuts are put through again.

This test provided statistics about the breakage rate – "breakage" being defined as damage to the nut's brown inner coat. The University's best technology resulted in a breakage rate of 40%, and the commercial mill's rate was 20%. The FBP sheller's was (and is) 5 to 8%; in fact, Illac's business plan reports it as 3.1%.[10]

The pedal-powered sheller, like other FBP machines, is designed to use locally-available parts. Besides incorporating the basic sheller – easily replicable anywhere – the pedal machine requires an oil drum and metal pipe, both of which are made (and available) in standard sizes world-wide. Bearings were locally made of hardwood so that they could be easily replaced. (There are many examples of a well-oiled hardwood bearing outlasting a metal one.) The belts and pulleys are of a kind commonly used in ventilating systems in developing countries. Molds can be replicated wherever

10 He states that the pedal-operated sheller had "a shelling efficiency of 96.9%."

there is someone working with fiberglass, and the metal parts for the innards of the sheller are easy to copy.

* * *

Other developments took place in the Philippines, such as a project to use the peanut shells for fuel. Jock had become interested in this when he found on the internet a very old report concerning the French colonial railway system in West Africa. The locomotives traveling from Dakar (Senegal) to Bamako (Mali) were powered on their trip inland by coal, and on the return trip by peanut shells. These, being very waxy, burn quickly and, pound for pound, have as much as two-thirds the thermal output of coal. Holcim Philippines Inc. set up a system in which the shells were used for fuel. By November 2006, Jock was able to report: "The shellers are made by the cement company and farmers pay for them with peanut shells which are used for fuel in the cement-making kilns of the cement company. And the [Holcim] head office in Zurich gets carbon credits (for not burning fossil fuels) that they can sell. Everybody wins." Again this project did not last.

In the Philippines, Jock also began working on a way to use the pedal machine as a platform for several add-ons, such as a simple cotton gin. He hoped and planned that it could be used to power a water pump and a grain processor as well. By then, the local people had already made adaptations to the sheller: they were the ones who put rubber around the rotor to shell coffee.

A couple of months after Jock returned home, Illac reported that he had been "terribly busy selling shellers (at a loss) to different parts of the Philippines …. The peanut sheller is about to take off." He also writes that the sheller can process jatropha nuts. However, three and a half years later he wrote to Jock that "the sheller died out ... in the north." I've been unable to obtain details.

Another project in the Philippines

A week before going to the Philippines, Jock had received what he called "a typical request." Mr. Joy Young, who identified himself as "consultant for education to the Mayor of Cebu City in the Philippines", wrote that 20% of the 150,000 students in the city's public elementary and high school system are malnourished. There is a food program – mostly funded by concerned but poorly paid teachers – but the food is porridge or bread, without protein. "I was therefore excited reading the story of Mr. Brandis when he went to Mali to help Ms. [Carrie] Young. Few people grow peanuts here because it is hard work to shell them. Instead they are growing corn which quickly and have in fact [sic] depleted the land already. With the peanut sheller we could encourage farmers or families to plant peanuts in their backyards even just for home consumption solving our malnutrition problems. The city schools can even plant peanuts as most of our schools have some space behind the buildings."

Jock replied that on his then-imminent trip to the Philippines he would provide information and molds to the ten agricultural colleges in the country and suggested that Mr. Young contact the one nearest to him. Young replied that there was no agricultural college on the island of Cebu and that he couldn't afford to fly to Manila, but he would ask friends in Manila to buy a mini-factory and ship it to him. By now his vision and his plans extended beyond the city schools: in the surrounding province, he says, "the problem of poverty is even worse." Even the farm families who are raising corn, usually just for their own consumption, can't have three square meals a day. "There is so much land out there that could be planted with peanuts. Instead this land are [sic] growing weeds!" Beyond that again, he is on the board of trustees of a non-profit foundation working with farmers and hopes to convince the board to adopt the sheller and promote peanut farming.

The story resumes in August, when Joy Young delightedly wrote to Jock to say that Illac Diaz was coming to Cebu in a few days "to turn over a set of molds and one working cement peanut sheller! ... I have just been re-inspired by you and Illac and you can rest assured that I will now work double time to promote your mission."

However, as I learned when I wrote to Mr. Young, this project also ran into difficulties. The school board's chief engineer, to whom Young had given the molds and the instructional DVD, resigned and so did four more engineers who followed him in (apparently) quick succession. In this upheaval, the DVD and some pieces of the mold were mislaid. By the time Young was writing to me, he had collected the parts of the mold and had found the DVD.

But that did not solve all the problems. It was difficult to persuade people to plant the nuts. Peanuts growing in a field were easy to steal. Moreover, farmers who did plant them sold the crop while it was still in the ground and therefore didn't need a sheller.

However, in northern Cebu island there were many people already planting peanuts. A friend of his, the manager (I gathered) of the foundation helping farmers, was going to look into the idea of sending a sheller to that location "if he can get the folks there organized." Young wanted to give shellers only to people who would use them properly. Also he wanted to "look for where there are many people already planting peanuts and distribute the sheller there as against trying to convince people to plant peanuts because we have a sheller."

This project is continuing.

Tajikistan and Cambodia

The sheller has been introduced in other parts of Asia, and here the "scatter-shot" aspect of its dispersal is very obvious.

An order came from Tajikistan. After the mini-factory was sent, FBP lost contact, but when CNN broadcast a story about Jock and the sheller, FBP received a short e-mail from Tajikistan: "We love Full Belly!" FBP, e-mailing back to ask for information, received a picture of the sheller mounted on a big industrial fan, and then contact was again lost.

In November 2007[11], Michele Tayler made plans to take a peanut sheller to Cambodia to help a community of battered women and former sex slaves to process the local peanut crop. After visiting Wilmington to learn how to make the sheller, she wrote: "Have some concerns

11 The date and quotation come from her e-mail to Full Belly of 13 November 2007. The brief note about her work in Cambodia is from http://www.starnewsonline.com. Accessed on 11/5/2008.

about getting the peanut sheller to Cambodia and figure there are 3 options. One is to take a pre-built one with me ..... yikes, how heavy is that? and probably prone to breakage?? ... option #2 is to take a whole kit with me ... repeat-yikes, how heavy is that? ... and option #3 is to wait until the timber is ready to ship (next year). I'd like to investigate options 1 or 2 as both the peanut farmers and the jatropha growers are anxious to see it."

Jock told me that Michele was a music producer based in Manhattan. She had never worked with liquid cement in her life, but after her training in Wilmington she went to Cambodia and made a perfect machine. She also got involved with jatropha-processing there. "The most unlikely people can learn to make this sheller," Jock remarked when he had told me about Michele.

In an update in April 2011, Michele (by then living in San Francisco) wrote:

> The peanut/jatropha project is in mothballs ... right now. We've had to steer our limited funds & attention to more direct action about gender-based violence and education. Our first peanuts venture was not wildly successful – problems with land, access, group dynamic – you name it. Lack of training and oversight were also problematic. I've lost track of my 'jatropha man' up in the north too. So while our initial flurry of activity was noteworthy – just getting the darned thing built will stay in my mind/heart for ever – we will have to look for other opportunities to put it into play.

Biofuel in India

In the quirky way so typical of the FBP's work, a project in India is proving to be very successful. It began with Dr. Paul Wilkes, a theologian who teaches in Wilmington and is Executive Director of an orphanage in southern India. FBP had given him a mini sheller (more later about this device) and a set of molds to take with him. There, to demonstrate what the machine could do, he threw in a handful of neem nuts.[12] The neem nuts came out shelled.

Dr. Wilkes took the sheller to the nearby Hassan Biofuel Park, of which Dr. Balakrishna Gowda is the Project Coordinator. Dr. Gowda was excited about the sheller and "within minutes," as Jock tells it, "there were fifteen PhDs clustered around with tape measures and cameras trying to figure out how it worked and how to duplicate it."

Then, in March 2008, Jock received an e-mail from Scot Frank, working in Bangalore, India. Scot wanted to apply for a position as intern with Full Belly, but Jock, in his reply, seized on another part of his e-mail: "You are in Bangalore? Perhaps for several more months?? What a happy coincidence. We have just attracted the attention of Dr. Gowda, who heads up the Biofuel Park Project, just north of you. He is very excited about using our 'mini sheller' to shell neem. He has already tested the machine and seems to be eager to move forward. There are about 2,500 villages in the park that would benefit and we would like to figure out a way to set up a

12 Neem grows widely in India, Myanmar, and Bangladesh. Its seeds, leaves, flowers, and bark are used in many different medicines. Growing on sandy soil and requiring little water, it is "is of great importance for its anti-desertification properties and possibly as a good carbon dioxide sink." It is also used as a biopesticide. http://en.wikipedia.org/w/index.php?title=Neem. Accessed on 1/3/2009.

small factory to make these very simple machines. The beauty of Dr. Gowda's plan is that he wants to keep production, processing, and profits at the village level, which is also our philosophy."

Scot asked Jock whether he had any specific requests or directions. Jock didn't pass up this chance to get information. He replied: "First, we are surprised that neem is being used as a biofuel, considering how expensive it is here and how much labour is involved. Is it being government-subsidized? How many litres per tree or hectare can be obtained? Compared to other economic activities, how will this add up? What other biofuels (jatropha, etc.) are in the works and what statistics does he have on the potential for them? How many farming families would benefit from this technology?"

Scot, after meeting with Dr. Gowda, answered all the questions. Prices of non-food oil crops appear to be lower in India than in the U. S., and both the production in the Park and the final biofuel price are subsidized. Young neem trees produce 1-2 litres [just under half a gallon]; 5-year-old trees produce 25-50 litres [roughly 5-10 gallons] , "and some species at a much older age yield 100-120 litres [22-26 gallons]." The villagers plant the trees on unused land. Dr. Gowda "is utilizing many different biofuel species …. In all, it looks like they are starting with about 6 primary varieties."

There are approximately 100 people living in each of 2,500 villages. "Initially Dr. Gowda would like 1-2 community shellers per village, and some individuals may opt to purchase their own."

Jock asked whether the mini sheller is what is needed for each village, or would a larger one, with more volume, work better. He asked whether Biofuel Park would be able to set up a small workshop for building the shellers. Did Dr. Gowda need molds and instructions sent by courier?

Scot's reply: "Dr. Gowda can see use for both the mini and the larger version. ... Initially, he is looking at 2,500-5,000 machines. I am unsure of the exact budget available, but it seems Dr. Gowda can find government funding for local production of these machines. He says he is already prepared to arrange for a workshop to be set up. ... He is looking to begin as soon as possible."

Jock asked what kind of press would be used to extract the oil from the neem kernels. Scot reported that he would post pictures. And in December 2008 Paul Wilkes told Jock that he had seen Dr. Gowda again, that modifications had been made in the sheller design, and that at least 60 of the shellers had by then been made and distributed.

Dr. Gowda himself reported to Jock: "Our people were very interested in this machine. We improvised [improved?] the machine in terms of fit and finish and also the movable metal parts for durability. It was interesting that this machine can now be used for making [sic] coffee beans after sun drying the berries. A good tool for small farmers and also ecofriendly minimizing/avoiding use of precious water for pulping."[13]

---

13 Dr. Gowda's comment about saving water refers to the fact that there are two techniques for processing coffee. In the "wet" process the berries containing the beans are soaked so that the pulp can be removed: this uses a great deal of water. In the "dry" method, which is the older one, the berries are dried in the sun; the resulting product

By November 2009 Dr. Gowda reported that they had built about 50 machines and that each one could process 25-30 kg [about 70 lb] of neem seeds per hour.

In January-February 2011 FBP received more information about the Bangalore project. Dr. Susan Bullers, who teaches a course on the Sociology of Food at the University of North Carolina Wilmington, and who was formerly one of FBP's Saturday-morning volunteers, took a group of students to visit the Bangalore Biofuel Park. On her return, she wrote a report for FBP.

> In addition to some use for food-crop peanuts, this Sheller serves mainly as a pivotal part of a unique agricultural research project [which] explores the feasibility of growing biofuel seed trees in areas of existing family farms that are not currently used for crops. The research station cultivates the saplings of several types of oil-seed trees[14] and provides them to local farmers. Farmers then plant the saplings along narrow strips of land along roadsides and footpaths or close to structures where they do not take up existing cropland. When the trees mature the seeds are then harvested and taken to a nearby community processing facility where they are shelled and refined into biofuel.

In an e-mail to me, Dr. Gowda says: "The machine is doing well. People are inquiring on this machine.

is called unwashed or natural coffee. Not only does this process save water – which is often in short supply – but the coffee produced is generally considered superior. http://en.wikipedia.org/w/index.php?title=Coffee_ processing. Accessed on 8/11/2009. As mentioned in the previous chapter, the sheller is used for removing the "parchment" from the coffee bean.

14 In an e-mail of 4 February 2011, Dr. Gowda reports that he is working with neem and jatropha trees, as well as coffee and groundnuts.

We could manufacture another 25 of the machines and provide it to the people in addition to the first fifty machines that were provided to the people and also kept for demonstration in our centers. Many new applications are coming up."

Shelling walnuts in northern India

Another project took a Full Belly device to northern India. This story began when Ariel Phillips, one of the instructors in the D-Lab at MIT, wrote to Jock with a question that's typical of the kind of thing he receives, and the subsequent correspondence gives a rare glimpse into the creative process. Because the chronology is an important part of the story, there are lots of dates.

It was on Monday, 24 November, 2008, that Ariel wrote to Jock: "I'm working with a group of MIT students this fall, and we'll be going to northern India in January to work with a community group. One thing the India people would like is a walnut sheller. They currently shell them by hand, one at a time. Have you guys tried shelling walnuts (English walnuts) with your sheller? Any suggestions would be great!"

Jock bought walnuts at a Wilmington supermarket and tested them. Later that day he e-mailed Ariel: he had found that there was a considerable breakage rate and asked, "How do you define breakage? I assume that you want two complete halves. Is there a market for smaller pieces?"

Ariel replied: "We're not actually sure if there's a market for smaller pieces, but we can email and ask. It may take a few days for an answer, but I'll let you know ASAP. Thanks for the quick work!"

Jock wrote the next day:

> So I spent the day looking at walnuts in the machine. The fact is that all they need is about 2 rotations and [then] the shell is shattered but still intact [attached to the nutmeat] and the nutmeat isn't broken. But it's still in the machine and that's where the damage occurs. It happens while the nut is escaping out the bottom. So if you cast an escape chute in the outer concrete part and all the walnuts enter the machine two revolutions upstream from the chute ....
>
> Then the nuts drop in at 12:00 o'clock, they drop to the right narrowness and catch. They [revolve] twice which gets them to 3:00 o'clock, at which point the shell is shattered but intact. Suddenly the vertical wide space, the chute, appears and the nut drops straight down without breaking the meat.
>
> I'll get volunteers to cast an outer piece this Saturday. ... We should have some numbers soon. Whatever, we'll have a set of molds for a test machine before you go. How much product are you thinking?

Jock continues inventing, and on Thursday the 27th he describes to Ariel what he has come up with:

> The design is a shorter, sturdier [version of the] peanut sheller with an "escape chute" cast into the concrete and a continuous column of nuts dropping into the machine an adjustable number of degrees ahead of the chute. This means that every nut falls to its level, makes two or three revolutions to shatter the shell, and then drops out before the nut meat is damaged. Tom cast our first test model yesterday and we'll have it working on Sat. afternoon.

Later on the same day, Jock wrote:

> By Saturday afternoon [after the session with the volunteers] I'll have a pretty clear idea of whether this thing is going to work. If we are getting good volume and

better than 50% breakage rate with supermarket nuts, we'll do a series of assembly instruction photos and some brief instructions on Sunday. Then we'll put the molds in a box on Monday morning. (With enough metal parts for 1 machine.) The guys in India will have to tweak it for breakage rate. … If we are prepared to take this overseas, I'll get you metal parts for 5 more machines that can be made over there.

His PS reads: "You definitely owe me a beer if we can pull this off!! – and Ariel replies: "WHEW! You're definitely right about the beer – quite a lot would be the correct amount. THANKS!" (The beer was consumed in 2009 in Ghana, where Ariel's and Jock's paths crossed.)

But there was still fine-tuning to do. On the Friday (the 28th), Jock wrote to Ariel:

I got it together and you can feed walnuts into two openings 180 degrees opposite each other. I think one person will be able to turn the handle with reasonable effort. I didn't have enough walnuts to do a volume estimate but I imagine that about two or three per second would be a good guess. Tomorrow afternoon will pin that down. The hope that the nuts of different sizes would each drop to its own optimum level before moving laterally seems to be well founded. But here is where I need more info.

The metering plate is stationary and it has two openings through which the nuts drop. By advancing the timing so that the nuts enter earlier and are exposed to stress longer, the shells tend to come apart completely and the nutmeat is less intact. If the metering plate is retarded, the shells are stressed less. They tend to be [cracked] and can be opened by hand releasing the two halves with the dried center membrane still in between. In any case there is still more hand processing/sorting to be done to the product after it leaves the machine.

What (if any) is the premium for perfect halves? Also you mentioned needing 40 or 50 machines. Is this based on the high volume or the fact that there are 40 or 50 individual villages/co-ops in the project?
Tomorrow is volunteer day and we'll get photos.

But it wasn't finished yet. On Sunday, 30 November, Jock writes: "I cast another outer piece with different design. Hopefully this will get better results."

In seven days, therefore, Jock invented a new device, made several test machines, had molds manufactured by Pete Klingenberger, produced the metal parts in the FBP's shop, took photos and prepared instructions, and sent the whole sheller-making mini-factory to Boston by courier. He wrote to Ariel: "You [the team going to India] can … make a machine … and test it before you go. Our experience with all of these designs that we have sent out is that they evolve rapidly once they are in the field, that the test nuts we buy in N. Carolina supermarkets are never what you will find over there. "

Later, providing me with the background to these e-mails, he explained that the walnut sheller is not just an adaptation but a new design. Walnuts vary considerably in size and, while the shell is hard, the fruit inside is fragile, whereas with peanuts it's the other way around.

As it turned out, Jock himself went to MIT a few weeks later to train the D-Lab teams. The walnut sheller was indeed taken to northern India, but that was not the end of the story. Ariel e-mailed Jock from there to say that the local people were excited about the prospects of the sheller but that the MIT team had not yet succeeded in making a working model, largely because the local cement didn't contain a quick-drying agent. The first cement parts broke easily. She asked Jock whether the freezing night-time temperatures could be an additional problem. Jock replied that "Frost is the worst possible thing", and also suggested a way to use thin rebar for reinforcement.

When she was back in Boston, Ariel wrote to John Fogg, the FBP treasurer at that time, that the D-Lab team had successfully made one walnut sheller during the short time that they were in Ranikhet.

To find out what has happened since then, I contacted Nathan Cooke, one of the D-Lab trip leaders in January 2010 (a year after the trip which introduced the sheller). He wrote:

> The device that was made in India is currently not in use by the community partner there (Pan Himalayan Grassroots Foundation). It … encountered a few problems. Hopefully Ariel has informed you about the process the students went through to make the device in 2009. In 2010, the feedback that we got was that the walnut shells are so hard that they break up the concrete of the sheller. As such, dust ends up with the walnuts, causing hygiene problems in the final product. There was some interest in making a metal sleeve to protect the concrete, but this has not yet been done.
>
> I recall that Jock originally wanted to make the peanut shellers out of metal, but was informed otherwise, because of concrete's wide availability around the world, as well as low cost. It seems that in the particular area of India we were in, while concrete was available, metal might be the preferable material. Both for the hygiene and durability aspects implied above, as well as the fact that many of the local fabricators seem to prefer it. There seems to be an aesthetic attribution to having things made out of metal, along with the ability of fabricators to handle it quite skillfully.

Afghanistan

In February 2011 Jock received an e-mail from Gayle Knutson in Kabul (working with Hope Worldwide) asking if the sheller would process pistachios and almonds. Jock replied that they had been experimenting with pistachios in the midi sheller (see later chapter), and that the device created for brazil nuts might be able to handle almonds. He also mentions the gravity water pump (more about that later), and Gayle asks for more information about it, which he supplies.

A few months later there came an e-mail, also from Afghanistan, from Tom Brown, working for an organization called IDEA/NEW. He was interested in the walnut cracker; Jock told him that the device needed further work and Tom said that he would send Jock some walnuts for testing. He was also working with peanuts and pine nuts. FBP sent him a UNS and a mini sheller adapted for use with pine nuts by having a rubber sleeve put around the rotor.

Indonesia

In the same month FBP received a request from Eco-Carbone, based in France, which "develops community-based jatropha projects in different countries including Mali, Indonesian Papua, Laos, and Vietnam." They had heard about the FBP jatropha husker from Mali Biocarburant and GERES, a group which had bought two kits for use in Mali. Now Eco-Carbone wanted to send a sheller mini-factory to Indonesian Papua. The e-mails exchanged in an attempt to arrange an economical way to transport the kit make a cliff-hanger narrative involving, in the end, a helpful Air France pilot who took it from Chicago to Paris on its way to Indonesia.

* * *

All this activity makes for scattered dots on the map, but gradually clusters and connections appear. This is how such an idea spreads.

FOUR

The Caribbean
and
Central and South America

In the Caribbean and in Central and South America, the Full Belly Project has a number of partners and projects, most of them quite successful, and as I write there is the possibility that the sheller may be adopted for peanut processing in Paraguay and jatropha husking in Peru.

Peanuts in Haiti

Haiti, even before the earthquake of January 2010, was "the poorest country in the Western Hemisphere and 80% of the people live below the poverty line."[1] There is widespread malnutrition, especially among children. Deforestation is catastrophic: it's estimated that only 2% of the forests remain, the rest having been cut down to make charcoal for fuel. The result has been vastly increased erosion, especially in the mountains, and also flooding. Serious soil degradation means lower food production and famine.[2] More peanut cultivation would help alleviate several of these problems.

---

1 *Random House World Atlas and Encyclopedia*. (New York: Random House, 2007).
2 http://en.wikipedia.org/w/index.php?title=Haiti. Accessed on 8/1/2009.

In October 2006, FBP was approached by Gerthy Lahens, a Research Fellow and Community Organizer connected with the MIT D-Lab, who worked with the Petit-Anse Women's Peanut Butter Maker Co-op. She wrote:

> The group is called cooperative "Fanm Fo" (strong women). These 5 very strong women have been working together for the past 5 years, the president of the group is Ms. Marie Druineaud.
>
> The only way of life or means of survival for these women is processing peanuts by hand to make peanut butter to feed their children and trying to make a little money by selling their product to the community. The peanut processing is extremely hard and time consuming. Ideally, these women would be able to produce enough peanut butter to be financially self-sufficient, as part of a microenterprise. Although they work hard for many hours each day, at the end of the day they really don't have much to take home to share with their family or make enough money to save to elevate [them] from their dire poverty.

She gives information about her organization: "Friends of Petite-Anse is devoted to helping the most destitute residents of the town of Petite-Anse by freeing them from helplessness, hopelessness, and exploitation. Our aim is to empower these rural poor with good nutrition, new jobs, and a sense of hope for the future. A stronger economy will aid in combating poverty, disease, child mortality, and illiteracy that plagues Haiti."

FBP sent molds and metal parts for four machines. In an update in December 2009, Gerthy told me that the co-op was indeed using shellers to process nuts which are then turned into peanut butter, enriched with moringa.[3] It also builds shellers to sell, using locally-made metal parts.

* * *

Also operating in Haiti is an organization called Meds and Food for Kids (MFK), founded and headed by Dr. Patricia Wolff, a St. Louis pediatrician and professor at Washington University School of Medicine. Pat Wolff had heard about the peanut sheller from one of her organization's major supporters, a Minneapolis-based NGO called Toddlers Food Partners, which itself had connections with CTI, the organization making the grinder which, in Uganda, was used in tandem with the sheller. Pat told Full Belly that MFK needed equipment to process peanuts to make Medika Mamba, a Ready-to-Use Therapeutic Food (RUTF) like the Plumpy'nut made by Project Peanut Butter in Malawi (see Chapter Two). They needed a better way to shell nuts: industrial machines were large and cost $10,000 plus shipping and couldn't process most of the small Haitian peanuts.

MFK received a hand-operated sheller from FBP and, finding that it worked well, asked for one that was electrically powered. Jock developed one (an adaptation of the pedal-powered machine) and, in November 2007, went to Haiti to install it. Shortly after that, Pat Wolff reported to FBP that the facility's output had quadrupled to about 400 kg [over 1,000 lb] of Medika Mamba per

3 "Moringa oleifera is a tree widely grown on poor soil in semi-arid tropical and subtropical areas. Almost every part … can be used for food or has some other beneficial property." http://en.wikipedia.org. Accessed on 27/6/2008. Being a legume, it enhances depleted soils, and it grows very fast.

day.[4] MFK is now (2011) using an industrial-sized sheller, but they would not have been able to expand their work to this point without having the FBP sheller as an intermediate stage.

* * *

The sheller is also being used in the Bayonnais Peanut Butter Project. Bayonnais is "an agricultural community located in Haiti's Artibonite Valley" where poverty and hunger are extreme. "It is common not to eat [on] one day of the week, and some people who live in the mountains may go an entire week without eating a proper meal. Most children have distended abdomens due to protein deficiency and malnutrition. ... Inspired by Project Peanut Butter [in Blantyre, Malawi], the Bayonnais Peanut Butter Project (BPBP) seeks to address hunger and malnutrition in Bayonnais, Haiti, by increasing consumption of locally-produced, quality peanut butter." They built an FBP peanut sheller from a mini-factory, which they bought because they were "interested in the possibility of making more and selling them. As our project grows, it may also be more efficient to use two."

Jatropha

In June 2008 Jock attended the JatrophaWorld2008 conference in Miami, where he had a display and spoke with those stopping to have a look. Drawing on his

---

4   http://www.fullbellyproject.org/haiti.php. The MFK website (accessed on 8 March 2010) reports that in 2008 100,000 pounds [about 50,000 kg] were manufactured and given to 4,000 children.

work with Mali Biocarburant, he gave information to delegates, most of whom knew far less about jatropha than he did. Among those attending, he writes in his report, were representatives from "million-dollar corporations trading on the London Stock Exchange with tens of thousands of acres [of jatropha] planted [who] came to the convention to buy the mechanical harvesting machinery, only to discover that it doesn't exist." Though at first not interested in the FBP sheller, "by the end of the event, when they realized they were going to be hiring an army of hand pickers, they were wondering how long it would take to make 2500 [FBP] machines in Indonesia [to process the crop]. Basically, all the bad news for the big mega-mono-crop guys is good for our 'village co-op' philosophy. Jatropha is a great idea when planted on marginal lands where it can be harvested by the world's poorest people. The yields per acre are less but so are the problems."

To explain why no one has so far invented a mechanical harvester, Jock describes the fruiting cycle of the jatropha tree.

> If you plant … jatropha along the edge of a desert, the arrival of the rainy season triggers the blooming and, thus, the fruiting. So [all the fruit] ripens at the same time. But the yields are lower because of low rainfall and you only get one crop a year. That's not a good enough economic model for [the big corporations], although it is fine for small co-ops. The [big corporations] have planted on good arable land, with big spacing between trees so that the [not-yet-existing mechanical] harvesters can move around. Very wasteful use of space. But if it rains all year round [one of the attributes of "good arable land"], the jatropha flowers all year round. So you always have both fruit and

> flowers on the same branches, very close to each other.
> The flowers are delicate, but the fruit is tenacious. So any
> harvesting that shakes ... or combs the ripe fruit [off the
> branch] totally destroys the flowers and you get a big
> delay 'til the next harvest. But the [big corporations] only
> found that out at this convention.

At the time of going to press (2011) there is still no satisfactory machine. Having fruit and flowers on the branch at the same time is not the only problem: another is that the fruit grows in tight clusters and that the individual fruit in any one cluster ripen at different times. A single cluster can contain fruit that is green, yellow, brown or black. Fruit should be picked when it is yellow, brown, or black;[5] however, a mechanical harvester currently being developed strips off all the fruit, including the green fruit that has yet to ripen.

I contacted Titus Galema, Technical Advisor to the Gota Verde project in Honduras (see below), to ask if he had any further information; he reported that there are experiments underway with "growth regulators" that will make all the fruit ripen at the same time. "Some harvesting technologies from grapes and berries have been adapted to harvest jatropha," he writes, but the results don't seem to be promising. In May 2011 Jock told me that a blueberry-picking device is sometimes touted as being suitable for harvesting jatropha but that there's still no way of harvesting jatropha nuts mechanically without also destroying the blossoms that are on the branches at the same time. He says that every video that is supposedly about the jatropha harvester

---

5 http://gotaverde.org/en_new_portal/ Accessed on
   21/8/2010.

shows it harvesting blueberries. (And he remarked that the lack of a harvester is a good thing for small producers because otherwise Shell or some other giant would move in.)

At the jatropha conference in Miami, Jock met several people with whom he was to do further work. One was Gerry Delaquis, a successful Miami businessman of Haitian descent, who was working with an NGO in southern Haiti. They were raising jatropha, and Gerry saw the potential of the husker which Jock was demonstrating at the conference. He told Jock that the mini-factory would not work in his project because he'd have difficulty persuading people to make the machine, and he asked whether FBP could ship him a finished one. So Jock developed a smaller-than-standard sheller and made it of crushed corncob mixed with binding glue. This machine – which the FBP people call the "granola sheller" because of its texture – was sent to Gerry and was a great success. No one knew how long the corncob-and-glue would stand up to the grinding of jatropha nuts, but it has lasted very well and is, at the time of writing, still in use. FBP later sent them a mini-factory and they are now making concrete machines too.

Also attending JatrophaWorld2008 was Kathleen Robbins, who works with an NGO called Partner for People and Place which "provides planning and technical assistance for humanitarian and environmental projects on the frontline of poverty." In Haiti, they "tackle the problems poor people face by creating solutions that are appropriate to who they are and where they live."[6]

6   http://peopleandplace.org. Accessed on 14/10/2009.

Their jatropha operation is in Terrier Rouge. "Founded in 2007, ... Jatrofa Pepinyè works with small farmers to grow Jatropha curcas and make biodiesel and other products from its seed oil."[7] Here, as in all countries where jatropha is grown, producing local biofuel reduces the outflow of currency to pay for petroleum. JP's principal product, in addition to biodiesel, is soap in both bar and liquid form, distributed in schools to promote hand-washing before the mid-day meal. Another is lamp oil. JP uses the biodiesel to run its own generator and other equipment, and solar panels to heat the seeds before pressing (heated beans yield more oil). According to the 2009 report, JP was expanding into a very poor area just east of Terrier Rouge. The soil there is so bad that food crops simply don't grow, but jatropha does; by cultivating it, farmers will earn cash to buy food, and at the same time improve the poor soil (because, among other benefits, the leaves dropping from the jatropha trees add organic matter). The JP nursery demonstrates agricultural practices, such as having sheep graze among the trees to keep the grass down and enrich the soil with their droppings. Waste jatropha shells are made into charcoal for fuel. And JP provides information about jatropha cultivation to "a steady stream of visitors ... as well as a steady stream of inquiries coming off the internet."[8]

When contacted for an update in October 2009, Kathleen replied: "Yes, we have several of the Full Belly

7 Rob Fisher, Executive Director, "Partner for People and Place, JP: Jatrofa Pepinyè, Terrier Rouge, Haiti. Progress Report-9, April-September 2009.
8 Rob Fisher's report.

dehullers in Haiti and the capability to make more thanks to Jock and Full Belly. They work great and are critical to our goal of bringing the economic benefits of jatropha to small growers."

Guyana

In 2004, contact was made between the FBP and Guyana. Jerry La Gra wrote to Jay Tervo saying that the group he was working with in Guyana had a grinder from CTI that they were happy with but were looking for "the best available low-cost sheller." He writes: "If you have a peanut sheller that is efficient, low cost and low maintenance we could use about 50 ...." Jerry, in a later e-mail to me, gives the background:

> Our project began in 1998 when I helped local authorities organize a workshop for Amerindians from 50 villages in the hinterland of Guyana [the Rupununi, on the border with Brazil]. By the end of the workshop they had prioritized the need to improve the productivity of peanuts for a cash crop and cassava for a food crop. Shortly after, we got some volunteer peanut specialists from the U. of Florida to train farmers and diagnose their needs. This led to a [five-year] Peanut Collaborative Research Support Program (CRSP) project in Guyana financed by USAID through the universities of Georgia and Florida [which began] in 2002. The Beacon Foundation was the local non-government organization that served as the umbrella for that five year project. I was the coordinator of that project and in 2004 had my first contact with Full Belly and learned of its peanut sheller. I didn't meet Jock until a year or so later. In 2005 we purchased a few Omega IVs [CTI's grinders], built our own shellers based on an old English model, and we built a barrel type roaster. With those three pieces of equipment we helped seven groups of women in as many indigenous villages set up cottage

industries to make peanut butter, cassava bread and fruit juice drinks. This later developed into the Ministry of Education's School Snack program. The seven groups of mainly women have supplied snacks to an average of 1400 nursery and primary students since April of 2005.

In December 2009 the School Snack program was expanded "to about 4,000 students in a total of 33 indigenous villages."

Jerry explains the importance of the program. "About 40% of children go to school without breakfast and eat whatever they can find along the trail (30 minutes to 3 hours walk) on the way to and from school. The thoughts of getting a free peanut butter/cassava sandwich with fruit juice was enough to motivate them to be [at] school on time and on a regular basis. This was determined by a survey of 280 parents, teachers, students and farmers conducted by S-SOS [Jerry's organization] in 2008."[9]

9 "Few incentives to get children into schools are as effective as a school lunch program, especially in the poorest countries. Children who are ill or hungry miss many days of school. And even when they can attend, they do not learn as well. Economist Jeffrey Sachs notes, 'Sick children often face a lifetime of diminished productivity because of interruptions in schooling together with cognitive and physical impairment.' But when school lunch programs are launched in low-income countries, school enrolment jumps, academic performance goes up, and children spend more years in school. Girls, who are more often expected to work at home, especially benefit. Particularly where programs include take-home rations, school meals lead to girls staying in school longer, marrying later, and having fewer children." Lester R. Brown, *World on the Edge: How to Prevent Environmental and Economic Collapse.* (New York, W.W. Norton & Company, 2011) 155.

"The government," Jerry wrote to me, "is very supportive of our peanut project because it is technically, economically, and socially sustainable. It has created about 50 jobs and buys cassava, peanuts, and fruit from about 200 small farmers. It presently generates about ... $100,000 US [of which] 98% remains to circulate in rural areas."

This is getting ahead of the story. As a consequence of Jerry La Gra's search for a peanut sheller, Jock went to Guyana in March 2007 with a group including Dr. Greg McDonald from the University of Florida, Dr. Glen Harris from the University of Georgia, and Jay Williams, an agricultural engineer from the University of Georgia. This tour was the concluding stage of the already-mentioned five-year project. A hand-operated FBP sheller and a pedal-operated one had been shipped ahead.

Jock, in his report on the trip, wrote that the other members of the group were "pretty high-tech oriented, with emphasis on chemical fertilizers, herbicides, and pesticides. A lot of what they talked about seemed to be out of reach, financially and supply-wise, for the Amerindian farmers there, and [the farmers'] lack of questions following the classes suggested that a fair amount of what [those members of the group] were teaching was not appropriate." There is no electricity in the region, and fossil fuel is expensive.

However, "the demonstration of the shellers was a big hit." Though most of the peanut crop was shipped to big processors in the shell, machines were needed locally to shell nuts for seed and for the school snack program. The local variety of peanuts is unevenly shaped, but in five minutes Jock adjusted the sheller so that it would process the nuts with only 10% breakage, which was considered very good.

The pedal-powered, fan-equipped sheller which he introduced was extremely popular. In December 2009, Jerry La Gra wrote to me:

> Jock's sheller/cleaner will help to increase the efficiency of processing by cutting down on the labor required to clean [winnow] the nuts. Jock sent us one sheller with electric motor and one pedal-operated. Our local fabricator[10] has built one of each and has made some adjustments in the process which should improve efficiency even further. Consequently, four of our seven cottage industries will soon have Jock's shellers and the fabricator will build three more pedal units by March of 2010. The importance of this machine is in the time it saves the women ... cleaning peanuts. ... We are presently increasing the size of one of the more progressive cottage industries and we are improving the technology by introducing Jock's mechanized sheller/blower and a stainless steel gas table to cook cassava bread, invented locally. We hope to install in each of the five sub-regions a model cottage industry for the adding [of] value to multiple crops. We will work to continue improving on Jock's ideas and pray that he keeps inventing useful tools.

When Jock was in Guyana, the local people told him that they needed a thresher to remove the nuts from the roots. "I will develop a peanut thresher attachment which will attach to the basic drum with the fan [of the pedal-operated sheller]. Basically [you would] lift the sheller off and drop the thresher on. ... This new thresher option will make the machine into a peanut 'system', and doing 'double duty' will make it financially twice as

10 This is a man called Jeffery Sankar, who will be referred to again later.

possible." The plan was to have a machine that would be towed into the fields behind a bicycle; the threshing would be done there so that the tops of the plants would stay in the field, where they would be ploughed in.

The device which he invented threshed four times faster than could be done by hand. In the spring of 2008, Jock took a prototype to the University of Florida at Gainesville, one of the two universities which partners with S-SOS in Guyana, for testing. The plan was to make several and send them to Guyana. But there were problems with this model. The basic issue is that there are two types of peanuts. Those most commonly grown in North America are the bunch type, in which the nuts grow in clusters. In the runner type more often cultivated on poorer soils and in harsher climates, the nuts are scattered along the root.[11] Jock's first thresher worked well with the bunch type but not the runner type: he is working on one that will thresh the latter.

In the conclusion of his report, Jock writes that the trip was "a BIG eye opener" for the people he was traveling with; "for the first time, [they] really did get excited by the possibilities of appropriate tech."

In December 2008, Full Belly received another e-mail from Jerry La Gra:

> We finally signed a five year agreement between our NGO S-SOS and the U [of] Georgia. A local peanut

11 Jerry La Gra, e-mail to Jock, 18 December 2008. "Greg says the thresher you left with him in Gainesville does a good job picking the varieties of peanuts that tend to grow in clumps. Randy says he tried an expanded metal table to pick the GuyJumbo and it didn't work well because on the runner variety the peanuts are spread out along very long vines. Do you have any answers for that situation?"

butter factory wants to purchase 220,000 lbs/year of shelled nuts from our Rupununi farmers starting with the 2009 crop to be planted in May. That means about 120 acres and 30-40 growers. Peanut CRSP will guide us on variety and production. We are wondering if you would recommend us using your pedal [sheller] with blower to do the shelling. We would probably need at least 20 units scattered throughout the growing areas. Karaudarnau continues to use your pedal sheller and seems to like it. They don't want us to take it back to Georgetown to use as a model in building others.

Questions:

1. Does shelling 220,000 lbs/year with your sheller sound feasible?

2. Will you authorize us to replicate your sheller here in Guyana?

3. What are the costs for materials per unit?

4. What's the best way to get our fabricator to build the 1st one: you send us plans and pictures or we buy another model from you without the cement sheller which we would build at the fabricator's place? Or you come down and help us build the first one?

This project would be the realization of Jock's hope that peanut production in rural areas could become a small but efficient industry.[12] The machines would be built in Georgetown, Guyana; FBP would ship the parts and molds and anything that might be hard to get in Guyana, and people there would obtain other parts such as oil drums and wood locally. However, so far it hasn't proceeded as planned because, as a result of drought, the peanut crop of Fall 2009 turned out to be only about 25% of what had been expected. However, Jerry reports: "We were able to ... purchase 40,000 lbs

---

12 One of his favourite sayings is: "You can't have prosperity without efficiency."

of peanuts to keep our seven peanut butter cottage industries ... going."

In February 2010 Jerry wrote to FBP that "the Jock shellers built by our guy in Georgetown" are being tested in the field. He adds that the drought continues and asks about the water pump that FBP has developed (about which more later).

In December 2010, Jock would write to another correspondent: "Our project in Guyana tells us that a sheller, [water] pump, and 200' of hose allows a family three peanut crops [per year] on 2.8 acres, totaling about 25,000 lbs of peanuts in a year, which is, frankly, revolutionary."[13]

* * *

Jerry La Gra's organization, S-SOS, was at that time also interested in jatropha. Jock had sent him information about Mali Biocarburant, and Jerry replied saying that S-SOS "has been considering putting in a trial plantation [of jatropha] ... and your on-farm oil extractor [a project on which Jock was working at the time – see below] will give the idea a big push forward. Guyana has at least 10,000 hectares [24,000 acres] potentially suitable for planting Jatropha where no commercial crops can be economically grown. These areas are inhabited by Amerindians ... who need income-generating opportunities." He asked whether Jock could advise him about where to obtain seed for the first five hectares

---

13 Translated into metric: "... a sheller, [water] pump, and 60 meters of hose allows a family three peanut crops [per year] on just over one hectare, totaling about 11,300 kg of peanuts in a year."

of test plots. Jock suggested which variety would be best, and Jerry asked how much the oil extractor would cost and how to get one. However, shortly after that he wrote that "the excitement from the initial jatropha high has dissipated."

Jatropha in Honduras

A jatropha project is, however, flourishing in Yoro, Honduras. Honduras is the second poorest country in Latin America; 100% of its oil is imported, costing 56% of its currency outflow. "In rural areas there is very little agricultural expertise and traditionally the crops are mainly survival crops like corn or beans, offering very little inputs for the local economy."[14] "A consortium of European institutions [Social Trade Organization, STRO] is developing Gota Verde ["green drop"], a project aimed at developing and testing an integrated regional economic development approach based on the promotion of small-scale production and local use of biofuels in Honduras." The project focussed on jatropha and castor beans:[15] farmers planting the crops would have a ready market, currency would stay in the country, and the dependency on fossil fuels would be reduced. The jatropha trees would be planted as hedges and also in pastures, in rows between which the cattle would graze while benefiting from the shade. The

---

14 "Gota Verde, Promotion of Small-scale biofuel production and use in Honduras." http://www.strohalm.net/media/pers/D_47_Gotaverde_Promotion_of_Smallscale_biofuel_production_and_use_in_Honduras.pdf . Accessed on 9/12/2008.

15 Castor oil is used for soap and biodiesel, and is being tested as a lubricant.

project would also help local farmers to improve their agricultural skills.

Jock heard about Gota Verde from Titus Galema, the Dutch Technical Advisor to the project, whom he met at the jatropha convention, and in September 2008 he went to Yoro himself. What he found was that the Yoro jatropha project was well-funded but was economically unsustainable because the hand-husking of jatropha took three times longer than the picking and the farmers were either losing interest or becoming hostile about having been persuaded to plant a crop that they couldn't sell for a reasonable price. [16] They seemed to feel that the profit potential of jatropha had been exaggerated. The processing was the bottleneck: as in Mali, the only village-scale alternative to hand-husking was to spread the nuts on the ground and flail them, and that was not an option because it produced "dirty" nuts.

Two days after Jock's arrival in Yoro, there would be a big meeting of the farmers' co-op. Jock promptly made two shellers. The farmers arrived for the meeting in a truculent mood; Jock was told that on previous occasions they had brought their hand-husked jatropha with them but when they heard what they would be paid they took it home again. This time, when they saw Jock demonstrating the husker, their mood turned to excitement. The FBP husker could do 250 kg [650 lbs] per hour, speeding up the process 60- or 70-fold. This would make the whole system economically viable, not only for Gota Verde but also for the farmers.

---

16 Realizing that the hand-picking is also slow, Jock is now working on a system that would double the speed of picking.

Jock in Honduras.

Photo credit: Titus Galema.

In March 2009, Titus sent me an update. "In our project we use [the shellers] for dehulling Jatropha fruits in a decentralized way. This is a great benefit in terms of organization, transport, and agriculture because there is no need to transport the nut shells; moreover, they can be applied directly to the field as an organic fertilizer. We already made six more of these [dehuskers] and the farmer-owned local business is distributing them among the farmers." During the following month's harvest, he told me, they would put about four of the dehuskers into use, and with the larger harvest expected in November they would probably use them all. And in August 2010 he wrote that the dehuskers were by then being made by the CEVER School, a vocational school in Yoro. There's a small building on the school grounds where the dehuskers and the oil are produced. "This week we made about four dehuskers. I think that we made a total of about 25 now."[17]

17 Information about the CEVER School comes from http://www.theceverproject.org. Accessed on 4/6/2011.

When he was in Honduras, Jock also continued his reflections on extracting oil from the jatropha kernels. In Mali he had seen Hugo Verkuijl's oil presses mounted on trucks and realized the advantage of doing the pressing locally rather than in a large central plant. However, he visualized something different: not a processor-on-a-truck, but a factory-in-a-container, the complete processing equipment built inside a shipping container, which would be moved from one area to another. He met with people at the Zamorano Agricultural School, and when he returned to Wilmington he began work on this.

Guatemala

Full Belly has had contacts with Guatemala, but it has been one of the less successful initiatives. In March 2006, Tom Triglione, working with people returning home after fleeing hurricanes and a civil war, wrote in an e-mail to a friend that the women in this group were making peanut butter with locally-grown peanuts. "The peanut butter is made totally by hand, with completely natural ingredients (less than 2% sugar and salt), and tastes as fresh as I have ever had." The hand-shelling of the peanuts was, however, limiting production. Tom contacted Jock who donated molds to the group; Tom made a sheller and then passed the mini-factory on to Mayapedal, an organization which had shown interest in using the sheller to process coffee. (But in the end the local people preferred to continue doing it in their traditional way.) Tom planned to demonstrate the sheller at a fair-trade fair, and he asked about a machine to shell pumpkin seeds. But here too there is a note of discouragement: he writes that "conversations with the

Junta Directiva reached another dead end, so my interest in this has waned."

There was some further contact with Guatemala. Jock learned that an organization called Nueva Alliancia had tried to use the sheller for macadamia nuts but that these were so hard that they damaged the concrete. Accordingly, he built a stainless-steel version, and in May 2007 he went to Guatemala to deliver it and also to build a pedal-powered unit. He left the sheller there and has heard nothing further.

Jock explains that Guatemala is not a very suitable country for Full Belly. True enough, being a very poor country it is a likely-looking field of operation. But FBP does not have a good partner there, no one who represents large numbers of farmers or deals with extensively-grown crops. These are among the many factors that contribute to success or failure. The projects in Haiti show what can be done when circumstances are more favourable.

* * *

The ways in which FBP collaborates with partners is crucial to its success; in the projects dealt with here, it's easy to see how the collaboration works. Locally-based NGOs tell Jock what is needed, and if it doesn't already exist he invents or adapts a device to do the work. In return, the partners on the ground provide feed-back. So there is a lengthening list of partners, devices, crops processed, and services provided.

FIVE

Focus on Malawi

It's a warm morning in May 2009 and I'm sitting on a wobbly folding chair in the wide doorway of a machine shop in Lilongwe, the capital of Malawi. Jock is assembling a sheller, watched intently by the owner of the shop and several workers who, this afternoon, will put together another one. As he works, Jock explains what he is doing; the men understand English because it's one of the country's official languages, but only the owner occasionally says a few words.

It's in the yard of this firm – C to C [Cape to Cairo] Engineering Foundry and Machinery Industries – that a shop will be set up to build shellers for Malawi. The shop's first task will be to make 900 huskers for this fall's jatropha harvest. [1]

The background

Malawi is in some ways a typical sub-Saharan country. It's mostly rural: "Agriculture ... is a mix of large estates

---

1 That was the figure on which the planning was based, and which drove the urgent need to set up the shop and start producing shellers; circumstances in the following months caused it to change.

(plantations), essentially monocultural, and smallholder farming for both subsistence and cash crops. The ... smallholdings ... have often suffered from unfair trading practices in which the middlemen cream off profits from the sale of cash crops giving little incentive to the small farmers to improve standards and productivity. The smallholders have also found that competition from the large estates has made the growing of some of the otherwise most attractive export crops [tobacco and cotton] uneconomic on the scale that they can hope to achieve."[2] All the same, small farmers (many farms are only an acre or two – less than a hectare) do grow cotton and tobacco for a cash income, though that diversion of land from food crops contributes to malnutrition and starvation, especially in bad years. Chemical fertilizers increase crop yields but are expensive and do further damage to already depleted soil. Traditionally it was the *variety* of crops that helped to maintain the fertility of the soil, but monocropping quickly exhausts it. The picture of African smallholders operating at subsistence level is largely out of date. Nowadays they are more likely to be part of a global system. Depleting soil makes fertilizer essential (hence the need for a cash crop) and that makes them vulnerable to fluctuations in the price of petroleum as it affects the cost of fertilizer. Growing more jatropha and peanuts would provide the villagers with food and alternative cash crops, and also improve the soil.[3]

---

2 John Douglas and Kelly White, *Spectrum Guide to Malawi* (Nairobi: Cameraprix Publishers International, 2003) 337.

3 "Since 1970, the population of sub-Saharan Africa has more than doubled. Land holdings have consequently shrunk in size, and many farmers, unable to leave their

Soil degradation has led to cutting down forests to obtain fresh land. "If one asks any Malawian, returning to the country after an absence of some years, what he first notices he will almost always reply, 'Where have all the trees gone?' The country is rapidly being deforested."[4] This – besides forcing the women to walk farther for firewood, which reduces the time available for other work – affects the climate and the water cycle. Forests are also felled to make room for the growing population. The result is "a demand that cannot be met if the forests are to be safeguarded. Fuel wood, for cooking and for tobacco curing, is in such short supply that even the posts erected to carry telephone wires are not safe."[5]

---

land fallow, now grow the same food crops, year after year, on the same plot of land. While the use of mineral fertilizers has risen tenfold in East Asia since 1970, it has remained stagnant, at very low levels, in sub-Saharan Africa. For most small farmers the use of fertilizers that could replenish the soils is not economically feasible, due to increasing prices and climatic risks. The result is land degradation, low yields, persistent poverty and widespread malnutrition." World Agroforestry Centre, "Creating an Evergreen Agriculture in Africa", http://www.worldagroforestry.org/evergreen_agriculture. Accessed on 13/3/2011. The "evergreen agriculture" project involves planting nitrogen-fixing trees in farm fields to improve soils, etc., and appears to be having significant success.

4 Douglas, 339.
5 Douglas, 339. More recent information is somewhat encouraging. Reforestation is taking place in Malawi, especially the planting of nitrogen-fixing trees "in preparation for the medium-term situation when fertilizer subsidies may have to be scaled back or withdrawn." [Report submitted to the U.N. Human Rights Council,

Linked to the disappearing forests is the problem of drought, which makes irrigation increasingly necessary. It can make the difference between starvation and survival. When William Kamkwamba, a clever Malawian teenager, used scraps of wood and metal to build a windmill which powered a water pump, his mother was suddenly able to grow – year-round – tomatoes, Irish potatoes, cabbage, mustards, soybeans, carrots, and spinach both to eat at home and to sell in the market.[6] Irrigation enabled William's father to harvest two crops of maize per year. Carl Scarbro, a Peace Corps volunteer, wrote to me that in the area of Malawi where he is located, "Irrigation is a no brainer …. They have substantial acreage near water during the dry season, the soils in those acreages are not depleted, and the year round temperatures are ideal for nearly all

20 December 2011. Report number is A/HRC/16/49. Report is submitted by Olivier De Schutter, the Special Rapporteur on the right to food. It cites D.P.Garrity et. al., "Evergreen Agriculture: a robust approach to sustainable food security in Africa," *Food Security* 2:3, 2010, p. 203.] "By mid-2009, over 120,000 Malawian farmers had received training and tree materials from the programme …." [p. 9 of UN report] Later in the report is this: "The use of such nitrogen-fixing trees avoids dependence on synthetic fertilizers, the price of which has been increasingly high and volatile over the past few years, exceeding food commodity prices, even when the latter reached a peak in July 2008. In this way, whatever financial assets the household has can be used on other essentials, such as education or medicine." P. 10. http:// slashfood.com/2011/03/08/u-n-small-scale-farming-could-double-the-worlds-food-production.
6   William Kamkwamba and Bryan Mealer, *The Boy Who Harnessed the Wind: creating currents of electricity and hope.* (New York: Harper Collins, 2009) 159 and 261.

the wet season crops they grow now. Our area is poor, but it doesn't have to be because of the above resources. The limiting factor is irrigation ...." Moreover, climate change is causing more drought.

As Carl indicates, this equatorial country receives enough sunlight for crops to grow year-round. But there is a dry season from May to October. At the end of the rainy season, when everyone is harvesting, crops fetch very low prices, but the same crop planted in May and harvested in September would earn five times as much.[7] And it's not just a matter of income: irrigation could deal with the seasonal spells of inadequate food, and the malnutrition and consequent illness. It would enable

7   The picture is, of course, more complicated than this. Year-round cultivation would further deplete soils which are already pretty worn out, especially if they have been used to grow tobacco, cotton, and maize. However, soil-enrichment strategies that don't depend on expensive chemical fertilizer are available. The cultivation of peanuts, which are legumes, fixes nitrogen in the soil, and jatropha shells and press cake are very beneficial. The leafy tops of peanut and maize plants, if dug or ploughed in, would add valuable organic matter to help hold moisture and reduce the need for irrigation. (As we were driving through the Malawi countryside, Jock pointed out that those tops need to be chopped up so that the farmers – who in that area have no ploughs but only spades – can dig them in more easily. "Something like a paper-cutter ...." Jock said with a speculative look in his eye, and I wondered if this was the genesis of another invention.) Another possibility (dealt with in the UN report and the Garrity article already cited) is agroforestry – the integration of trees and shrubs with agriculture and/or livestock – which leads to "more diverse, productive, profitable, healthy and sustainable land-use systems." [http://en.wikipedia.org. Accessed on 7/3/2010]

farmers to grow and eat more vegetables. If farmers' incomes improved and fewer child-hours were taken up with shelling peanuts, more kids would be able to go to school and, being better fed, would be better able to learn. Better-educated children would benefit the whole country, and better-educated women would help to reduce family size.[8]

The staple food crop in Malawi is corn (maize), introduced to the continent in colonial times. Like cotton and tobacco, it's hard on the soil.

> In better watered areas, maize became an increasingly preferred crop over traditional African grains such as sorghums and millets. Maize ... matured much faster, and offered better protection against birds, but it also carried a greater risk of failure if rainfall proved inadequate. ... By the middle of the [20th] century, [maize] hybrids developed in South Africa spread throughout the subcontinent. Smallholders switched to maize because of its potential for higher yields and because maize brought a far higher price than sorghums and millets. In many areas of unpredictable rainfall, [however,] it remained a gambler's crop.[9]

And on many farms it replaced at least a large part of the crop diversity which had formerly characterized the smallholding and produced both healthier people and healthier soil.[10]

8 "Around the world, people got to work figuring out how to slow population growth. Educating women turned out to be the best strategy." Bill McKibben, *Eaarth*, 92-3.
9 Gregory H. Maddox, *Sub-Saharan Africa: An Environmental History*. (Santa Barbara, ABC-CLIO, 2006) 134.
10 Some of my information about village agriculture in Malawi comes from Dick Wittenberg, *Binnen is het donker, buiten is het licht* ["Indoors it is dark, outside it is light"]

Apart from the advantages already given, maize keeps well because of its waxy coat. After a good harvest, a family can be sure of having food for twelve months. It's used to make a stiff porridge called *nsima*, the basis of every meal and sometimes the only food. Unfortunately *nsima*, being mostly starch, is very low in nutritional value; when possible, people supplement it with peanuts or vegetables. But the need for a cash crop, and the crucial importance of maize for feeding the family, mean that often there is no room to grow other food crops.

These problems interact and affect the environment and the farm families' lives, and problems for the environment and for farmers affect the whole country.

This is the image of sub-Saharan Africa that's familiar to many of us from the media and the appeals by aid organizations. But there's another one, sent to me by Sarah Pedersen, a Peace Corps volunteer whom I met in Malawi. At my request, she wrote a word-portrait of one of the villagers in the area where she and her husband Austin were based. It's a reminder that within the large framework of serious economic, environmental, and human problems, there is a kind of normality where crisis – until it strikes – is in the background.

Grace lives in Gomatz village, Malawi, with her husband and four children. Each day she wakes up with the sun around 5 a.m. to work in the field and care for her family. After drawing water from the borehole and preparing maize porridge [*nsima*] for her children, she walks to the

(Amsterdam, Atlas, 2007). It is a chronicle of the author's experience of living in a village in Malawi. Wittenberg mentions almost no crops except maize and tobacco. (See page 39 and elsewhere)

field to begin her long morning of cultivation. Grace is a progressive farmer. Uniquely, she understands the value of the soil she cultivates. She plants a diverse selection of crops on two hectares of land – groundnuts, hot peppers, tomatoes, cassava, sunflowers, maize, rice, beans, and pumpkins. She practices sustainable agriculture, aquaculture and agroforestry. She uses a treadle pump during the dry season to produce watermelon, jalapenos, tomatoes, bell peppers, cabbage and cucumbers. When the sun is high in the sky, Grace walks back to her home to prepare lunch for her husband and her children who have just returned home from school – a four kilometer [2.5 mile] walk. On a three-stone fire Grace prepares pumpkin leaves with tomatoes and *nsima*. When her husband is at the home of his second wife, Grace and her children eat together on a straw mat on the floor in their three-room mud-brick house. When he is home, her oldest son and husband eat in the house while she and her girls eat outside on a mat on the ground. After eating, washing the dishes, and drawing water, Grace escapes the hot afternoon sun by sitting on a mat under the trees. Many villagers come to her home throughout the afternoon to buy produce from her garden such as tomatoes, cucumbers and cabbage. Throughout the week, Grace and her family make a profit of about 500 Malawi Kwacha from their produce – an equivalent of 3 dollars. She uses this money to purchase seeds, soap, and cooking oil and hopes to save enough each week to send her children to secondary school one day. Once the sun is lower in the sky, Grace rides her bicycle to the homes of local farmers to teach about sustainable agriculture and provide support to farmers who are implementing various techniques in their fields. Around 6 p.m., Grace returns to her home to begin dinner. She prepares dry beans and *nsima*. After eating and cleaning up, she sits with her children and neighbors to relax and chat before going to bed.

At first glance, this is a picture of poverty. But look again. Grace "understands the value of the soil she cultivates," and she plants a remarkable variety of crops. She practices sustainable agriculture and teaches it to others. The technology she has available is minimal – a treadle pump, a bicycle – but she uses it effectively. Sitting under the tree selling her produce to the neighbours she is, in a tiny but significant way, an entrepreneur. This short narrative, as well as giving a wonderful glimpse into the life of an African family, resonates with issues that are important for the planet because it links traditional farming with a forward-looking image of sustainability.

The Project in Malawi

The Full Belly Project's serious connections with Malawi began, as we've seen, in 2006 when Brian Connors, the Assistant Peace Corps Director for Environment there, began making shellers and spreading the word (and the shellers) through the Peace Corps network.

Then, in early 2009, FBP received a grant from the Change Happens Foundation, headed by Doug Troxel. Change Happens is "a private organization committed to helping motivated groups with pioneering research and forward-thinking projects that benefit humanity."[11] Jim Nesbit, a member of the FBP Board, met Troxel when they were both on holiday in Bali. At breakfast in the hotel one day, halfway through a cup of bad coffee, Jim noticed a man at another table brewing his own

11 http://www.changehappens.us/message.aspx. Accessed on 31/8/2010.

Kona coffee. They got into conversation, and the upshot was that Doug invited Jim to send to Change Happens a proposal about FBP's plans for Malawi. This led to FBP receiving a grant for $40,000, designated specifically for use in that country.

The FBP Board and Jeff Rose, the Executive Director, formulated what they called the "Acceleration of Innovation" plan (AOI), whose goal was to promote entrepreneurship there. From then on, Jeff and the Board decided, FBP was "officially" active only in Malawi, even though in actual fact the work in other countries continued. The problems with AOI and this "all eggs in one basket" policy will be dealt with in a later chapter, but at the time of our trip to Malawi this was the course which had been set.

At the same time, FBP had learned that Malawi – a country completely dependent on imported petroleum – was moving into jatropha production. A Malawian company called Bio Energy Resources Limited (BERL) was working with small farmers to plant jatropha seedlings: BERL told FBP that 24 million had been planted and that ultimately they expected to have 250 million.[12] The first crop would be harvested in September 2009 and the oil sold to petroleum companies. They had heard about the FBP sheller-husker and requested 900 of them for September 2009, one to be given to each of the "clubs" of jatropha-supplying farmers which they had set up so far, and with many more required later.[13] To fill such a large order, FBP would set up a shop in Lilongwe.

---

12 Information from Sander Donker, BERL official.
13 Information from a leaflet published by BERL.

The project was divided into two phases. In the first, Jeff Rose and Jim Nesbit would go to Malawi to find an organization which would manufacture and distribute the machines. This would lay the foundation for Phase II, the work which Jock would do when he arrived a couple of weeks later. Jim and Jeff went to Malawi in mid-April. I would accompany Jock to get first-hand experience of the FBP's work in a developing country.

I joined Jock in Wilmington and spent a few days there observing the operation of the shop and meeting with several volunteers and members of the Board. Then he and I travelled to Malawi, arriving in Lilongwe on Thursday, 30 April. Jock's friend Gregor Wilson, a free-lance production manager in the film industry, arrived the next day. Besides filming the project, he poured concrete, drove the borrowed Land Rover, and did a lot of other useful and necessary things. All five of us used all our luggage allowance (beyond one suitcase each for our personal needs) to take FBP equipment. This included two mini-factories, one each for two new designs of sheller (the midis – see below) and one for a water pump, as well as parts, some tools, and other things which might be hard to find in Lilongwe. Some additional equipment was sent by diplomatic pouch.

From then on, the two phases were interwoven. Jeff and Jim, the business-management people, set up meetings for Jock, who then came – usually with Gregor and me tagging along – to talk about engineering, agriculture, and other technical matters.

Jeff reports: "In those 21 days we saw 21 organizations and 38 people. They ranged from NGOs to the largest food processor in Malawi. Every group we met with was very enthusiastic about [the program]. Our main idea of setting up a self-sustaining system run by Malawians for Malawians to manufacture, distribute, and maintain our Universal Nut Sheller (UNS) was well received. After this is up and running, we will develop new technologies to solve other problems that the farmers identify."

One way in which farmers' needs would be identified would be through Total Land Care (TLC), a Malawian NGO which promotes sustainable community-based natural-resource management, and also strategies relating to crop production and marketing, reforestation, and irrigation.[14] Jeff, Jim, and TLC formulated a memorandum of understanding by which TLC would distribute the sheller, train farmers in its use and maintenance, and collect data for FBP's guidance.

The "largest food processor in Malawi", RAB Processors Ltd., "agreed to purchase every peanut that is shelled by the UNS, graded and sorted." They also pledged to "collaborate with FBP in the development of a Peanut Butter and Moringa leaf" RUTF.

C to C, which would build the shellers, was already manufacturing appropriate technologies: cassava peelers, maize shellers, tobacco presses. It met FBP's requirement of having a western business model: the CEO, Lameck Makutu Sr., had grown up in Africa but had worked in Poland, India, and England.

---

14 http://www.totallandcare.org. Accessed on 26/2/2010.

In the shop

Jock and I, having arrived on the plane from Addis Ababa at about noon on Thursday, 30 April, went to C to C that afternoon for a quick look around. The next day the five of us met with Lameck Makutu and his son, Lameck Jr., who was the plant manager. Following the meeting, Jock assembled one of the shellers, as already described, all his years of experience in teaching others, some of whom knew little or no English, investing his hands and his words. The workers understood the language of Jock's hands, watched the precise degree of tightening a nut, the hands testing for tension, the fingers brushing off dust or stroking grease around working parts. That afternoon, they assembled another machine themselves, with Jock watching closely. (A few days later, he trained these metal-workers in the handling of concrete. They listened closely as Jock talked about the qualities and "habits" of concrete at different seasons of the year, and told them that working with concrete is not a cut-and-dried process but one that requires judgement, sensitivity, and experience.)

In the following days, one of the buildings in the C to C yard was designated to become the shop where the 900 shellers would be built. The sheller-making began: there was none too much time if the deadline was to be met. But focussing on BERL's order proved difficult because the machines were in demand for processing peanuts. Brian Connors, who would be connected with the shop as an outside observer and the purchaser of machines for the Peace Corps, told Jock that these shellers were much better made, and much more accurately adjusted, than those he had built. He "bought" C to C's shellers (in fact, obtained them in exchange for bags of concrete) and took them to the villages to replace his home-made ones.

Jock told me then that the FBP people had known for some time that machines made by workers he had trained were of better quality and would spread good news about the usefulness and performance of the shellers. He also explained that peanut-shelling requires more precise machines than jatropha-husking because of the peanut's delicate inner coat and because, with sun-dried nuts, the kernel fits so snugly inside the shell. One task of the C to C workers would be to test each sheller and decide whether it should be used for peanuts or jatropha.

In his report on the trip, Jock describes the set-up:

> We have a space cleared out where the machines are now being made and which, when we expand production, will just be the metal-working area [the concrete-casting would be done outdoors]. Right now it has no electricity and we have got a bid for 90K kwachas [roughly US$500] to set up wiring for power tool welding. I recommend that we find a source for that money and get it done before my return [which would be in three months]. If I return and there is no electric hook-up I will have to totally compromise the assembly-line expansion. I had hoped to build some work benches and shelves. Africans generally work on the ground but it is tiring and chaotic. Our Uganda push [in 2007] to get Western-style shop furniture paid off well. We'll do the same [here in Malawi] when I return. I did, however, have time to make jigs [patterns to guide the welding] to insure consistency in the metal parts. We also built a lathe to turn each rotor to ensure perfect centering.

Using funds from the Change Happens grant, he also bought steel and cement, lots of tools, and a welder's helmet. And he assessed the local cement and investigated the availability of tools, parts, materials, and skilled workers. For instance, the slow-to-harden local cement would limit the speed at which machines could be turned out. All this information, besides being needed for setting up a shop routine, meant that when he was back in Wilmington he would be able to guide the work and solve problems by phone and e-mail.

On the road

To return to the beginning of the trip: the shellers assembled on that first Friday were destined for a group of villages where Sarah and Austin Pedersen, the two Peace Corps Volunteers already mentioned, were stationed. They were packed into the Land Rover loaned by Brian Connors – packed very carefully, because on rough roads the concrete could break. Also we took a peanut thresher which, dismantled, had travelled in one of our suitcases and had to be tested under local conditions. We took a few simple, hand-held devices for stripping corn kernels off cobs. Some of this was packed on the roof of the Land Rover, because we also had five people (Jock, Jeff, Jim, Gregor, and me) and our overnight bags, along with some edibles and drinkables for during the trip and in the place where we would spend the night.

And so we set off on Saturday morning, heading east. From time to time we passed trading centres, the clusters of small shops which serve the off-the-road villages where people actually live. Before reaching Lake Malawi we turned north and, shortly after that,

A trading centre.

Photo credit: Marianne Brandis.

left the paved road. This smaller road was sandy, with huge potholes, and riven with deep gullies made during the just-past rainy season and with tracks left by the few motor vehicles that ever came this way. For about three-quarters of an hour we travelled at little more than walking speed, jolting and lurching. At a pre-arranged spot we met the Pedersens and Andrew Mailosi, a local man. On their bicycles they led us further, along tracks so narrow that the Land Rover ploughed through the tall grass on both sides. This took us to the first village, a group of probably no more than a dozen small houses of home-made brick. (Jock, in a quiet aside to me, said, "This is just about as poor as it gets.")

In a later e-mail, Sarah gave me information about the area. The greater community (a total of 40 villages) was called Chipelara. Within that region are villages called Chipelara 1, 2, 3, and 4; other villages have names

The village of Jojo.

Photo credit: Marianne Brandis

not including the "Chipelara" component. The Senior Group Village Headwoman was responsible for all 40.

The one to which they had led us was Jojo. When we arrived, most of the villagers were sitting on the ground awaiting us, and three women immediately got up to sing and dance a welcome. Then Jock gave a short speech explaining that we had come from America to bring them a present that would make their lives easier – a machine for shelling groundnuts. The machine would stay in their village forever. Also we had come to test – for the first time in Africa – a tool for taking the nuts off the plants.

The thresher, when assembled, looks like a small table with a top made of expanded metal. (In developing countries, Jock told me, it would be easy for local people to make the mesh from bamboo.) The operator, while dragging the plant across the surface with one hand, presses the roots onto the mesh with the other; the detached nuts drop onto a sloping trough which funnels them into a basket. Two people can use it at the same time, one standing on each side. Jock had been unable to test it properly in Wilmington because he couldn't get enough plants with the nuts still attached. So now he asked for some and, while testing the device for his own information, asked the villagers what they thought. In his report he wrote: "... they all said it worked well and was faster [than threshing by hand]. ... What we agreed was that the table design was nice but perhaps a bit more complicated than necessary."

Then he brought out the sheller and showed the villagers and the Pedersens how to adjust it for different sizes of nuts. And he gave them one of the corn-strippers, which delighted them.

Gregor Wilson filmed all this, and when he showed the villagers how they appeared on video there were hoots of laughter.

Andrew Mailosi's family, who lived in another village a kilometre or two away, had prepared lunch, which provided interesting insights and experiences for me, the only person in our group who had not been to Africa before. The younger members of our party sat on a grass mat on the ground; Jock and I were given very low stools. The menu was *nsima* together with meat-with-sauce and a boiled vegetable; the old Africa hands ate with their fingers, but I was given a fork. The host came around before and after with a small bowl of water in which we could wash our hands. When we had finished we went out to thank the family (who had not eaten with us) for their hospitality; this was a more luxurious meal than they'd normally eat themselves, and there were seven guests, so it was a big undertaking for them.

After lunch we went to Gomatz (Grace's village, though we did not meet her), which already had a peanut sheller. Sarah and Austin had reported that the women were dissatisfied because too many nuts came out broken. Jock found that the sheller was working properly; with Austin Pedersen translating, he explained that possibly it was on a too-narrow setting. He explained that they could put each batch of peanuts through twice, setting the machine first to fit the larger nuts and then, after making a quick adjustment, putting the unshelled ones through again. Or it could be that the nuts, at the time of shelling, were old and therefore brittle.

However, when he asked for details about the breakage rate he was told that it was only about two nuts out of every fifty, which is 4%. This is in fact very low. Only hand-shelling produces less breakage, but probably the broken nuts – and quite a few more – are eaten by the people doing the shelling. The FBP group, talking it over later, thought that perhaps there were other issues involved, such as personal rivalries.

After spending the night at the Nkhotakota Lodge, on the shore of Lake Malawi, we went the next morning to Sarah and Austin Pedersen's house, which is like those of the villagers and has a walled garden where food plants flourish. After delivering the second sheller to another village, we returned to Lilongwe.

Jatropha in Malawi

Two days later we met with officials at BERL. Since setting up a shop to build their 900 jatropha huskers was a big part of the Malawi project, this was an important meeting.

But in fact – so far as we know now, two years later – nothing has come of that project. The company's website is long on plans but short on statistics about what is actually being achieved. Jock explains that that kind of failure is very common in Africa.

Developing a smaller sheller

In the following days, we focussed on building and testing more machines. In Wilmington, Jock had been working on two new versions of the sheller, both smaller and both called "the midi" to distinguish them from the "classic" and from the even-smaller "mini" version, to be discussed later. One model of the midi is precisely three-quarters the size of the classic with all its proportions the same, and the other is about two-thirds as big as the classic and has a shallower angle. Jock described the latter in an e-mail to David Campbell, who was going to test it in Senegal: "We are eager to test the `midi', which is about 2/3 size. It has a greater taper on the rotor and hollow outer piece. This means that a much smaller up and down adjustment allows a greater range of nut/pod size to be processed. In addition, the hopper at the top is not part of the concrete outer piece but is an add-on made from a locally purchased plastic bucket or bowl." We had brought molds for both versions of the midi, and Jock built and tested them in Lilongwe. He hoped that the midi would be stronger than the classic, as well as small and light enough to be moved around on the back of a bicycle. In third-world villages, bicycles are most people's only wheels and are used even to carry bulky and heavy loads. Tim Strong, the Peace Corps Volunteer who had such success with the sheller in Malawi, moved the sheller – and this was the classic, the big one – from farm to farm on the back of his bicycle.

Like the thresher, the two versions of midi had to be tested in real-Africa conditions. Jock built them in the Connors' back yard and ran peanuts through them. Disappointingly, there was a very high breakage rate, partly no doubt because the nuts were a year old and very dry. In his report on the trip, he wrote: "The midi became the orphan of the expedition. ... I believe that final testing will show that midi's have to be crop-specific. The ... shallow-angle that had my hopes way up ... will become our new coffee machine and ... peanuts will go through the 'old geometry' machine [the midi 3/4] which will do nothing else."

There's a postscript, however. In October 2009 Brian Connors wrote to Jock that the security guards at his compound – one of whom, Peter, had been working closely with Brian to make shellers – were using the midi to shell nuts for oil. "... the nuts my guards shelled this morning [with the midi] were 98% perfect." Jock's reply: "Well, that is weird because I got lousy results from both machines in your back yard [in May]. I was getting up to 33% breakage. I must have had a very horrible batch of nuts." In 2010, David Campbell's tests with the midi in Senegal (see Chapter Two) also gave good results but by then, Jock told me, the design had been improved. The shallow-angle is now the only kind of midi being distributed.

While in Lilongwe, Jock significantly improved the design of all the shellers. Up to now the stands had been made of angle iron. When machines were transported over rough roads, these rigid legs couldn't absorb the shocks and sometimes the concrete broke. So now, in Malawi, Jock developed a stand made of rebar and shaped so as to be springy.

The rocker water pump

If the midi was the orphan of the expedition, the water pump proved to be the almost-unexpected star.

Knowing how important irrigation is for sub-Saharan Africa, Jock had invented a simple, portable water pump (more about this in Chapter Nine) which now needed to be tested on an African farm; the molds and parts had come in our luggage. On the day after our return from Chipelara, Jock and Gregor cast the concrete parts; two days later they were taken out of the molds and the device was assembled.

The pump consists of three shallow cylindrical chambers, with an intake hose and an outflow hose.[15] Across the tops of the cylinders is a horizontal board: the operator stands on this and simply shifts his or her weight from side to side. The device is called the rocker pump to distinguish it from an entirely different one that Jock would invent later.

That first pump, when tested, leaked everywhere; because the concrete was still unseasoned and fragile, Jock had deliberately not tightened the nuts. Also the design was still under development. Jock discussed it

---

15 Two chambers are for intake, one for outflow.

Jock assembling the rocker water pump.

Photo credit: Marianne Brandis.

with Gregor and Brian Connors, and with Bryan and Keah Payne, who joined us on that Wednesday. Bryan and Keah were Peace Corps Volunteers who had already been in Malawi for several years. In the next couple of days, while Bryan and Gregor made another pump, Jock worked on the design: the pivot supporting the centre of the board (allowing the teeter-totter movement) was not stable enough, and some kind of carrying handle was needed. (Portability is one of the pump's advantages.) Because the group decided that operators would probably like to have something to hold onto while rocking, Jock added an upright bar.

On the road again

Brian Connors had decided that we should test the water pump in Kwende Village, where Bryan and Keah Payne were stationed. This was south of Lilongwe, where the Shire River empties into Lake Malombe. Jock and Gregor and I would take it there; the Paynes had gone on ahead. It would again be a two-day trip; we would spend the night at the lodge in Liwonde National Park and, by way of a tiny holiday in the midst of a busy work-schedule, take part in two short safari-type outings, one at the end of the afternoon of the day we arrived, and one the next morning.

The testing of the pump took place on the second day, on the farm of Medson Chabwera. Here cabbage, carrots, peppers, tomatoes, onions, and okra were being grown on plots bordered by tall grass.

On the farm was a fish pond. Using an early model of KickStart's MoneyMaker – operated with a "stair-climbing" movement – the farm people pumped water from it into tiny irrigation ditches alongside the vegetable plots. By means of little dams made with a few handfuls of earth and then removed, the water was directed into one row of plants after the other.

The FBP pump was set up on a small ledge partway down the sloping side of the pond. The intake hose, its end encased in a perforated plastic soft-drink bottle to act as a filter, was let down into the water, and the end of the outflow hose was taken into one of the vegetable plots. Jock stepped onto the board, "rocked" fast for a moment to prime the pump, then settled into a steady back-and-forth movement. Water flowed from the outlet hose.

When one of the villagers tried it, the water flow was weaker, but Jock showed him that he had to press down harder on one of the intake chambers, and then it improved.

About the whole procedure of testing the pump, Jock wrote:

> There was so much excitement over the pump that it overshadowed [the other machines]. ... The reason people all took to it instantly was that they were all looking for something between drip irrigation and irrigation-ditch irrigation. They all wanted a machine that had more pressure and less volume. Drip irrigation is endlessly fussy, with the little holes getting plugged up all the time. Ditches work only in a pretty small radius and they are very [wasteful of water] ... and the [water] saturates the ground [so that] it turns brick-hard at the end of the season. That makes preparing the soil for the next crop very difficult. What our pump offers is spot watering. ...
> My big design error was that, since the pump works with your body weight, not your muscles, I had created a good design for the average Wilmington volunteer's body weight. Everyone [in Malawi] was much lighter, and the natural rocking speed didn't fit with the water flow. I'll start from scratch with a smaller unit that will fit their body weights.

That pump was left in Kwende Village for further testing under Bryan Payne's supervision; when we got back to Lilongwe, Jock and Gregor made another one. Word spread in the aid community, and in the next couple of weeks Jock demonstrated it over and over again. When the intake hose was put in a pail being filled from a tap running full speed, operating the pump kept the level of water in the pail constant. An area of the Connors' garden got well watered.

Jock also demonstrated the pump to representatives from Alliance One, a firm which buys tobacco from 100,000 small farmers[16] in Malawi (as well as others

16 The figure comes from Jock; I haven't been able to verify it.

in many different countries). In Malawi at least – and perhaps elsewhere – Alliance One struggles with a see-saw fluctuation of supply. When prices are high, farmers plant more; the resulting large harvest causes the prices to drop and in the following year farmers plant too little. Alliance One told Jock that they'd like to persuade the farmers to make the supply more consistent and to reduce their dependence on tobacco by planting other crops; irrigation would allow for that diversification and for growing crops year-round. They were therefore also extremely interested in the water pump; there was talk of pumps being distributed by their representatives – thousands of them – who regularly visit all the farmers whose tobacco they buy.

Connecting and collecting

Besides making and testing new devices in "real" circumstances, another goal of a trip like this is connecting with local people and aid workers, and collecting and giving information. One day, over a lunch of sandwiches at the Connors' house, there was a meeting which included Brian Connors, Bryan and Keah Payne, our group of five, and Nick Lea, a development economist working for the World Bank. Jock described a percussion well-drilling device that his volunteers were working on, explaining that something similar was used in the American West in the 19th century to drill water wells and even the first oil wells. (More in Chapter Nine.) A pipe is driven into the ground by means of a weight dropped from the top of a tripod set up over it. Jock estimated that it could probably drill a well of up to 150-200 feet deep [50-60 metres] for $400 compared to the $10,000 which it costs to drill one with modern technology. To draw up the water, there would be a simple pump at the bottom, and probably a Savonius wind turbine.[17] Everyone discussed the need for irrigation to raise farm income. They also expressed the hope that the sheller would encourage farmers to shell nuts when they're fresh because in storage they're more likely to develop aflatoxin. As part of the discussion, Jock described the benefits of jatropha.

The group talked about how the local people's traditional thinking and family structures sometimes prevent the adoption of new technology even when it's affordable and is seen to work. This applies even to FBP's simple devices, which are designed to be as non-invasive as possible. There is more about this in Chapter Seven.

A few days later, Jeff Rose, Jim Nesbit, and Jock met with Brian Connors. Jeff reported on agreements reached with Total Land Care (TLC), who would do a survey of farmers to help shape future technology, and with the Citizens Network for Foreign Affairs (CNFA),

---

17 Savonius turbines – invented by Sigurd J. Savonius in 1922 – are vertical-axis "drag-type devices, consisting of two or three scoops. Looking down on the rotor from above, a two-scoop machine would look like an 'S' shape in cross section. Because of the curvature, the scoops experience less drag when moving against the wind than when moving with the wind. The differential drag causes the Savonius turbine to spin." http://en.wikipedia.org. Accessed on 3/8/2011. Jock would make the turbine of two halves of an oil drum sliced vertically and reconnected to create the "S" shape – another example of using what's available in the developing world, where oil drums are easy to find.

who would help pay for training and do bookkeeping. There was talk about various organizations who might train people to build the machines, but Jock stressed that training must be uniform if they're to be made correctly. Brian suggested a training video, which could be taken to the villages by the Peace Corps Volunteers.

Jock reported on the state of his inventions-in-progress and on modifications planned for existing ones: for instance, the classic sheller would be modified to make it easier and cheaper to build. He described a hand-washing station which he had developed for schools where the shortage of water prevents children from washing their hands after using the squat-holes. (Because schools rarely have toilet paper, children are told to bring their own from home, but most homes have none either, so the children wipe their bottoms with their hands.) Plastic bottles containing water are suspended over an old truck tire sliced in half and with a drain hole so that waste water can be collected in a bucket. Lifting the valve on the bottom of the bottle (think of a soap dispenser in a public washroom) produces enough water to wet one's hands and, if there's soap, to work up a lather. Touching the valve again provides a bit of water for rinsing. The device uses perhaps 10% of the amount of water required to wash one's hands in a basin. The components can be found in any third-world town.

Brian remarked that such a thing is needed everywhere in the developing world because inadequate sanitation spreads disease. [18] As for soap – he himself makes it with

18 From the FBP newsletter of Winter 2011: "Every year, untold thousands of children in Africa die from diseases they contract at school. With each of those children go the hopes for a better life for the next generation." Hepatitis, parasites, and polio are mentioned as diseases that spread

peanut oil, palm oil, and jatropha oil and teaches the craft to Peace Corps Volunteers who can then teach the villagers.

Information obtained during a trip like this helps Jock to invent new devices and work out how they can be manufactured and distributed in poor countries. The developing world's problems are of course well-known but there are local variations – not to mention the effects of weather and climate change, and of politics in both the developing world and the aid-granting countries.

The talk among us all – standing in Brian Connors' back yard, driving through the countryside, drinking a beer at the end of the day – touched on other questions. If irrigation allowed farmers to grow more vegetables, how could that produce be transported to markets such as restaurants? What kind of distribution network (marketing boards, regular pick-ups) would be needed?[19] Regular pick-ups from the farmers would require better side-roads, as well as reliable trucks and therefore repair shops and supplies of parts. If more

---

in this way. "Rotary International has spent more than 1 billion dollars to eradicate polio worldwide, and hand-washing is a key step along the way. But how do we [FBP] get the simple design of our solution out to the thousands of health-care and education professionals? Cape Fear Rotary answered the call with a generous grant allowing us to write clear instructions and produce a video of how it's done." This video is now on YouTube and the device can be made by anyone, anywhere.

19 When Jock and I were growing up in northern British Columbia, our parents started a marketing board to collect the produce of several farms in our small valley; a truck regularly came to our farm to pick up the collected produce and take it to Prince Rupert and Kitimat. Even though we were not involved in the work, Jock and I saw and absorbed the operations of a small, simple distribution system.

vegetables and peanuts were grown, would the villagers themselves actually eat more of them or would they sell them? (In the trading centres we had seen small displays of vegetables for sale and recognized that the growers had made the difficult decision of trying to sell them for a few kwacha rather than using them in their own families' meals.)

My own collecting of information went on just as constantly, and what I came home with was a similar dense amalgam of facts, impressions, and the insistent impact on the senses of things that were entirely new to me.

Sarah Pedersen writes from Malawi

Collecting information continued after I left the country, because I wanted to know what happened next. I had established friendly contact with Sarah Pedersen; her e-mails – which began a couple of weeks after I returned home – supplemented what I'd been able to collect, and she answered the innumerable questions which occurred to me in the following months.[20] In August she wrote to me:

> The first women's group we visited [Jojo] is doing
> very well with their sheller. We trained them how to
> appropriately use the sheller and we received funding
> through Peace Corps to purchase an oil press for them

---

20 Another invaluable source was Danielle Wiegel, a Dutch woman whom I met on the plane when I left Lilongwe and who had been working for several months with a Dutch aid group in the south of the country. In the e-mail correspondence which developed, she gave me information about life in that village, and she mentioned the Wittenberg book about a Malawian village, referred to earlier.

on loan[21] to use in their value-added business. They have been pressing oil since June and have made over 10,000 Malawi Kwacha ($66 [US]) so far. We trained them on how to keep books, market their product and how to manage running a business as a group. Although it's a learning process, I think they are doing very well and are very grateful for the sheller and the time and efficiency it affords them.

The second women's group we visited [in Gomatz] is currently doing nothing. As we discussed with them, ... (because of the breakage) people are fearful to go to them to have their groundnuts shelled so the sheller is currently sitting in someone's house I'm afraid. We've been working with TLC to provide them/us with an oil press so that we can develop a model business plan consisting of a sheller/press combo. As you can see, the sheller on its own (at least in broken-peanut-fearing Malawi!) isn't worth it for individuals (because of the expense) and for groups (because of the breakage issue). But if the sheller is coupled with a press as a means to add value, then the sheller is incredibly helpful and vital to a successful business.

In October Sarah reported that the combination of sheller and oil press, in Jojo, was a big success. "In three months they made about 12,000 kwacha (around $85 – a lot for the village in a short amount of time!). Currently, we are in the process of planning for the future. In December

---

21 In reply to my question for clarification of the "purchase ... on loan" phrase, Sarah wrote: "Austin and I received a grant through Peace Corps to allow us to purchase an oil press for this women's group. However, because we are working with several women's groups, it wasn't possible to simply give them the press. Instead, we gave them the press and after harvest in May, they will repay the 'loan' we gave them. With the money, we will assist our local community-based organization to purchase a battery for their cell phone charging income-generating activity which will benefit the greater community."

they will plant two acres of groundnuts to shell and press next year. We've been working on the cost/profit breakdown with them and assisting them with record keeping and management. They are very grateful for the sheller and the opportunity to save time and earn money." By then, the group in Gomatz was also making progress: "The other group you visited (the group that already had a sheller from TLC) is in the process of also designing and implementing an oil press business. Although they experienced many obstacles with the sheller alone, they were not ready to give up on it. With the help of TLC, we are designing a business model for them to use for future groups and entrepreneurs."

These nose-to-the-ground pictures provide an invaluable supplement to the larger one: it's essential to know how the machines are actually used. Along with the portrait of Grace given earlier, this puts a human face on life in an African village.

Sarah provided other information as well. I had been mulling over Brian Connors' telling us that he taught the PCVs to make soap. Soap is something that we in the industrialized world take almost completely for granted. It's inexpensive and omnipresent. In my reading about Africa I had learned that it was one of the necessities that villagers bought with their tiny income. But Brian talked about people being able to make it themselves. If it was so easy, why weren't they doing it? I asked Sarah, who replied:

> No one we encountered in our community made or knew how to make soap. I think this is the case for the majority, if not all, of Malawi. The materials such as palm oil and caustic soda were expensive and only available in

northern Malawi in cities such as Mzuzu and Karonga. So villagers had to buy soap in trading centers for about 30 Malawi Kwacha. As Brian mentioned, volunteers were taught how to make soap during training so that they could teach others if the project fit the needs of the community. Because the materials were not easy to access or transport, this project was not a good one for our community.[22]

What followed

I've told the story of our trip as it happened at the time, but problems began almost immediately, which meant that some of what appeared so promising came to nothing. There was a time during the following winter when Jock flatly declared that the Malawi project was a failure. Since then there have been some good developments but it's been a rough road and the results are different from what had been expected.

---

[22] Sarah also wrote to me about a project that wasn't directly connected with the peanut sheller but that provides another glimpse into the life of the village. "Austin and I assisted our community to open a community center and library in early July. We began the building in February/ March with the assistance of Peace Corps and USAID. It was a long process with many rewards and challenges but the final outcome has been more than successful and fulfilling for the two of us and our community. The center holds many different community functions and is a positive contribution to many of the community's various groups – women's groups, youth groups, Positive Living groups for those living with HIV/AIDS. In addition, the library has been a huge success. With the funding, two volunteer librarians were trained in Lilongwe with the National Library Service (NLS). We have also received many books from NLS as well as Peace Corps and family/ friends from home. It puts a huge smile on our faces to drop by the library and see people of all ages reading."

When Jock left in May 2009, about a week after my departure, it was obvious that he'd have to go back soon, and he did so in August. What he found, and what developed during the following months, led to a major crisis in the FBP organization (see Chapter Eight).

One sign that all was not well had come to light even before he went back. When we were there, the shop at C to C had no electricity, so it was impossible to install the metal-working equipment to make metering plates. For the time being, therefore, these would be made in Wilmington and shipped to Lilongwe. Word came back that the plates were too big, which meant that the rotors were too short.

When he returned to Lilongwe in August, Jock found a discouraging situation; he describes it in the report he wrote. About 50 pairs of stators and rotors had been made but the machines had not been assembled. "They had completed some machines but only to supply the needs of the Peace Corps." So in the next days, while Jock set up a small assembly line to make the 900 jatropha machines for BERL, the workmen put together the shellers. He found also that the urgency to get the shop operating up to speed had diminished because the BERL deadline had been extended to the summer of 2010. But it could not be left to languish: so far as anyone knew at the time, those 900+ huskers would still be needed.

By now, the shop had had wiring installed, and it was equipped with a drill press and "a high-speed saw that could cut several hundred pieces of metal per day." Jock bought steel, and the workers started making parts.

When they grumbled about working on an assembly line, Jock explained that it was an assembly line for machines, not for the men themselves, who could swap tasks.

Jock's report gives insight into the training he was providing. As he knew from setting up the shops in Uganda and Mali,

> ... it was essential to change the basic way that metal workers do things in Africa. Centuries of 'making do' had them working on the ground, with no work benches, no shelves for inventory at various stages of completion, and no racks for storing tools. So building shop furniture was a first priority. Next was the need for volume to create efficiency. [I trained the workers] to plan the week, not the next 30 minutes. So that if 50 short pieces of pipe would be needed for that week's production target, 50 pieces should be cut at the same time, the sharp edges ground off, and they should be placed on a shelf for that purpose only. The next issue was the idea of a minimum inventory. The first few days indicated that there was no policy of reserve inventory. The first attempts at a smooth assembly line were interrupted by the habit of buying a small amount of, for example, welding rod. When the last one was used, someone had to find the boss, get some money, get some transportation, and get another small amount. During that time, the skilled welder sat and waited.
>
> ... All the skills are there in various people but there is no management system within C to C that comes in on Monday morning, plans the week and makes sure that materials and manpower are there. That might start happening when profits from sheller production become an essential part of C to C's continued operation.

Jock assessed how the partnership with C to C was going. "I think that C to C is a good partner choice. They are now totally under-using their space and talent, but in many ways that's the story of African entrepreneurship.

The point is that they have the talent, the machinery, and the space to expand, and I think that once the BERL shipments head out and the money comes in, shellers will be a priority."

There was, however, another major problem. Lameck Makutu Jr. explained that in May he had been promised by Jeff and Jim "that FBP [would] handle all the selling and distribution" – which he assumed would happen when Jock returned. An alternative version was that the Makutus had been told that TLC would do this. Because this never happened, FBP had to hire a Project Coordinator (see below).

During this trip, the making of connections continued. Jock and Brian Connors met with UNICEF, which was establishing centres where "AIDS grannies" could work. Brian suggested that the women might make peanut oil, using the sheller and a small, hand-operated oil press. He showed that a woman could make 1 litre [just under a quart] of oil per hour. By selling this at the trading centre where she now bought her oil, she could earn a profit of the equivalent of 50 cents per hour. In a country "where incomes are around 50 cents per person per day,"[23] that's a huge increase. And producing more cooking oil in Malawi – even if, initially, only on a local scale – would start to decrease the country's dependence on oil imported from Asia. [24] (So far as I've been able to discover, this

23 Jeffrey Sachs, *The End of Poverty: Economic Possibilities for Our Time.* (London: Penguin Books, 2005.) 9.

24 Cooking oil is important in Malawian villages; like soap, it is one of the absolute essentials that people buy. In Malawi, Jock told me, they used to make cooking oil from peanuts. Now they buy soybean oil imported from India and China, so Malawi has become dependent

promising UNICEF project has gone nowhere.)

Jock also met with Energem, a big fuel-oil company active in the development of biofuels. Like BERL, they were encouraging farmers to grow jatropha on marginal land.[25] And he met with a busload of small farm-equipment retailers from Tanzania who came to see the FBP equipment and wanted to know if there was a wholesaler in Tanzania. Jock was told that there would be no way of getting completed machines to Tanzania because the transportation system was so poor.

A Project Coordinator

Even before Jock returned to Malawi in August, FBP had decided that they needed a person based in Malawi to oversee operations. This would be a major change in the way FBP operated; they had never had an employee stationed in a developing country but had always worked with the overseas staff of NGOs like the Peace Corps. A Project Coordinator was needed because FBP had not found a completely suitable partner in the country.

---

on those imports. If peanut growing and processing in Malawi could produce cooking oil that is cheaper than the imported oil – as is now starting to happen – Malawi would regain self-sufficiency in this area. But if the peanut oil is to be competitive, it has to be produced efficiently, and it's essential that it be done in the country. If it can be done in the villages, either in the home or by co-ops or village-level industries, so much the better because it keeps more profit from the crop in the rural area. That is one of the things that the Full Belly's machines are intended to achieve.

25 Jock delivered one jatropha husker to Energem when he was there, and they bought two more from C to C.

The Project Coordinator would be on a six-month contract, his salary covered by the Change Happens grant. Jason Colvin, the person hired, had a BA in international business and had worked in Malawi for two years as a Peace Corps Volunteer establishing business plans for rural farmers, including doing market research, budgeting, and bookkeeping.[26] There had been a sheller in "his" village, so he had first-hand experience with it. His work as FBP's Project Coordinator would involve supervising the manufacture and promoting sales of the FBP machines and doing a survey of farmers to find out what help and tools they needed.[27] He would make sure that shellers moved out of the C to C shop and that money came in. Jock, concerned about how well the C to C shop would continue operating after he himself returned to Wilmington, wrote in his report on the August trip: "Although his duties will lie more in sales and promotion, I will strongly urge him to set up Monday morning meetings where the issues of inventory and shipping targets get dealt with on the spot."

Jason arrived in Malawi a day and a half before Jock left. It was a very short overlap time, but Jock did what he could to fill him in. Some months later Jason was joined by Amanda Shing, an MIT graduate and Fulbright Scholar. Under the direction of Jeff and the FBP Board, the two of them began work on the preliminaries for the survey. In a report of December 2009, Jeff wrote that they would be "meeting with a variety of different groups (farmers, merchants, bankers, NGO workers, etc.) to … hold some informal conversations to find out what are

26 http://thefullbellyproject.org. Accessed on 19/1/2010.
27 *Ibid.*

the priorities for rural Malawians. The reason for this exercise is so that as we craft the [planned] needs-based survey we don't impose our priorities on those who will be interviewed. This way the survey tool can be closer to actual priorities rather than assumed priorities." Their preliminary findings, and those of the survey to follow, were intended to guide FBP in the development of new machines and the structuring of new projects.

This survey was never to be completed; it is part of the story of the Full Belly's crisis in Spring 2010 and will be dealt with further in Chapter Eight.

Jock's third trip to Malawi

In January-February 2010, Jock was again in Malawi. What he found shows how a situation changes over time.

In his report he first writes about the sheller. Sales had been disappointing, and he gives possible reasons for some local farmers' reluctance to adopt it. "Groundnuts are wrapped up in a complex social web that makes farmers' responses to the machine seem illogical to us. For example, if a farmer shells all his nuts at once and gets cash, he is considered wealthy and there is an obligation to share that with his relatives." However, Jock sees good prospects for the jatropha shelling, where these issues don't exist. He believes that, in Malawi, FBP came into the field one year too early for jatropha (witness the postponement of the BERL deadline), whereas the success of Mali Biocarburant shows that in Mali the timing had been perfect.

"The [water] pump, however, seems to be arriving right on time. Meetings with the Clinton Foundation and Heifer International created much excitement and early orders for testing, and, perhaps more telling, requests from staff members who wanted to send one home to family." Alliance One "want 50 to test out for crop diversification by their farmers." When tested in a village where a Peace Corps Volunteer was located, with a 200-foot hose [60 metres] they watered a corn field "at a rate which we calculated would amount to 2 acres [just under 1 hectare] in a day."

But he found many serious problems. He questions the value of the survey, of which there was still no sign. "The survey may or may not give us valuable information about how to chart our course in the future but there are pitfalls aplenty when people from a dominant culture survey the poorest members of another. I understand that great effort is being made to take into account how the answers will be affected by the many other economic pressures on our farmer subjects and their natural desire to give the answers that gain them respect in the eyes of strangers." Later he remarked that a more reliable source of information is the NGO personnel who have constant contact with the local people, and have wider knowledge and experience than the farmers themselves so that they can imagine and invent solutions for their needs.

He questions whether C to C is after all the right partner, in light of the fact that "they have made it plain that they will never get involved in marketing and sales and delivery arrangements." It was this that made it necessary to have a salaried FBP staff member in Malawi permanently. He contrasts this situation with the one at Mali Biocarburant, where "the sheller project seems to be on its own steady course with no financial drain on us. [As well as manufacturing the ones they need themselves] Mali Biocarburant is selling shellers to the competition and even training Peace Corps to make machines. The country essentially takes care of itself."

He considers finances. The ticket price of each machine is just over US$60, but when Jason's salary is factored in it costs much more than that to get it from the C to C shop to the user. In fact, FBP is subsidizing the shellers' cost, which "is in direct contradiction to our end goal of creating entrepreneurial independence for our partners so that we can move on."

The work of the Project Coordinator was not having the results that had been hoped for. During Jock's previous trip, in a meeting that he and Jason had with C to C, Jason "totally agreed that he was their marketing and sales guy. He offered good ideas on how to proceed. Then the BERL deal was suddenly put on hold, but I knew that there were at least 75 smaller jatropha producers who should hear about our machine. I had set up a meeting with the Minister of Energy, a big jatropha promoter, but he died suddenly before my arrival." At that time, Jock had worked out procedures for Jason to follow, designed to help C to C to turn out good-quality shellers at a reliable rate. Every Monday morning, Jason was to meet with Lameck Makuto Jr. to review inventory and also orders for shellers. Jock showed Jason how to supervise quality-control procedures in the shop. But when he was there in January he found that there had been no regular Monday meetings. The quality-control checklist which he had posted in the shop had disappeared. Jason had, it appeared, not visited any

Ministry or obtained a list of people interested in or working with peanuts or jatropha.

According to reports from the Peace Corps Volunteers, some villagers were unhappy with the machines – which, indeed, had major flaws. Stands were breaking because, it turned out, the steel rods being used were thinner than the size called for in the design. At the very moment when Jock, on his first day in Lilongwe in January, arrived at the C to C yard, Brian Connors was there loading several shellers into his truck. Jock saw at a glance that they were defective; he pulled them off the truck and recalled as many as possible of the ones already sold. Ten had gone to UNICEF. "They haven't been handed out to farmers yet and I think someone should check them out before that happens."

The problems were serious enough so that Jeff immediately went to Malawi to help solve them. Jock, in the covering e-mail for the report which he wrote after his first few days there, says: "This will read like we are in big trouble. The fact is that between Jeff and I, we can sort it out. We just have to be pretty hard on ourselves to get there. And I believe we should not look at Malawi as a series of smaller problems. We should all talk about a realistic path to sustainability and away from the big monthly cash infusion [Jason's salary] for which we have no option now. There is the danger of becoming the NGO that we used to make fun of two years ago. One where surveys are more important than product."

Call it what you will, we have an all-our-eggs-in-one-basket policy, and it seems we are committed to it for three to five years. That basket is in Africa, a place where even well-conceived, well-nurtured projects have a discouraging history of withering and fading away. Right now, I believe that the most important person in the entire organization is Jason, because we need good numbers to bring to future funders. He's the only guy in our only country and our future success depends on his success there. We can't say, "We've had some set-backs in Malawi but wait 'til I tell you about Haiti and Guyana." [These success stories were, at the time, not on FBP's official map. More about this later.] Unfortunately, the four days I was planning to get him up to speed on pump manufacture and material sourcing, he needed to renew his driver's license and car registration.

Jock recommended that Jason be instructed to submit reports weekly instead of monthly and that his work be micromanaged from Wilmington. He suggested that each sheller or water pump be tested in the shop before being sold.

Jason, at my request, provided comments on the Malawi project. Asked about his job description, he says that it was "vast" and that he couldn't do it all. "For me," he writes, "my primary job was to promote FBP technologies and assist the licensed manufacturer with any organizational development issues they might like addressed." His assessment: "By the end we realized that the UNS was just not a good device for Malawi. Labor and time are too cheap, not to mention several cultural reasons: people keep their savings in goods like groundnuts, not cash; nut shelling is a social activity for women and children; and the device didn't save enough time (e.g. it did not winnow the nuts from the shells)."

From this point on, the Malawi project will be dealt with in Chapter Eight. Briefly: Jason's contract was extended but he was put on a reduced salary because

FBP was by then very low in funds. When he was let go, no replacement was hired. Jeff resigned when it was discovered that there had been mismanagement in his operation of the office. The AOI program with its "all eggs in one basket" policy was eventually dropped and Jock was again able to work wherever people needed the technology. The Board, as part of the usual rotation of membership, was somewhat revitalized by new members. But it took another year before things began to work better.

* * *

Contact with Malawi is now fragmentary, partly because Brian Connors was transferred to Tanzania during the summer of 2010. Such news as reaches Wilmington is mixed. Jock learned in May 2010 that C to C was cranking out pumps; they had had more molds made so that they could build pumps faster. They sold 50 to Alliance One, the tobacco-buying company, and seem to be selling some to other organizations. This is what Jock hoped would happen, that a local outfit would just take off.

Information also came from a report on C to C written by Michael Brugger, a volunteer with the Citizens Network for Foreign Affairs (CNFA), who was assigned to work with C to C in order to develop and promote the FBP technology. He visited Malawi in April 2010. His report – detailed and full of fascinating information – states that C to C was making shellers and water pumps, and it brings up the question of using peanut shells to make briquettes for fuel.

And information came from another direction. In the fall of 2010, the BBC included the Full Belly Project in its World Challenge campaign. They filmed in Malawi as well as Wilmington, and Fiona Melville, the filmmaker who went to Malawi, sent a quick report to Jock about how the filming had gone.

> The guys at C to C came up trumps, taking me to Chilombo village as well as to some of their customers – a lady who uses the peanut sheller to make peanut butter to help support her family (she supports lots of orphaned relations), your friend Nick who makes briquets from the peanuts he shells and uses them to roast his coffee beans. I also went to the Makutus' village in Lizulu to film a farmer using his Full Belly water pump. He's been able to buy cattle with the money he's made from his increased crop of cabbage.

In March 2011, however, Full Belly learned that the shellers and pumps being made by C to C were very poor in quality. This information came from Nick Ford (the "Nick" mentioned above), who is working with small-holder coffee farmers in Malawi. The sheller that Nick bought from C to C was very badly made, so when he was in the U.S. in early 2011 he went to Wilmington to learn how to make his own and took a mini-factory back with him to Malawi.[28]

---

28 The coffee-producing co-op he works with – REMAP (Responsible Management Approaches Company) – sends coffee directly to Port City Java, a chain of coffee shops in North Carolina. This direct-trade arrangement is described by Jock as "a kind of door-to-door system which achieves the fair-trade ideal without all the bureaucracy that by now is making fair trade very expensive and complicated and intimidating."

The Full Belly Project's involvement with Malawi is currently focussed on the need for a device to screen peanuts and maize for aflatoxin, a subject that goes far beyond this one country. That whole topic will be dealt with in Chapter Eleven.

PART II

Inside the Full Belly Project

SIX

The Hub

The Full Belly Project's vision is huge and is being realized by means of a growing network of people working with the FBP technology. But the hub is tiny: the shop in Wilmington, and the little group of staff (Jock and the Executive Director), Board, volunteers, and interns.

The shop is, in floor area, about the size of two tennis courts. Besides open work-space, there's a small office and a room with a table for Board meetings and general paperwork. It's a few blocks from Jock's house, and just around the corner from Folks, a café where the FBP people are regular customers. It's in this neighbourhood that the large vision is turned into reality. Here the minds and the imaginations of the FBP people range back and forth between the vastness of the developing world's problems and the immediate matters of how a particular device works, and how it can be built and repaired in developing countries.

The shop. Creative clutter.

Photo credit: Marianne Brandis.

The technology

In the shop, visitors such as potential customers or funders can see many of the "finished" inventions (almost nothing is ever *really* finished) and others that are in progress. Groups of high-school or university students come; so do media people filming the work and interviewing Jock. A local Rotary group met in the shop, bringing its own coffee and doughnuts and being joined by Jock, the Executive Director Daniel Ling, and several members of the Board. (Rotary, which is deeply involved in the eradication of polio, supported the cost of disseminating build instructions for the hand-washing station described in the previous chapter.)

The current and most popular devices are usually on display - devices for processing food and other crops, for pumping water, and, in the case of the hand-washing station, for water-related sanitation.

Visitors might see, first of all, the various forms of the Universal Nut Sheller, most of which have already been described: the classic, the midi, the walnut sheller, the "granola" sheller, and the pedal-powered and electrically-powered versions of the classic. At the time of writing, the brazil-nut sheller is away being tested on cashews. Mentioned earlier but not dealt with is the mini, which is half the size of the classic. Jock wrote in an e-mail: "It is SOOOO cute, you just want to hug it and take it home. It weighs in at 20 lb. [9 kg.], including the wooden base, which, considering the dimensions, means we have actually gotten our post-harvest processing equipment down to being hand luggage. It will fit into an overhead bin on an airplane. We tried using sisal (manila) fibre as a re-enforcing additive to the concrete. Cost of materials is down significantly. The mold has only 3 fiberglass[1] pieces so it will be cheaper as well." The mini is good for coffee – it's the model used at the Biofuel Park in Hassan, India – and to shell peanuts for seed because, although the volume is lower than with the classic or midi, the breakage rate is also very low.[2]

---

1 Now plastic.
2 Jock is in fact working – partly in his head and partly in the shop – on a whole peanut-processing system: planting, threshing, aflatoxin-scanning, shelling, and oil-pressing. The setting up of an entire system is important because if only some of the stages are speeded up there will be bottle-necks at the points which are still less efficient.
   For planting the nuts, Jock is recreating a device used in the American South in the 19th century. It's a tube with a flap at the bottom and a cross-bar partway up the outside. When the farmer inserts it into the soil, the

Related to processing peanuts – as well as corn and other crops – are two devices for screening out aflatoxin-contaminated nuts or corn cobs. There's more about them in Chapter Eleven.

Under development is a press to extract oil from peanuts (and perhaps also from soy). The main component is the kind of drill bit used for drilling concrete; Full Belly gets these bits when, on account of the tip being work out, they are discarded. There are lots of discarded ones around, and this would give them a second career.

As for processing other food crops: we've seen that Dr. Gowda in India uses the sheller for coffee, and so does Nick Ford in Malawi. I've already mentioned the simple corn-stripper that we took to Malawi; it's a wooden ring with a handle, like a magnifying glass without the glass. Screws are driven in from the outside of the ring towards the centre so that the sharp points project into the open space; when the operator twists a cob of corn through the ring the projecting screws scrape off the kernels.

There's a device to crack corn (maize) for livestock feed: uncracked, the kernels are too hard and smooth to be digestible. It consists of two rotating concrete cylinders, adjusted so that they crack the corn without

---

crossbar both helps him to push the tube down with his foot and stops it at exactly the right depth. He drops a nut in, pulls up the tube, and scuffs the hole closed with his foot. In developing countries nuts are usually broadcast and then raked in, but this results in a great deal of wastage because they don't germinate well (or at all) if not planted at precisely the correct depth.

pulverizing it.[3] Such a corn cracker would be useful in Africa.[4] Corn is a staple crop all over the continent but, as we've seen, the *nsima*[5] made from it is not nutritious. The corn cracker would enable farmers to crack corn to feed poultry which, in the form of eggs and meat, would supplement people's diets. Moreover, poultry and eggs could be sold year-round for income. Poultry produces manure. The corn cracker is currently in use in North Carolina (see Chapter Ten).

A recent addition to the list of inventions is a device for opening cocoa pods. Jock had been asked "to make a machine to cut open the cocoa pod as the first step in making chocolate. Apparently it takes between two and five minutes to get all the seeds out of the pod. This creates a huge need for labour and has resulted in what is virtually a slave trade in labourers." Ivory Coast, the world's largest cocoa producer, "is also the centre of human labour traffic just to support the industry."

---

3   An interesting wrinkle: the kernels are hard enough so that they would wear down the concrete, except that by a fortunate chance their slight waxiness gradually coats the concrete. Waxed concrete, Jock says, lasts forever.

4   In the developing world, women use a mortar and pestle, or some other pounding device, to process corn (maize) but that produces corn meal, not cracked corn for animal feed. Industrial corn crackers are too big for small villages. (Jock tells me that the steel cylinders in these crackers *are* worn down by the hardness of the kernels because the wax – see preceding note – doesn't stick to steel.)

5   The Wikipedia lists other names for it, and other foods very much like it: nshima, bidia (Zambia, Malawi, Democratic Republic of Congo), ugali or posho (East Africa), sadza (Zimbabwe), pap food (South Africa), fufu (West Africa). http://en.wikipedia.org. Accessed on 7/6/2011.

Many of those labourers are children: there are "200,000 children working in Ivory Coast."[6] A village-sized device would enable farmers to do this stage themselves (in humane ways) and sell the results to fair-trade organizations so as to bypass the chocolate cartels who employ the children and own the slaves.

When he received this request, Jock – knowing about the power of the cartels – was wary. He tried to obtain information about the people who had approached him but couldn't learn very much, and he was afraid that he "might just be finding a way for the child slaves to make more profit for the cartels" by being made to work harder. His contacts did, however, send him pods for testing the machine.

Jock's first creation was a quite complex device that reduced the processing time per pod to twelve seconds. The next – simplified – version did it in eight seconds. Since then he has gone a step further, making the simpler device slightly more sophisticated but also safer to use. Even though nothing further was heard from the people who approached Jock, FBP is continuing to develop this technology. A D-Lab team from MIT took it to Ghana in January 2011, and it has also been tested in Costa Rica.

Several non-food devices are at various stages of development. One is the jatropha-processing factory in a container, already described in Chapter Four. Another is a village-sized, foot-operated cotton gin. Like a roller

---

6   http://en.wikipedia.org/w/index.php?title=Children_
in_cocoa_production. Accessed on 8/12/2010. The
statistic comes from a story prepared for the BBC. The
Wikipedia article states that up to 12,000 of those children
"may be victims of human trafficking or slavery."

gin, it pulls rather than cuts the cotton fibres off the seeds. Cotton that is pulled off is of higher quality because the fibres are longer, and it earns more on the international market; moreover, because less fibre is left on the seed there is more to be sold. On the political side (almost all of FBP's work has a political dimension) decentralizing the ginning would diminish the power of foreign-owned cotton-ginning companies and keep more of the crop's value in the villages. And, since two-thirds of the shipping weight of the cotton is seed, it will cost far less to ship a crop that is already ginned. The oil-rich seed makes excellent cooking oil, so that keeping the seeds in the village and pressing the oil there will result in more locally-produced cooking oil and less need for the imported kind. The press cake can be fed to livestock.

Water technology includes the rocker pump already discussed, a gravity-powered pump, and – the latest addition – a portable solar-powered pump. Until recently, work was being done on the well-drilling device mentioned in Chapter Five, and on a well-bailer, a deep-well pump, and a windmill, but this cluster of devices has been superseded by the solar-powered technology. The hand-washing station has been described in Chapter Five. Chapters Nine and Ten give more information about these water-related inventions.

In a category by itself is a simple and inexpensive wheelchair. "In developing countries there are lots of handicapped people," Jock says. This one allows the occupant to ratchet himself or herself up steps, with another person needed only to balance the chair. The ratcheting replaces much of the muscle-work demanded of an attendant and therefore enables less muscular people to assist their handicapped relatives and friends.

* * *

Not all of these devices are being actively worked on. The initial idea – the "Eureka!" moment – starts Jock thinking and experimenting, but the full development of a machine takes a great deal of time and work. Jock doesn't control all the steps; he relies on Pete Klingenberger and Accu-form, the plastics manufacturer, to make the molds, and everything depends on obtaining funding.

Equally important is the fact that for the development of each device Full Belly needs an in-country partner. The corn cracker is an excellent machine but for some time the prototype sat rusting behind the shop. No matter how useful such an invention is, if no organization has been lined up to help FBP to develop it, find opportunities for testing it, build it in a developing country or find a shop that will do so, and promote and distribute it, nothing happens.

The advanced levels of testing have to be done in developing countries. The machines have to be compared with any similar devices already available there. The testing has to take place at the right time of year: peanuts are best shelled soon after the harvest because old nuts don't give useful results, and the date of the harvest varies from one region to another. The jatropha sheller should also be tested with freshly-picked nuts. The rocker pump ought to be tested in the dry season, which also varies from place to place. But Jock's trips to developing countries can't always be made at the right time of year: testing may take second place to other reasons for the trip, such as setting up a shop, training workers, or attending a conference. So a machine may sit in the shop for some time, waiting for field tests.

Volunteers, interns, and the community

In Chapter One I described how crucial volunteers were in the Full Belly Project's early stages. They still do about 80% of the work. There have been several hundred by now, 20 to 25 of them at any one time, of all ages and from a wide range of backgrounds. Many come with useful skills or aptitudes; Jock finds that women make particularly good welders. The late Diana Rohler, a stock-broker who became secretary of the Board, began her association with FBP as a Saturday-morning volunteer doing metal-work. High-school students learn to work with wood, metal, and concrete and are given design and engineering projects. Recently, under the guidance of Jock and of Tom Ellsworth, himself a volunteer, a group of high-school students has been working on the oil press mentioned earlier. The project leader is Nathan Hansen, a high-school student. Some projects are done entirely by volunteers.

Tom Ellsworth – a retired Senior Vice President of Sheraton Hotels, whose hobby is restoring and racing antique sports cars – wrote to me: "I have worked with Jock in the shop for the last three years while my wife Jane and I winter in Wilmington [their summer home is in Massachusetts]. I average about 2 full days per week. Jane supports the organization by handling the donor data base, annual appeal and thank-you notes on a [year-round] basis."

Volunteer Sami Herbert was for a time the Local Events Coordinator and leader of the team that organized the 2010 version of FBP's big fall fundraiser. Other volunteers work on the annual February fundraiser, a complex event featuring exotic cuisine, a silent auction, and entertainment. Yet another group of volunteers set up a display at the Wilmington Children's Museum comprising "a power point telling the FBP story, the UNS, a functioning rocker pump, and child-oriented posters showing how our gear helps others." Volunteers have also restructured FBP's computer database.

A number of volunteers and interns come from the University of North Carolina at Wilmington. There is an FBP chapter there, and FBP people regularly take part in promotion and information events about volunteer projects. Students with special skills – a major in anthropology, or computer expertise – might serve as interns; in 2010, intern Susan Smith worked with Jock to prepare build instructions for the rocker water pump.

One volunteer, Colin Pawlowski, sent me this:

> The R&D department at the Full Belly Project is unlike any other. They are not the typical group of engineers/grad students who you would expect to find doing cutting edge research and trying to save the world. Instead, most of the people on the Full Belly design squad are Wilmington locals who volunteer at Full Belly a few days a week as a fun part-time hobby. While some of the volunteers are professional welders or mechanical engineers, many volunteers come with no previous training and are taught everything onsite.
>
> The core of this community-based volunteer organization is the "Saturday morning crew" …. This group of Full Belly volunteers is very informal and non-exclusive; anyone is invited to come join them on

Saturday mornings since there is almost always some new project going on at the Full Belly workshop. I found out about the Full Belly Project and their Saturday morning volunteer sessions two summers ago as a junior in high school when I had no previous experience in machine shop or engineering; I had used a power drill maybe twice before. The first time I showed up to volunteer at Full Belly one Saturday morning, the Full Belly founder Jock Brandis gave me a tour of the workshop, and then I was immediately asked to join a group of Full Belly volunteers who were testing a new well-drilling apparatus in the backyard. It was a group of high school students, and they had built a pulley system with a metal drill-bit and bailer to break up the dirt and pull it out of the well-hole. By lunchtime, everyone on the well-drilling testing team was completely covered in mud and sludge, because each time we dropped the bailer down the hole a large geyser of loose dirt debris and water from the well would spray everywhere. After that, I started coming every week because it was so much fun.

As a student interested in math/science, I was able to apply the concepts that I learned in school and get first-hand experience in engineering and mechanical design. Jock Brandis has been a really great mentor for me and the other high school volunteers who are in the Saturday morning crew. Not only have we learned from Jock the basics of engineering design and machine shopping, but also how to take the initiative to make a positive difference in the world. Jock encourages the experienced volunteers on the Saturday morning crew to step up and lead some Full Belly projects themselves. For example, another Saturday morning crew regular, Conner Brex, led the well-drilling team during his senior year in high school. As a result, the high school students who volunteer at the Full Belly Project typically have high aspirations for colleges and beyond, and many of them go on to study at top universities such as Yale and Cornell. In this way, the "Saturday morning crew" also acts as a launching pad for Full Belly volunteers to be successful in the future.

One intern was Ming Lueng, an MIT student, who was there in the summer of 2008. She came to develop the midi sheller and did interesting design work, but her biggest contribution was to draw up instructions for building the sheller – instructions which Jock calls "fabulous." In 2010, intern Anne-Cecile Besson – who had heard of Full Belly in France and asked to work with them without pay – developed a communications strategy and did other office work; she also translated the build instructions for the UNS, mini, and rocker water pump into French. Every week she updated the FBP Facebook page, and she coordinated with the UNCW chapter.

In a 2010 grant application, Jock wrote: "One of FBP's greatest successes is the remarkable series of young people who have been part of our design, testing, and assembly-line teams. ... FBP's 'graduates' have been accepted into some of the best colleges, often with generous financial support. They credit it to the extra-curricular essay they have to write. It's always about their part in FBP's worldwide projects and the hands-on engineering experience they get along the way."

* * *

Everyone in the organization is a channel between FBP and the people of Wilmington, who are the source of private funding and donations of services and materials. Tom Ellsworth wrote:

> Jock is the "Pied Piper" of Wilmington. How he does it I do not know, but somehow he has been able to generate a following that has enabled Full Belly to survive and grow. He has numerous volunteers (including my wife and I)

who work for the organization only because of our respect for this man. He has a relationship with the community that enables him to obtain free labor and free or reduced rates on many materials for [the] projects. ... Most of the steel and much of the lumber is donated. The Full Belly vehicles have been donated, Pete Klingenburger provides all the fiberglass plugs and molds at significantly reduced prices and is willing to wait long periods to be paid, Accuform provides all of the plastic molds at no charge. If Jock needs back-up on one of his projects he can pick up the phone and call friends at Georgia Tech, MIT or the like.

The weekly updates that Daniel Ling, the current Executive Director, sends to the Board indicate the extent of the support that FBP receives from the community. Local people and organizations stage fashion shows and a "Pedaling for Peanuts" cross-country mountain bike race to raise funds for it. A bookstore gave 10% of its net profits for one weekend to FBP. Someone donated the networking of the FBP office computers, and another organization designed FBP's new website at a much-reduced rate. A 1999 Toyota pickup truck was donated, and someone else helped to design and distribute the newsletter. The Wilmington Fire Department provided facilities for testing the gravity water pump. A former Peace Corps Volunteer and FBP supporter left Full Belly a $5,000 bequest in his will. These – a small selection from a very long list – show FBP to be the hub of another network, this one in the community itself.

* * *

When I was in Wilmington in April 2009, on my way to Malawi with Jock, I joined the group for a Saturday work session. They and Jock met at nine o'clock at Folks

Café. Then, with cups of coffee, they strolled around the corner to the shop.

That morning, in the metal-working area, three men worked on the percussion well-drill. Elsewhere in the building several volunteers cut up old inner tubes to make gaskets for water pumps. With the team leader who would run the sessions while Jock was away, Jock reviewed the work in progress, and then they discussed an idea which the team leader had come up with regarding the cotton gin. A volunteer came to collect T-shirts and brochures that had to be delivered to a church which was raising money for FBP. Jock circulated, making observations, answering questions, explaining things to me, helping people to find parts and tools. A photographer came to take pictures of the electric jatropha sheller; while he talked to Jock, a couple of volunteers removed clutter so that it could be photographed from all angles. Three visitors dropped in: Jock showed them the wheelchair and the "granola" sheller, and told them about the percussion well-drill. In the background, softly, a radio permanently set to the local PBS station played classical music.

One of Jock's tasks that morning was to pack for the imminent trip to Malawi (we would be leaving on the Tuesday). Besides the thresher to be tested, which he dismantled and packed in a suitcase, he was taking a set of molds for each of the two midi models of sheller and one set of molds for the rocker water pump. He was also trying to guess which of the required tools and parts would be available in Malawi and what he should take with him. Washers, nuts, bolts, a steel brush and other items went into the two large, shabby suitcases used for this purpose. The overflow was packed in his personal luggage, wrenches and screwdrivers mixing with the socks and the malaria pills. He always takes gifts for the local people, such as half a dozen pairs of drugstore reading glasses for the village chiefs and the elderly, and on this occasion he had two baseball caps specially stitched with "Obama" on the front, explaining that Barack Obama was a big hero in Africa.

That was the Saturday morning. In the previous and following days I also spent many hours at the shop. This gave me a sampling of the variety of activities, including the phone calls and e-mails, the visitors, and the dropping in of a Board member and a team leader. I also went with Jock to buy tools, parts, and gifts.

Funding institutions and partners

Besides the income from community donations and other regular donors, FBP applies for grants to foundations and other funding institutions. For a time (2010-2011), Jock was writing the applications (details in the next chapter) but now Diana Woolley, a professional grant-writer who is a new addition to the Board, has taken this over. (It was under Diana's tutelage that Jock learned how to do it.)

The sale of mini-factories and additional parts brings in some income, though some are given free. Organizations such as universities or well-funded church groups are charged $700 for a mini-factory for shellers or rocker water pumps, but in other cases the price is adjusted to what the customer can pay.

Jock's air fares are paid by donors or USAID-funded organizations. Overseas accommodation and in-country travel is covered by the hosting group; someone picks him up at the airport, drives him around, and organizes everything.

FBP always works with partners – American-based NGOs like the Peace Corps, funding agencies such as USAID, universities like MIT and N.C. State and the University of Florida, organizations in the developing world like Total Land Care in Malawi and S-SOS in Guyana. These connections are helpful to both sides: the FBP machines enable the partner organizations to bring practical, low-cost aid to people in need, and FBP keeps its core small and economical by linking with existing networks. FBP looks for partners that have goals and philosophies similar to its own.

Inventing

At the heart of FBP's work is invention – not only inventing machines but, in most cases, designing them so that they can be made in developing countries from mini-factories. Devices originate either with FBP's observations in the field or with requests from aid workers for solutions to specific problems. Some – the peanut planter, the percussion well drill, one of the water pumps – have their roots in pioneer times in the U.S., when agriculture was not so very different from what it is now in parts of the developing world.

Invention requires knowledge as well as experience. To be taken seriously – as he is – Jock must be well-informed. His anthropology degree is a good start, but he's had to develop his engineering and inventive skills and to research soil science, tropical and semi-tropical agriculture, international aid and development, construction materials, and many other subjects. All this, added to his and FBP's experience with past inventions, and to his work in the field, generates new ideas; at every stage Jock exchanges information and suggestions with aid workers, especially those already using the machines. He needs to know what equipment, materials, skills, and services are available in developing countries. He is particularly pleased when – as with the hand-washing station – all materials are available *in* the developing country. No molds or specially-made parts are required for this device: the instructions for making it are on YouTube.

In the process of developing a new device, there will be experimental models that don't work. This is an essential part of inventing; Jock, aware of the danger of *talking* about a projected machine for too long, starts making it early on. His approach – "fail early, fail often" – comes from the film business. "'Take 1' is no good? Do another one immediately." This is how it's done in the FBP shop. Building and testing the machine early speeds the process up, and if the first prototype is a failure ... well, then, you learn from it, build another, test and assess it, on and on, until you have one that works. Even then there'll be refinements, and experiments with the design or with different materials, or with a variety of ready-made components – always bearing in mind what will be available to people in Lilongwe or Port au Prince. Because most of the machines are so simple, this process is comparatively easy, fast, and inexpensive.[7]

7 Full Belly's move into inventing low-tech devices for use in the industrialized world is a new departure and will be discussed later. The machines are still mostly simple and low-tech but will not be made by people themselves.

A 2007 e-mail from Jock to correspondents in Guyana shows part of the process of invention taking place. Jock had been asked to create a peanut thresher (see Chapter Four) but had been sidetracked. Now, six months later, he was getting back to it and wanted to check a few points to make sure that he wouldn't "head off in some foolish direction."

> Peanuts are dried in the field. And, by weight, the nuts are about 5% of the total plant. This suggests that the threshing be done in the field. …
> Combing the roots with a sturdy comb works, I am told, but the farmers don't seem to want to do it. Perhaps that is because the comb tends to get stuck in the tangled roots. So if we go with a rotating comb, it will need to have considerable momentum for that first moment that the roots hit the comb.
> The attaching root tends to break at the point where it joins the nut. Although I have seen somewhere that [this] does not seem to be the case.
> The fields can be very far from the farmers' home/storage so the thresher should be light and mobile.

Would a rotating comb work? How would you drive it? Leg power is stronger than arm power, and legs tire less quickly than arms. He considers mounting the thresher on a trailer, which farmers can tow to the field behind a bicycle, and then the bicycle can be attached to the thresher itself so that the rear wheel – driven by pedaling – operates it.

We've already had a close-up look at the thresher he came up with; it's the one we tested in Malawi in 2009 and it doesn't use a rotating comb or bicycle power. But it's not perfect: it works well for the kind of peanuts – most common in North America – which grow in bunches, but not for the varieties, more often grown in developing countries, where the nuts are strung out along the root. So this is still a work in progress.

* * *

One significant technical development was in making the molds from plastic. Plastic has advantages: concrete sticks less to it than to fiberglass, and the new molds are a fraction of the weight so that more metal parts can be put into each box. They're also much cheaper. Because "dimples" are built in to show where holes should be drilled, there's less chance of inaccurate assembly. They're safer because cutting plastic doesn't produce the fine dust that cutting fiberglass does. And they carry the Full Belly logo.

* * *

An ongoing aspect of FBP's work is contact with people in the field who are using the machines. We've seen examples of this already, and here is a vivid snapshot. In March 2008, Jock received an e-mail from Chee in Ghana[8].

> I wanted to check in with you about what you'd like me to do on behalf of the Full Belly Project. There are lots of options, and I want to be sure to do what you think best. … I have a little sheller at Frances's house in Accra, I have a set of metal parts at Abraham's office in Amasaman, near Accra, I have molds in New Longoro, I have two shellers in New Longoro. We have peanuts primarily being grown in the North. We have shea nuts, also largely in the north. We have palm kernels, grown largely in the south.

---

8 I have no further information about this person: there is only the single e-mail with its vivid picture.

Chee appears to be in touch with Peace Corps personnel:

> David seemed like he might be interested in doing a follow-up training …. Do we show the little [sheller] off there? Do we built a big one? Where should the little sheller end up? Should I borrow the big molds from New Longoro so that we can make a sheller for Abraham? Should I borrow the metal parts from Abraham so that Crossman and John can duplicate them? … I need to be able to take care of this tomorrow, as I'm heading up to Kumasai on Wednesday.

This shows us how the hub connects with the people in the field. Success stories confirm FBP in what it's doing, while problems with design, manufacture, or distribution lead to modifications.

And so the work goes on, a constant flow back and forth between the core and the periphery.

Connection, promotion, and recognition

Part of the "wheel" is the connection between FBP and people and organizations in the U.S., such as universities with outreach programs in the developing world. There are also occasional contacts with corporations like Coca Cola, Pepsico, and the tobacco company Alliance One. In the case of the corporations, exchanges with the head offices can be very different in tone and content from those with the same corporations' staff in developing countries. Alliance One's field workers in Malawi are very interested in the water pump, but the head office in Raleigh, N.C., is not. Nonetheless, attempts are made to interest the head offices because, if successful, that might lead to the wider adoption of the FBP devices.

Jock also goes to universities, industrial firms, and other organizations to learn what he needs to know. In the Winter 2011 newsletter, he wrote that it was the staff at Accu-form Polymers who had taught him "how to make thermo-forming molds for our shellers and pumps." (He adds that they also provide "truckloads of plastic parts for our mini-factories. And we're still waiting for the bill to arrive" – another instance of the support that FBP gets from the community.)

He is regularly invited to speak and to give media interviews. Not only is he Full Belly's front-line figure, but he's a teacher and promoter of appropriate technology. He instructs MIT students as well as the volunteers and interns in the FBP shop, and he teaches concepts as well as technology.

In October 2009, FBP acquired its first corporate sponsor: Port City Java, a Wilmington-based chain of coffee shops featuring fair-trade and organic coffee. In the words of the press release:

> The Universal Nut Sheller can shell a variety of crops, coffee just happens to be one of them at a rate of 125 lbs of coffee beans per hour. It can also shell a number of other crops such as peanuts, jatropha, shea and neem nuts. The Universal Nut Sheller costs about $50-75 to make in a developing country, depending on the price of local materials, and can serve the needs of a village of 5,000 people. The Full Belly Project is working to link Port City Java® with organic coffee farmers in Malawi. These farmers will use the Universal Nut Sheller to remove the sun-dried pulp that seals the coffee bean into a rock-hard encasing.[9]

9 http://www.portcityjava.com/secondary/pressrelease_100609.html. Accessed on 13/6/2010

The web page continues: "The partnership takes the concept of Fair Trade to a new level." This "new level", called "direct trade", means that the coffee goes straight from the Malawian coffee co-op to Port City Java coffee shops. Jock told me that there was talk about having a "Full Belly Blend", which "would come with a brochure explaining the process. It would be in effect fair trade without all the bureaucracy."

* * *

Awards and honours are certainly a sign of success. Jock and the Full Belly Project have won a number of important ones. Money prizes are, of course, always welcome. The 2007 Geoffrey Roberts Award of $6,000 provided FBP with travel funds. The $5,000 MIT Ideas award for the pedal-operated peanut sheller paid for Jock's and Illac Diaz' plane tickets to the Philippines.

In 2006, the manually-operated sheller won one of the *Popular Mechanics* "Breakthrough" Awards that "recognize individuals, teams, and products that are helping to improve lives and expand possibilities in the realms of science, technology, and exploration."[10] In connection with the award ceremony, an exhibition of all the prize-winning inventions was held in New York.

In 2007, the University of North Carolina in Wilmington recognized Jock as an "Albert Schweitzer Honor Scholar", an award given annually "to a person from the Cape Fear area who exemplifies the attributes or interests of Albert Schweitzer."[11] In 2008 Full Belly

---

10 Press release from *Popular Mechanics*.
11 http://uncw.edu/honors/schweitzerbrandis. Accessed on 27/10/2008.

was named a Tech Awards laureate by the Tech Museum of Innovation.

Also in 2008 Jock was declared a CNN hero. Short videos showed him using the mini-sheller to process peanuts and coffee, and operating the pedal version of the sheller. Unfortunately, as Jock wrote in an e-mail at that time, "… our recent appearance on CNN International gave us very little money [in donations] because our website crashed and we were unable to restore it during the broadcast cycle." Nonetheless, the videos were very widely seen.

In December 2008 Jock personally won one of six Purpose Prizes, each for $100,000, given by Civic Ventures, "a non-profit think tank on boomers, work and social purpose."[12] This organization's goal "is to mobilize the time, talent, and experience of older Americans, thereby providing a strong sense of purpose to individuals and advancing the greater good in areas such as education, health, and poverty. [It] aims to make the Encore Career a powerful norm for Americans in their 50s, 60s, 70s, and beyond. … The Encore Career is a form of practical idealism, bringing together the practicalities of making ends meet over longer lifespans with the spirit of service typically associated with volunteering."

This is the most important prize that Jock has won to date; the prize money enabled him to keep working through the lean times of being on the "normal" (low) salary and then on half salary. (More about this in Chapter Eight.) That was the period in which he worked on the gravity water pump, the cocoa-processing device,

---

12 http://www.encore.org/about. Accessed on 27/6/2011.

and the aflatoxin scanner. Moreover, it was in connection with the Purpose Prize that he met Tim Will, whose support (which included help with grant applications) saved FBP from going under in Spring 2010.

In the fall of 2010, FBP was one of twelve finalists in the 6th annual BBC World Challenge competition, the goal of which is "to reward social entrepreneurs who [are] making a difference in the world, but not harming it." Following the event – which featured short videos of various organizations' work – FBP received innumerable requests from around the world for information about its technology.

At about the same time, Jock was profiled on National Public Radio in the U.S. and was contacted by people interested both in obtaining information about the technology and in offering help.

As part of the 50th anniversary celebrations in 2011 of the Canadian University Service Overseas (CUSO, now merged with Voluntary Service Overseas to make CUSO-VSO), Jock was featured in the newsletter as an early CUSO volunteer who is now doing work resulting directly from his service with the organization.

In 2011, FBP was invited to include the Universal Nut Sheller in the 2011 Gwangju Design Biennale in Korea, "the world's largest design exposition."[13] The UNS would be exhibited "as a representative of the field of technology for empowerment."

The flow of information and energy back and forth between the hub and the wheel's rim keeps the work moving forward.

---

13 Letter from Ai Weiwei, Artistic Director of the 2011 Biennale, to Jock, dated March 16 2011.

SEVEN

What Works and What Doesn't

As I suggested in the Introduction, the big question about foreign aid and development is why, with so much effort and money being put into it, there are still such serious problems in the "poor" world. Evaluating success in this whole area is a necessary exercise, but it's complex and difficult.

In the case of the Full Belly Project, one way to define what has worked and what hasn't is to look at the extremes. The greatest failure was the attempt to set up a sheller-building shop in Uganda; the greatest major successes have been Mali Biocarburant, S-SOS in Guyana, Meds and Food for Kids in Haiti, and Dr. Gowda's project in India, though several smaller ones rate as successes because they perfectly achieved what they set out to do.

In a 2007 e-mail to Hugo Verkuijl, Jock wrote that Mali Biocarburant was exactly the kind of project that FBP liked to work with.

You are
- partly owned by the farmers. This is very important to us because our mission is to keep as much of the crop value in the producing villages as possible.

- oriented to Western management techniques. This provides management efficiency and alignment with modern technology and markets.

- focussing on renewable energy sources to keep energy profits in the country instead of ending up in the pockets of the planet's wealthiest people and corporations.

In December 2010 Jock told me that this "still says it all." Successful projects are those where there is a partner on the ground who needs the equipment and who will pay to bring Jock over to give instruction in building it or to help set up a shop for its production. These partners want well-built, efficient machines and will make sure that that's what they get.

Mali Biocarburant is successful because Hugo absolutely needed the sheller for his jatropha operation and was committed to making it work. He's now selling the shellers widely[1] and FBP is helping to set up a competitor so that the price remains reasonable. The sheller is important in Mali, where biofuel is "big": because the country is landlocked, petroleum from the nearest sea-port has to pass through neighbouring countries, and the bribes that have to be paid all along the route raise the price of the oil. Mali Biocarburant may now be producing as much as 10% of the country's fuel needs.

S-SOS in Guyana has embraced the FBP technology and improved it. Jeffery Sankar, who builds the

1 Josh Litwin, in an e-mail of 8 March 2011, mentions that Mali Biocarburant has 40 shellers in operation; we don't know how many were sold to other people.

equipment, has modified the pedal-operated sheller so that the fan is in the base, which is safer and more effective. The shellers are an essential part of the school-snack system already described in Chapter Four, improving children's motivation to go to school as well as their learning ability and therefore, over the years, raising the level of education in the country as a whole. The program provides a market for local farmers. And the entire operation was set up by the partner on the ground.

Meds and Food for Kids is a success *because* – paradoxically – it is no longer using the FBP sheller: the operation is now so large that it has an industrial-sized one. But it was the FBP sheller that enabled it to grow to its present size.

Some of the smaller successes involve mini-factories. Robin Saidman trained in the FBP shop and then took a mini-factory to Senegal where he built a sheller and created a small but highly successful operation. What led to this success – one that mini-factories alone, without such sponsorship, rarely achieve – is that there was a direct pipeline from Wilmington and that the project was driven by a strong personality. The same driving energy can be seen in the work of David Campbell in Senegal, dealt with in Chapter Two. In Malawi similar successes were achieved by Tim Strong, Brian Connors, the Pedersons, and the Paynes.

Failure

One of the clearest causes of failure is a bad choice of partner, like Henry Masagazi in Uganda. His mission and vision were totally at odds with FBP's, and he had no interest in serving the local people.

The C to C operation in Malawi can't at this point be called successful. The big mistake was choosing a partner for whom building the FBP machines was a sideline, and who declared from the beginning that they would do no marketing. The fact that a Project Coordinator was needed – and that his salary was a serious drain on the FBP finances – was part of the near-collapse of Full Belly, dealt with in the next chapter. C to C is still doing no marketing, but organizations like Alliance One that know about the equipment can – and do – go there to buy it. But the fact that at this time the shellers and pumps being built by C to C are of such poor quality is also an indication of – at least – a very dubious situation.[2]

Some projects, therefore, failed because they were badly designed, probably through FBP's lack of experience or of relevant information. The connection with Rotary in Uganda came to nothing because Rotary – not being made up of farmers or people working closely with farmers – was not a good partner. An adequate vetting of Henry Masagazi beforehand would have shown that he didn't have the same mission as Full Belly. FBP and Nourish International, having set up the shop, gave it to him; he did not pay for what he received and had no financial interest in recovering his investment.

---

2 Jock remarked to me in April 2011 that "in Malawi, our name is mud." It's possible (and to be hoped) that FBP's devices – still under development – for scanning peanuts and corn for aflatoxin will improve its image in the country. See Chapter Eleven.

Another cause of failure in the early years was FBP's naïveté in thinking that building and distributing shellers was simply a matter of technology, with no social or economic angles. They thought that introducing the sheller or mini-factory to a particular location would lead to immediate adoption, and that distributing enough of them would change peanut production around the world. But for the first several years, at least half of the mini-factories just disappeared. The fact that the one sent to Dr. Manary in Malawi was eventually "rescued" by Brian Connors and put to such good use is a miracle, but its roundabout and accidental nature shows how difficult the miracles can be.

Even working out the mechanical aspects took time. For several years, the machines made with mini-factories were defective and the instructions "terrible" (Jock's word). It has taken years of further R & D, including Jock's experience making shellers in different parts of the planet, to solve those problems. Because, these days, people making the shellers can stay in touch with FBP by means of e-mail, internet, and cell phones, Jock now hears about problems and provides guidance. The much-improved instructions also help: it was Ming Lueng, the MIT intern who worked with FBP in 2008, who first prepared good instructions and started the FBP people thinking about the importance of language. Ming's focus on language has led to FBP's replacing the term "kit" with "mini-factory." This better reflects the reality: the boxes sent out from Wilmington are precisely that.

And then there are the more or less unexpected consequences. Tony Lumu achieved little in Uganda: the mini-factory he took was one of the early, defective ones, and the shellers he built probably didn't work very well. Even those made by Jay Tervo during his trip in 2005 may not have stood up well. But – this is the unexpected consequence – the video that Rex Miller made was sent out by the hundreds and helped to get things going. Tony was the essential link.

The example of Brian Connors shows that it's possible to learn to make shellers from just the mini-factory and the video instructions. Encouragingly, his first one worked, and enthusiasm carried him through a period of experimentation. However, when he saw the ones made under Jock's direction at the C to C shop he recognized that they were better. This is an example of the mini-factory model *almost* working: its complete and triumphant success is seen in the achievement of David Campbell in Senegal. Jock says now that if he and his colleagues, early in FBP's history, had been asked what they visualized would happen with their technology they would have "told the David Campbell story." But David's success is exceptional, and it came about because many factors merged into a useful and creative whole: the failures of other initiatives and projects indicate how rarely that happens.

David's work vindicates the mini-factory model but even now, with improved molds and instructions, there's still room for failure. FBP is trying to prevent some of these failures by a new approach: when contacted for information about the mini-factories, they first send out the build instructions and ask whether the recipient has the resources to do the manufacturing. This is increasing the success rate.

For a while the FBP Board was thinking of abandoning the mini-factory system: they thought that, when requests came in, Jock should travel to the destination in person. But that was clearly impracticable – for one thing, Jock was needed in Wilmington to develop new machines – so it was decided to keep the mini-factory system but to create fool-proof instructions.

* * *

Some of the failures result from encounters – which are sometimes collisions but also sometimes complete non-events – with the larger world.

Big industry and big research institutes have not been interested in the FBP technology, perhaps because it's not high-tech, perhaps because it's made mostly of concrete, perhaps because "big" just can't see "small." For example, FBP attempted to interest Coca Cola in supporting the rocker water pump. Coca Cola claims to have three major initiatives: food security, the wiser use of water, and package recycling (discarded soft-drink bottles are an enormous problem in Africa – and, of course, elsewhere). They have a huge presence in Africa and, Jock tells me, are one of the biggest single employers on the continent. The plastic or half-plastic version of FBP's rocker water pump (more information in Chapter Nine) would have connected with all three initiatives: it would be made partly of recycled soft-drink bottles and would use water more effectively to grow dry-season crops which would increase food security. But they turned it down. Talking about possible collaboration with such companies, Jock says: "What they do is not very honourable, but they have such incredible resources that if their mission happens to coincide with ours there is no reason not to work with them. But it's important for us to discover whether being 'green' is really part of their mission or just window-dressing."

Relations with universities have been better. The D-Lab program at MIT continues to be important. The link between the University of Florida, the Peanut CRSP, and the S-SOS project led to the success in Guyana. Dr. Rick Brandenburg at N.C. State brought about the success of the sheller in the Ghana villages with the new high-yielding peanut varieties. These three universities also support FBP's work by buying machines and providing feedback about how they work in the field. Once again, the common element seems to be that one key person – Amy Smith at MIT, Greg Macdonald at UFL, and Rick Brandenburg – seizes on the concept of appropriate technology and integrates it into the university's projects in the developing world.

Brief vignettes

Many promising openings go nowhere. A partial list illustrates the diversity of inquiries – and, incidentally, of the potential for FBP devices.

In May 2006, Late Lawson, "a Senior Technical Advisor for the Economic Development Unit that oversees CARE's projects in Africa"[3] saw the sheller operating in Uganda and was so impressed that he recommended the technology to all his field representatives throughout Africa. Nothing came of this because – as Jock explained – the focus of

---

3 http://www.fullbellyproject.org/history-php. Accessed on 17/3/2008.

a number of organizations at that time was not on post-harvest processing but on irrigation.

Also in that spring FBP received a request from Todd Reese, working in Togo with Adventist Development and Relief Agency (ADRA); he asked for information about the sheller and said that it would be helpful for women's co-ops in rural areas.

In October 2006 came a request for information about the sheller from Peru Projects, a church agency. Information about the mini-factory was sent but nothing further happened.

We've seen that one of the best uses for the mini-sheller is to process coffee. FBP was contacted by the Jane Goodall Institute, which was working on fair-trade coffee in order to enable villagers living in forested areas – important wildlife habitat – to grow coffee and process it in a small-scale, low-tech way; if the local people could make a living sustainably, it would help to preserve the habitat. In an e-mail, Jock wrote: "[The mini-sheller] ... could be what gets the Jane Goodall people excited." But it didn't.

In May 2007, Jock received an e-mail from Anja de Boer, a Dutch anthropologist working in Honduras for MOPAWI, a Honduran NGO focussing on sustainable economic development and conservation of natural resources. She had been told of the FBP website by Professor Prabhu Kandachar at the Technical University in Delft, the Netherlands. She asked Jock whether the sheller could be used for shelling the nuts of the Ojon palm tree to extract Batana oil. Jock replied that the stainless-steel sheller which he had made for macadamia nuts might be better; he asks for further information and says that he will research batana. Nothing more happened.

An e-mail from David Ware in Portugal requested information about using the sheller for pine nuts. "I would like to set up a foundation that could go to small villages once a week with the Sheller and the farmers would bring their pine nuts to the meeting point, as this is part of the Portuguese culture. They are not looking to profit from this but to use the nuts for themselves." Beyond that, he hopes to spread the word of the sheller throughout the Portuguese-speaking part of the developing world, which consists of "200 million people, including many African countries." FBP sent the mini but it broke in transit and there has been no contact since.

We saw in Chapter Three that in India there has been one notable success and several that haven't made much progress. There's another that looked promising but came to nothing. In October 2006 Roey Rosenblith wrote in an e-mail that "a group of students from the Massachusetts Institute of Technology … will be traveling to Gujarat, India, for the express purpose of introducing the sheller to India." He was responding to a request from Mary Sudhaker, working in Hyderabad with the organization Seguna Seva Trust, whose focus was on skill development for women and other community programs. Mary wrote: "It was my dream to introduce the sheller to the Indian farmer, ever since I saw it being used in Africa on link TV in 2005." Roey mentions that FBP has "received an e-mail from an Indian mechanical engineer who also lives in Hyderabad and is very interested in building these shellers." Nothing further was heard.

In 2006, much effort was made to get a set of metal parts to Simon Cooke, who wanted to send them to Zambia; he needed only the metal parts because he intended to use the molds left at the university in Lusaka by Allen Armstrong (see Chapter Two). As it turned out, Simon was sent a complete mini-factory. He discovered, however, that in the area where his charitable organization was located "there was little growing of groundnuts (indeed my villagers had not come across them!) so the mold was not utilized. I asked my manageress in Lusaka to find out where in Zambia it would be of use and I believe she transferred it or perhaps returned it to the university. [That] manageress ... has subsequently left and we do not know where she has gone to so the 'mystery' is proving difficult to resolve."

Intermittent contacts between Jock and organizations in Zimbabwe about the jatropha sheller have come to nothing, but in this case the decision was Jock's because the organizations were linked to the corrupt Mugabe regime. "You don't want to be part of a set-up that will use the equipment just to get more work out of the slaves," Jock said.

The "imponderables"

And then there's a whole group of factors relating to life, society, and customs in developing countries.

Even when a village is interested in obtaining a sheller, it might not be able to afford it. The sheller, while inexpensive for people with dollars in their pockets, is a costly investment for an African community where, as Sarah Pedersen reported, village earnings of $85.00

in three months were considered "a lot … in a short amount of time." The sheller which Tim Strong used to earn enough money to have a well drilled was *borrowed* from the Peace Corps, not bought. The peanut-shelling season is short, and to create a small local industry based on processing peanuts the crop would have to be safely stored so that the processing could be done over a longer period. Or the village might lack the organization to use it effectively. A sheller which could be the basis for a family-scale or village-scale industry might stand idle because the entrepreneurial ability and drive are missing, or because of illness or death in the family.

Many people in the developing world are so impoverished and stressed that they lack the energy to see as far as the next month, or the next harvest. "For as many generations as anyone can remember," Jock explains, "they have just survived. If they take a chance, they may lose what little they have." The very act of looking ahead, whether it's practical planning or visionary dreaming, requires a sufficient standard of living so that there's mental space left over from the absolute need to get through today and tomorrow, to postpone starvation, to cope with illness, to find water and fuel. The woman in Woroni could speculate about better ways of shelling peanuts because she did after all have a pile of nuts in front of her.

Because most of the world's hungriest people live in sub-Saharan Africa, Jock has done most of his work there; his understanding of local conditions, his talks with people there, and his study of anthropology have led him to reflect on their way of thinking. On the subject of the environment, for instance, he makes this comment: "The Africans had been good at long-term thinking until the Europeans came with their religion and science. The traditional way was for the wise old men in a village to warn against cutting too many trees because the spirits of the forest would be angry, and against polluting the water because the spirits of the river would be angry. Christianity taught them that there were no such spirits, thus opening the way for exploitation of the environment. Western science taught them about 'progress' and about the possibility that it could fix everything."

Joan Baxter, a Canadian journalist working in Africa, discovered this too. She quotes the chief of a village in Ghana: "My grandfather ... said that we should never cut a living tree for firewood .... He said that we should be careful when we cleared the land for crops and always leave trees in our fields. That is how we always did it. He said that the young people with their foreign ideas would cut down all the trees and then we would be hungry. The rains would stop. The crops would wither and die. ... That day has come. You see the trees are almost gone. The rains don't come as they used to. The soils are poor. And we are hungry."[4]

Many Africans are also fatalistic. In Mali in 2001, the rains were late arriving and Jock heard the local people saying, "Maybe this is the year when Allah decides that we will die." This acceptance of a difficult reality is not universal, of course; many of the poor and hungry do look for help. But where it is present it creates resistance to innovation, both in technology and in methods of

4   Joan Baxter, *A Serious Pair of Shoes.* (Lawrencetown Beach, Nova Scotia, Pottersfield Press, 2000.) 75.

doing things. Again, mental space is needed for even imagining the possibility of change.

Jock has also observed that in Africa good news does not travel fast, while bad news does. A single defective sheller spoils the prospects for the adoption of other machines, but a properly working one is something that its owners might keep silent about because it gives that village an advantage over its neighbours.

Sometimes introduction of the sheller is hampered by personal dynamics in the village, such as resentment of one person having something that gives him or her an edge. When aid workers encounter this, they suggest that the local co-op buy the sheller, but if there is no such mediation the resistance will not be overcome.

When a sheller is demonstrated in a village there's often, initially, a great show of interest. But, as Jock points out, poor people are inclined to be polite to the rich, and some are flattered that people from America should come to help them. Or, though watching with great interest, they're unable to imagine owning such an object themselves – and, indeed, they will *not* be able to, on an income of $1.25 or less per person per day.

Many villagers may lack the skills to work with concrete, which is another good reason for setting up a shop and distributing the machines from there. Jock can in fact not think of any instance in which local people made *good* machines from mini-factories without instruction from him or from someone like David Campbell.

Regional differences play a part: the sheller seems to be more acceptable in West Africa than in Malawi, perhaps because more peanuts are grown in West Africa. Also, because life in West Africa is much harsher – more extreme climate, more drought – villages are larger and the co-operative movement is stronger. One machine in such a village would likely be very well used – and indeed it is in West Africa that David Campbell has had his success.

Frequently the adoption (or not) of the machines has nothing to do with whether they work well, or whether they will help the farmers, or even with their cost. In the Philippines, as we've seen, Joy Young reported that farmers didn't want to grow peanuts because it was too easy for people even hungrier than themselves to steal them.

Sometimes we can't even guess at an explanation. In N'dem in Senegal, the bakery has the perfectly working sheller that Robin Saidman built. Vast quantities of peanuts are grown in Senegal and the villagers must be aware that this innovation would increase their incomes and make all their lives easier. But, although the molds and parts are available for anyone wishing to use them, there is only that one sheller in the area. So far no one has built more.

In Mali, Jock observed something else which discouraged people from initiative and innovation. He met a farmer who was doing well raising chickens. But as the farmer became more prosperous, his family and neighbours expected him to share his prosperity with them. Such sharing has many benefits, especially in times of hardship and shortage, but for the innovator and entrepreneur it's a kind of penalty: in the end, his innovation and hard work bring little benefit to him personally, though they help the community as a whole. In fact, Brian Connors reports from Malawi that farmers who grow peanuts don't like to shell their crop all at once because then they're regarded as being rich and are expected to share their wealth.

To counterbalance this, there are two stories about women farmers in Ghana who saw the sheller's potential. They were part of the 2009 project in which N.C. State and Jock introduced shellers to the farmers who had the much increased peanut crops.

> Yaa Adu, 45-year-old peanut grower in Hiawoanwu, said the sheller would help her in two ways: The first was reducing the fatigue of hand shelling peanuts. The second improvement was more economic: Being able to quickly shell peanuts would allow her and other growers to take advantage of times when the market price for peanuts is high. Hand shelling isn't fast enough to allow growers to rush peanuts to market to take advantage of a price premium.
>   Grower Janet Serwaah, 46, who tried the peanut sheller during the demonstration, said she has wanted to expand her peanut operation, but hand shelling limited her capacity to handle a larger crop yield. With the sheller, she said, expansion is now an option for her.[5]

Carl Scarbro, the Peace Corps Volunteer already quoted in connection with irrigation in Malawi, wrote to me: "Full Belly is making products that have use in the village. If the villagers buy these products and use them they will benefit. It is important to find the local risk takers to lead the villagers into more productive farming. Once the villagers see those people's success then they will follow. Most Malawians are very conservative and risk-adverse."

---

5 Natalie Hampton, "Cultivating Efficiency".

There is, however, often resistance to the ideas and technology offered by aid workers from the industrial world. Joan Baxter, doing a survey about firewood consumption, reported a conversation she had with an elderly woman in Ghana.

'You people with your education and foreign ways, we don't understand you …. When I was a young girl, you came here and you told us to cut down the trees we always left growing in our millet and sorghum fields. You told us to cut them down and plant maize. Only maize. You told us not to plant it with beans or around the trees the way we always planted our millet and sorghum. You said we should grow it by itself. You told us to buy tractors and to use modern farming methods. So we did. We bought fertilizer. We cut down our trees, even the economic trees we need for protecting our soil and for sheanut butter and our foods. We bought your maize seed. We did everything you said. Our tractors broke down and we couldn't get fuel. You sent the tractors but not the means to run them or repair them. Next thing, you people came here and told us never mind the tractors; tractors were not good. You said we should go back to using bullocks to plough our fields because it was better than tractors after all. Then we couldn't buy fertilizer any more because it became too costly. So our harvest just get[s] poorer and poorer. We don't have our own seed any more and we cannot afford to buy the seed you sell us. You come again and tell us we should use manure and trees to fertilize our fields. But we don't have any of the trees left that used to feed us and make the soil rich because you told us to cut them down. And so we can't find fuelwood. We spend our days walking, walking, walking to get some small firewood and water. Now you strangers come again and tell us we should plant plenty of trees, not cut them down.'
     She paused, finally eyed us each carefully. Then she ran her tongue over her lips and said, 'Why don't you make

up your minds? We are tired of this. Why do you bring
your mistakes here?'[6]

This moving and disturbing passage helps us to put
ourselves into the minds of the villagers. Maybe the
peanut sheller is an answer to prayer, as it was for the
woman in Woroni, and maybe it's just an unwanted
and almost incomprehensible intrusion from a world
which – with tact and helpfulness, or perhaps bossiness
and condescension – continually tells them that they are
doing things wrong. "'Just another stupid white man's
idea,'" as Jock muttered to me one day, quoting an
imaginary disgruntled villager.

It's impossible to generalize about a billion poor
farmers in dozens of countries: the imponderables
vary from place to place. Many – perhaps most – of the
failures have less to do with the technology itself than
with the circumstances. Some seeds fall on good ground,
some on unwelcoming soil. As Jock wrote in February
2010, Africa is known in the aid community as "a place
where even well-conceived, well-nurtured projects have
a discouraging history of withering and fading away,"
and the causes are complex and subtle.

Reflecting on the FBP's progress to date, he uses the
phrase "the vine of success" – not a tree, but a vine, a
single strand with few branches but with a strong
forward-growing energy. Inventing and making the
machines is the simple part.

For the Full Belly Project, assessing success and
failure, and analyzing the causes, is an ongoing
process. In these early years, driven by the enthusiasm
of creating something which has the potential to do

6   Joan Baxter, *A Serious Pair of Shoes*. 77.

so much good – and driven too by the awareness that starvation is, every day, killing people who might have lived had they been able to benefit from these machines – FBP has been concentrating on the invention, development, and distribution of the sheller and other devices. Because their staff is small, choices had to be made about how to spend the available time; gathering follow-up information has not always had a high priority.

Jay Tervo, ruminating on my question about FBP's successes and failures, told me that he prefers to think in terms of "what worked and what didn't." He wrote:

> We have no formal measures of success that we have agreed upon as a Board. We are clear that we know them when we see them – i.e. a certain number of machines made using a set of molds, requests for more machines or for consulting, the increase in income in an area because of the introduction of the machines. ... Every attempt [which initially appears to be unsuccessful] adds to [Jock's] and our body of knowledge about how to be effective and successful. ... To me, the most clear measure of success is whether or not our efforts are sustainable, both here and in another country. Overseas, my metric is whether the machines we cause to be built are being used and, most especially, whether new machines [are] being made and distributed.

And Jay adds a useful reminder: "The biggest part of the question [is that] so much depends on the personal philosophies of who is asking the question and who is answering it."

Unfortunately, by 2011 the Full Belly Project's assessment of its own successes and failures had strayed far from the reality. It had set itself on a course that did not work, and a major redirection had to take place.

EIGHT

Inventing a Non-Profit, Stage 3

In the previous chapter, I showed that the Full Belly Project itself contributed to some of the failures that mark its history. But that's not the whole story: in the spring of 2010, as a result of fundamental internal problems, the organization nearly collapsed.

Founded in November 2003, FBP is still young. It began with nothing except a bright idea, and what exists now – the hub in Wilmington, the wheel of connections, the stream of new inventions and their increasingly widespread use – shows that it's a success. Jay Tervo wrote in January 2010: "[When we started] we knew of no other organizations we could look [to] to model ourselves after;" in other words, there was no small organization which designed equipment for use in the developing world but had no staff overseas. The conviction that they had an "awesome idea,"[1] which became embodied in an extremely practical tool – now a number of tools – provided the enthusiasm and energy that, in spite of setbacks, have kept them pushing ahead.

Declaring FBP to be in general a successful operation does not, however, explain why it very nearly died.

---

1 Jay Tervo's phrase.

* * *

In the beginning, Jock and Jay and their colleagues had envisioned a small, adventurous, "fly by the seat of your pants" organization, and Jay set it on that course. After his term as president ended in 2007, he was replaced by two co-presidents, both of whom were risk-aversive. (One worked in nuclear energy, the other in state insurance regulation.)

When Jock returned from the jatropha convention in Miami in June 2008, he was told that FBP was going to become more corporate. The Board had decided that all the machines would be patented, a move that Jock opposed because he regarded the "open technology" status as a way of passing donors' generosity on to users.[2] Furthermore, users would have to sign a complex legal document which would make them, in effect, partners of Full Belly. Jock opposed this too, pointing out that if you buy a car you don't become a partner of the manufacturer – you just want a car. In any case, people making machines in developing countries can't cope with anything so legalistic. The document stated that, in case of unresolved disagreements, the partner/user would have to appear in a court of law in New York State – a clear impossibility for virtually all of them.

Part of the reason for considering patenting was that FBP was short of funds. The profit from the sale

2 Jock has modified his position on patenting. When he mentioned the rocker water pump to UNICEF in Malawi, they asked him whether Full Belly had control over the design, because they didn't want to support an organization that didn't have the legal ownership represented by a patent. See below for more about the issue of patenting.

of mini-factories doesn't nearly cover the overhead, salaries, and other running expenses. Arrangements with customers have to be flexible because most buyers are small-budget operations; some mini-factories are given free of charge. A non-profit organization like this would normally derive most of its income from grants and private donations. For FBP, whose work touches on so many issues of concern in aid circles, obtaining grant money ought to be easy.

But the Executive Director at that time, who should have been writing grant applications, was either not doing so or was writing unsuccessful ones. Little money was coming in except from private donors. There were no current official projects which could serve as the basis for grant applications: a vicious circle, with no money coming in and no grant-attracting work taking place. This inactivity also provided little basis for local fund-raising, the kind that involves asking for money for a specific project.

The two Full Bellys

"No current *official* projects"? Well, one wrinkle was that Jock's R&D projects often didn't come under the umbrella of the Executive Director and Board. This resulted from the way in which FBP had been set up. In its by-laws Jock is designated as staff – he is the Director of R&D – and has no vote on the Board. Officially, therefore, he is the junior employee, subordinate to the Executive Director; in Spring 2010, in the middle of the crisis, he was told by the President that he "worked for" the Executive Director and had to obey orders. In fact, of course, he's the central figure in the organization and his work is the reason for its existence. Jock's way of dealing with this uncomfortable anomaly, and also of doing his work creatively and quickly, was to treat his inventions as a series of R&D projects which produced new technology and got it out to developing countries as fast as possible. This was the continuation of his and Jay's original vision of a small organization that would respond rapidly to needs.

Jock called this arrangement "the two Full Bellys." To test prototypes of the inventions he was currently working on, he'd set up small, fast, efficient projects such as the one in Mali to test the jatropha sheller. Usually the invention was his response to a request for a solution to a specific problem, and it was natural to test the machine in collaboration with the person who had requested it. He raised funds from regular donors who liked his approach. On paper they were R&D projects, but they often developed into successful free-standing operations, like those in Mali, Guyana, and Honduras, and several of the ones in Haiti.

Having done the R&D, Jock would present the results in a report to the Executive Director. Because these projects usually required no further financing, the issue of Board approval never came up, and the report went into the files.

The Executive Director and the Board disliked this split, but it existed because of Jock's frustration with policies and decisions which limited both his creativity and the wider dissemination of his inventions, as well as causing a slow response to urgent requests.[3] The

---

3 He had learned his approach in the film business, where assignments had to be done very quickly.

Executive Director and Board moved much more slowly and ponderously. The operations in Uganda and Malawi, which were typical Board projects, required large amounts of money and involved official fund-raising, extensive planning, and many meetings. There were, in fact, very few such operations and they have a poor record: Uganda is a complete failure, and in Malawi there has, at the time of writing, been too little achieved for the time and money spent. After the expenditure of $30,000, the latter project has not progressed nearly as far as the ones in Mali or Honduras.

What aggravated the split was the fact that the normal Board turnover gradually eliminated the original members, most of whom had been Returned Peace Corps Volunteers. Fewer and fewer Board members, therefore, had actually worked in the "poor" world. "With [these] changes in the composition of the Board," Jay wrote, "many times lessons learned in the early years are lost, and [have] to be relearned. (Those who don't know their history are doomed ....)"

Because of the "two Full Bellys" arrangement, the Board was never good at analyzing FBP's successes and failures. It considered only the official projects and ignored Jock's R&D ones, most of which are self-sustaining, therefore successful, and therefore pretty well off the radar. As far as the Board was concerned, they were merely reports in a filing cabinet. Newer members frequently knew nothing about them; upon joining the Board they were briefed by the Executive Director, and from 2008 to 2010 he told them that FBP operated only in Malawi. Some Board members in that period looked blank at any reference to the projects in Mali, Guyana,

Haiti, Senegal, Honduras, and India – precisely the ones which, being successful, should have been used as models. At a strategic planning meeting held in early 2010, when Board members were given a list of all the countries where Full Belly had worked and was working, they were amazed at the range of activities.

Acceleration of Innovation

Part of the move to become more corporate was the Executive Director's "Acceleration of Innovation" plan (AOI), already mentioned in Chapter Five. It led to heated discussion about where FBP was going. This was, of course, its purpose, but it caused a great deal of turmoil – and waste of time and money – as well as pushing FBP to the brink of collapse.

Malawi only for five years

A crucial element of AOI was that for five years FBP would operate only in Malawi. This country was chosen "as our pilot project because of its relatively small size and varied ecological zones." Jock opposed this "all eggs in one basket" proposal, pointing out that if you set up projects in three countries, and one of them never takes off, at least you can go back to the funders and talk about your other successes. As he wrote in an e-mail of 19 March 2010 which was a last-ditch attempt to prevent the adoption of AOI as official policy:

> The fact is that we are *not* in one country, and it will be tough to turn our backs on people just because that might become our policy. Our local funders would be very unhappy if we refused to support programs for needy

people where there is no cost and little hassle for us just because the poor people are in the wrong country. If we get dogmatic, and [then] Heifer International offers us an all-expenses-paid chance to set up water-pump production in 30 African countries, we [would, under AOI] have to refuse. ... Our donors believe we are committed to helping poor people everywhere.

Jock was not the only one to object. FBP's president at the time was Jack Slattery who, as a retired USAID Project Manager, had a great deal of experience in international development. He also warned against it. In fact, by the time Jock was writing the just-quoted e-mail, one very serious effect of the "all eggs in one basket" policy had already showed up. Shortly after the January 2010 earthquake in Haiti, Slattery was approached by a friend in USAID, which had instant funding available for the country. The friend knew that FBP had partners there, any or all five of whom would have benefited from an infusion of money by being able to expand its work in the devastated country. Slattery took this offer to the FBP Board but – sticking to the AOI position of operating only in Malawi – they rejected it. Jack Slattery resigned and FBP did not get the funding to pass on to its Haitian partners.

Survey

To find out what Malawian farmers needed, AOI stipulated that a Technological Needs Survey would be prepared and administered. Jock wrote:

The plan was that Jason Colvin [the Project Coordinator] would be working with Amanda Shing, who arrived with her own $26,000 Fulbright scholarship, and they would, working with Total Land Care, do the survey. But after five months, it all fell apart because FBP had not even been able to come up with the wording on the survey. [What they had worked out up to that point] was so intrusive into so many personal aspects of the farmers' lives that it would probably have been met with some resistance or returned false data. Poor Africans tend to tell white people what they want to hear.

Jock – experienced in finding out what such farmers need – knew that much more reliable information could be obtained from FBP's dozens of contacts who are working in the field and are in constant touch with the farmers. Moreover, as Jay Tervo pointed out in an e-mail to his colleagues on the Board, "We have basically no experience conducting surveys, which is a highly specialized activity."

Invention

Then these machines would have to be invented. In the words of the Acceleration of Innovation Plan, they would be invented not just by "The Experts": "The AOI recognizes that engineers will always be needed but seeks to break down the wall between designers and supporters by offering an interactive online space where anyone can share their ideas in an international collaboration. This system invites the ideas of all who choose to participate, which will open the door to 'outside-the-box solutions'." Jay's comment: "When this was first shared with the Board, it seemed so far-fetched to me as to defy belief. In a nutshell, groups of folks in this country would help solve problems identified by groups of people in other countries utilizing unproven/ unwritten programming on our website." Jock also considered this process unworkable. As he put it, "FBP staff and volunteers or people around the world in internet chat-rooms [would] develop the machine, if [it is] possible, if it doesn't already exist."

Promoting entrepreneurship

The machines would then be manufactured and distributed by entrepreneurs which FBP would set up in Malawi. In fact, while dealing in a minor way with inventing and disseminating low-tech tools, AOI concentrated on promoting entrepreneurship. Jock explains that such promotion had been tried in the aid community ten years earlier and had not succeeded. It was transmuted into microfinance, which did succeed, at least for a time.[4] Even had the fostering of entrepreneurship still worked, FBP had no expertise in it: "None of us has spent enough time researching why previous attempts at fostering entrepreneurship in Africa have done so badly. We know machinery. We are engineers. We don't know economic systems." The attempt to set up an entrepreneur in Uganda had failed,

---

4 There are now problems with microfinance. "Done right, these loans have shown promise in allowing some borrowers to build sustainable livelihoods. [But] most borrowers do not appear to be climbing out of poverty, and a sizable minority is being trapped in a spiral of debt. ... Even as the results for borrowers have been mixed, some lenders have minted profits that might make Wall Street Bankers envious." Vikas Bajaj, "Microlenders, Honoured with Nobel, Are Struggling." *The New York Times*, January 5, 2011.

and by the spring of 2010 the prospects for the operation in Malawi were not looking good.

Moreover, Jock pointed out that setting up entrepreneurs does not necessarily help poor farmers: in North America, helping the John Deere Corporation would not benefit the small farmer. Africa, he remarked, has a lot of entrepreneurs driving around in Mercedes. Specifically, the choice of C to C was by then recognized to be a bad one; the Project Coordinator's salary was a constant drain on FBP's finances, and the need for one constituted an open-ended commitment to subsidize C to C's production of FBP devices.

Unfundability

AOI was, of course, intended to be the basis for grant applications, but it was most unlikely to appeal to funders. Aside from general declarations of vision and purpose, applications have to consist of hard facts. Granting organizations want to know about the applicant's business plan and up-coming projects, with the focus on a specific undertaking for which a budget, time-lines, and names of partners are provided. The fostering of entrepreneurship, no longer regarded as a workable form of aid, would (and did) gain no support from any funders except Change Happens, and that grant was based on the personal contact between Jim Nesbit and Doug Troxel, not obtained through normal grant-application channels. In the "last ditch" e-mail already cited, Jock wrote: "My impression is that there is more money available for food security than for promoting entrepreneurship." Later, looking back, he wrote to me:

[AOI] is a completely un-fundable idea because it breaks every rule in grant-writing. It doesn't identify the final beneficiaries nor estimate how many of them will benefit. (Will they be chicken farmers or AIDS grannies?) It doesn't give any assurance of final success (is this machine even possible?) or any timeline for the project. It doesn't allow a real budget because you have no idea of what you will have to accomplish or how long it will take. ... And the donor will have no assurance that FBP will have any real control over the process.

Jock felt strongly that Full Belly should continue doing what clearly worked: inventing new machines and co-operating with partners who either would themselves be the end-users or were in close contact with them. He pointed out that their current practice was in fact an indirect promotion of entrepreneurship. "Example: S-SOS becomes our partner in Guyana. They choose Jeffery's metal-working shop to build all their machinery. We sell them models which get copied. Jeffery is now making our most sophisticated [pedal- and electrically-powered] machines ... at no expense to us and without me getting on the plane. I have never met Jeffery but we have fostered his entrepreneurship. That is a model we can duplicate rapidly, especially now that we are putting a major emphasis on fool-proof directions [to go with the mini-factories]."

Adoption

Jay told me that, when AOI was brought before it, the Board decided "to vote on one part of it (the five-year focus on one country, Malawi) and work our way into the business plan one bite at a time, testing it as we went along. We also voted to allocate money to fund the website programming upgrades. … As time passed, Jeff and … Board members became convinced that someplace along the way the Board had voted to adopt the entire AOI program as the business model for FBP. This became a huge issue … A record of any vote of this kind does not exist [in the minutes] until just before 'the crisis'."

As the chair of the Strategic Planning Committee, Jay decided to try "for once and for all to end all the sources of conflict we have had over the years. My committee met several times and came up with a very extensive strategic plan that we all compromised on. The vote was unanimous on the part of all 6 members [of the committee]." What was suggested in this compromise plan was a two-pronged approach: one would be AOI and the focus on Malawi, and the other would be a continuation of existing practice. It also aimed to bring into the Board's line of sight the successful R&D projects which were unknown or ignored.

The Board rejected the plan.

* * *

AOI was adopted as Full Belly's official business plan in March 2010 but some of its elements had been shaping decisions since at least early 2009. The timing of our trip to Malawi in spring 2009 should have been determined by the date of the peanut harvest because the midi shellers and the thresher had to be tested using fresh peanuts. However, the Board delayed it, with the result that, although the new technology was tested, the trip focussed on setting up the shop at C to C – a shift away from developing new technology and in the direction of promoting entrepreneurship.

Effects of AOI

AOI was, then, a serious change of direction. Filling me in on the background, Jock mentioned that thousands of projects have been taken into Africa, projects which were expected to work there because they worked in the industrialized world. But most of them don't work in Africa. Jock felt that AOI would make Full Belly too similar to those projects. None of them sufficiently considered the complexities of African social behaviour and agricultural traditions; he wanted FBP to design projects that did take those factors into account, so that he could say, "We're new!" The highly flexible mini-factory system is part of what makes FBP different and innovative, and is the basis for most of its successes. AOI bypassed and marginalized that system. Most importantly, perhaps, AOI limited FBP to only a tiny fraction of what it could potentially do.

The project in Malawi, which was the realization of AOI, became the crux of FBP's near-collapse in the spring of 2010. It was too expensive to be sustainable. Because it was not fundable, little grant money was coming in. The Project Coordinator in Malawi, rather than focussing on promoting and selling shellers, had been instructed by the Executive Director to work on the survey. Amanda Shing, the MIT graduate who was in Malawi on a Fulbright Fellowship, waited for months for the wording of the survey so that she and Total Land Care could proceed.

The very fact that a Project Coordinator was needed was a sign of trouble: with self-sustaining projects like the ones in Guyana, Mali, India, and Haiti the partner supervises shop personnel, quality control, promotion, sales, everything. In Malawi, apparently no real attempt had been made to find such a partner.

Jason Colvin, the Project Coordinator, told me that he considered that "the Malawi project was too ambitious for FBP. Everyone had to do more than they feasibly could. Also, because we each have our own specialties, we lacked the skills to do these additional assignments well. … we took on something that required more staff, skills, and money than we had."

By the spring of 2010 Full Belly was very nearly broke. The only money coming in was small amounts from local donors who supported Jock's work. In an e-mail to the Board on 5 April, Jay wrote: "In three months we will close our doors unless we take drastic measures now." Besides suggesting ways to cut costs, he talked about the need to obtain more grant money. The fact was that, except for the $40,000 Change Happens grant for the operation in Malawi – which by then was spent –

> no one else has given us any money for the project.…
> Logically,… it seems that maybe we need to consider that
> the kind of grants we have been writing are not the kind
> of grants that are fundable. Overall, I would say that the
> grants we have been sending out have been really general,
> and maybe even theoretical in nature. I believe we might
> be more successful if we started sending out grants that
> were highly specific in nature, i.e. that identified the
> exact population base, the exact technology we will
> be introducing, and the exact local partner we will be
> working with. … Jock is of the opinion [that] we might
> have more success if we focus our grant applications
> in the arenas of food security, renewable energy, child
> nutrition, and water projects.

Jay also suggested other ways of bringing in money, such as trying to get consulting jobs and revising the website so that it would reflect the FBP's work more accurately.

As a cost-cutting measure, Brahm Fischer (who had briefly been Jock's assistant) was let go. The word at the time was that Jason had also been let go, but later evidence showed that he had not. Jock was put on half-salary and told to spend all his time on fund-raising, not R&D, and the only thing for which he was allowed to raise funds was AOI. In fact, fund-raising is something he always does, but until now he had not been actually writing grant applications (as mentioned, he learned how to do this under the tutelage of Diana Woolley).

While all this was going on, there was a glimmer of light on a new front. Tim Will, Executive Director of an organization called Foothills Connect based in western North Carolina, was looking for low-tech agricultural devices. Details are in the next two chapters, but its relevance here is that funding was, it turned out, readily available for any project which would aid poor farmers and unemployed textile workers in North Carolina.[5] Jock, his awareness of the empty coffer sharpened by the fact that he was now writing grant applications, and instantly visualizing ways to help people close to home, was enthusiastic. But this would not fit under the "Malawi only" aspect of AOI and would require a

5 Tim Will helped FBP to obtain emergency funding. On 3 May 2010 he wrote to Jock: "Brother, Appalachia needs for you to stay in business. Jock, humanity needs you to stay in business. You came here with your crew to help us. We will do anything we can to help you because that helps us."

change in FBP's mission statement, which at that time specified that FBP worked only in developing countries. The Executive Director decreed that no change in wording would be allowed.

Jock resigned and so did Jeff Rose. The treasurer locked the shop for five days, intending to deny Jock access; Jock, of course, had his own key, but the fact that the building was officially closed prevented him from doing a demonstration to potential funders, an event that he had worked hard to set up and that likely would have led to FBP's receiving financial support. Jay Tervo and Jim Nesbit – who shared Jock's vision of FBP's potential and responsibilities, and his ideas about how to help the developing world – were dismissed from the Board, but only just before their terms were due to end.

Then Jock was taken back, on half-salary, still to do only fund-raising. Jeff's resignation was accepted, and in the vacuum Jock undertook some of the Executive Director's work. He ignored the Board's orders to do no R&D: the half of his time for which he was not being paid was his own. Foothills Connect was eager to have a low-tech water pump for irrigation and livestock-watering, and Jock set about inventing one – a device which turned out to be quite different from the rocker pump. By the fall of 2010 this gravity-powered water pump was being tested in the Appalachia area of North Carolina. And, during these troubled months, Jock was also working on the cocoa-processing device mentioned in a previous chapter.

Tom Ellsworth, the volunteer already mentioned, wrote to the Board in February 2011:

We realize that Jock is difficult or impossible to control and we sympathize with the board. Like it or not, for the time being, he is "Full Belly", he is your franchise and should be supported. The board should figure out how to maximize his assets not squash them.

I am a retired Senior Vice President of Sheraton Hotels and have been on the board of two corporations and two non-profits. I have dealt with all sorts of smart people, but Jock is one of the brightest and most creative that I have encountered. Give him a mechanical problem and he will find a solution.

....

A large portion of your funds come because of Jock. Individuals donate because he has either asked for money directly or because they know who he is and what he is doing. He is the one who has won numerous awards. He is the one who is asked to promote Full Belly on radio and TV. It is his relationship and intellect that has brought Z. Smith Reynolds[6] to the table and will generate more money as you expand into Western North Carolina. He is the person who receives phone calls and emails from all over the world asking for help with agricultural problems.

All of the above is generated because of Jock – not for the love of Full Belly or its board of directors. If he goes, so go his supporters.

Recovery

At the time of writing, the situation has improved greatly. AOI has been dropped, and so has the complex legal document mentioned earlier. Patenting is done with devices that have been significantly supported by tax-payers' money, to protect future manufacturing investment. This would prevent a large manufacturer

---

6   This is a foundation which awarded FBP $30,000 in response to one of the grant applications that Jock wrote. Another application, to the North Carolina Rural Economic Development Center, was also successful.

in North America from making the devices more expensively than FBP can do, or one in China from doing it more cheaply and shoddily. (Very simple devices like the hand-washing station or the cocoa-pod opener will not be patented.) Work in North Carolina is progressing quickly and funding is coming in for it – funding which, by covering operating costs, supports the invention of new technology for the developing world as well.

There is a new Executive Director, Daniel Ling, and the Board's normal turnover has led to the acquisition of several new members. The Board is smaller, and the Executive Director now has a seat on it so that the linking between the staff and Board is greatly improved. The "two Full Bellys" are now one: there is no more need for Jock to set up separate R&D projects because the Board supports everything he does – in fact, besides paying him a good salary they have allocated him $1,000 per month as a "crazy idea fund" so that he has instant financing for the "crazy ideas" that in the past have turned out to be such extremely fruitful projects.

One new Board member is Diana Woolley, the professional grant writer already mentioned; she is writing FBP's grant applications, allowing Jock more time for R&D work and the outreach and promotion that are so much a part of what he does.

That the forward-driving energy continues can be seen in an e-mail which Jock sent to Daniel Ling in July 2010. After briefly outlining what had worked in the past, Jock looked towards the future. This was the first attempt since AOI at formulating a strategic plan.

FBP has three promising paths to explore for future growth that comes with its own funding. And that comes with its own exit strategy so that we don't get into that trap we had in Malawi, where we promise the guys with the Mercedes (C to C) an endless and high-priced subsidy [in the form of the Project Coordinator's salary] that never gives us a funding return.

1/ If we look at our successes overseas, they all came from partnering with a Western-oriented, self-funded NGO ... with its own infrastructure and long-term commitment to work directly with women, farmers, whoever the end beneficiaries would be, on a co-operative basis. Not with entrepreneurs who have a profit motive to sell our product to the very poorest people on the planet. That's why Mali, Guyana, Ghana, and Haiti were successes. We paid virtually none of *our* funders' money to make those projects happen. The NGO partners themselves came up with the cash, yet we can take the credit for being part of a successful team, and that can be our basis for fund-raising, especially direct-asks, here at home.

2/ Here in North Carolina, there is a lot of money available to any organization that can solve the engineering problems that separate our local demographic, [which is] small-acreage farmers, from financial prosperity. Here, either we sell ourselves as an engineering-solution organization for a wide range of simple tech problems, livestock-watering, kudzu-harvesting for animal fodder, animal-feed processing, etc. That involves letting others write the grants and contract us. Or we identify the problems and write the grants ourselves. Our mantra is rural prosperity through small-farm efficiency, and job creation in under-utilized manufacturing firms that have suffered from the collapse of textiles and tobacco. We steer clear of any human-food processing or human-water projects because of huge potential FDA [Food and Drug Administration] and legal pitfalls. Every grant will have a timeline and a completion point.

3/ There is also great potential to co-ordinate a lot of academic semester-based engineering that never goes anywhere because it is designed to be an educational experience. It is a short-term intense effort which then gathers dust. We can pick these projects up and find another semester, perhaps in another school, to move them forward. There is foundation money to figure out how to turn this kind of academic achievement into real-world solutions.

The Full Belly Project's near-collapse and recovery might provide some insights for other NGOs and for anyone interested in the subject of providing aid. The next chapters return to the process of inventing and developing new technology.

PART III

Moving Forward

NINE

Water

The planet's current and intensifying water problems have focussed attention on this resource. Drought is a global issue, and since so much of the world's food production requires irrigation, food depends on water. In the "poor" world, food shortages are often caused by a lack of water, and the same situation could develop in industrial countries as glaciers melt and aquifers run dry.

Water is also a very local issue, farm by farm, household by household: *this* field is dry and the corn crop is dying, and so we won't have enough corn to last until the next harvest. In developing countries, water for household use often has to be fetched from far away. It's heavy work and takes time; the hours spent carrying water aren't available for other tasks. The water is not always clean. Contaminated water spreads disease.

When discussing drought, Bill McKibben quotes a small farmer in Uganda as saying, "We've stopped seasonal planting. Now we just try all the time. We used to plant in March and that would be it. Now we plant again and again. We waste a lot of seeds that way, and our time and energy."[1]

A farmer in Tanzania describes other aspects of climate change:

> I have observed climate change and weather changes in my village for the last five years now. I am a small-scale farmer and I produce and sell banana, vegetable cassava and pawpaw fruits. … I have kept record of these changes from the harvest I make from the farm and the loss I incur due to change of seasons.
>
> The weather pattern has changed. The level of water we used to irrigate our farms has reduced drastically and the

---

1 McKibben, *Eaarth*, p. 155.

Chris Wood in *Dry Spring* writes: "Drought [poses a great danger] to wealth, health, and communities. Losses to drought cost the world economy at least $42 billion U.S. a year. Famine brought on by drought affects scores of millions of people each year, taking an incalculable toll in death, suffering and the lasting effect of malnutrition. Relief agencies reckon it the most socially destructive natural disaster of all, with a corrosive effect on the ties of family and community greater than that of fire, flood, earthquakes, tsunamis or windstorms." Chris Wood, *Dry Spring: The Coming Water Crisis of North America*. (Vancouver: Raincoast Books, 2008) 46.

Another aspect of the global water situation is reflected in an article from the BBC News website: "Key to the report [prepared by "the Engineering the Future alliance of professional engineering bodies"] is the concept of 'embedded water' – the water used to grow food and make things. Embedded in a pint of beer, for example, is about 130 pints (74 litres) of water – the total amount needed to grow the ingredients and run all the processes that make the pint of beer. A cup of coffee embeds about 140 litres [about 30 gallons] … of water, a cotton T-shirt about 2,000 litres [about 440 litres], a kilogram of steak 15,000 litres [3,300 gallons]." Richard Black, "UK water imports 'unsustainable'". http://bbc.co.uk/mapps/pagetools. Accessed on 18/4/2010.

small stream that used to feed us with water has changed its course. I now harvest water in big tanks and sand dams in my farm. I use it for domestic purposes and small-scale irrigation around my compound. The rich vegetation along the streams that comes from Ruaha River to our village is no more. We don't see several birds that used to take water from the streams.

The area is getting dry and sometimes we experience droughts whereby the vegetation gets dry, trees shedding their leaves and wild animals such as monkeys and rabbits straying into our villages in search of water and pastures.

At other times of the year flash floods affect our farms, causing displacements. We have also incurred a lot of expense in buying malaria drugs during the warm seasons as we see increase in mosquitoes unlike before.[2]

Yet there is often water nearby – in a stream or a fish pond – obtainable with simple technology. In many places a 15-foot well will produce water for household use and irrigation. In Lilongwe we saw a farmer who had planted crops along a stream – the beds being only as wide as what he could irrigate by splashing water from the stream onto his plants.

The rocker water pump

Jock, aware of all this, began developing a low-tech, portable, concrete water pump.[3] The first version was

2 Siwema Prosper, short article in *Living Planet, Magazine for Canadian WWF supporters.* Spring 2011, p. 5. Siwema Prosper is a young woman farming in Kisiwani, Morogoro, Tanzania.

3 A story from Jock's past work shows the byways and serendipity which can have such important results. In 1999 a TV movie was made about the CSS Hunley, the Confederate Army's manually operated submarine which was the first such boat in history to sink an enemy ship (during the American Civil War, in Charleston harbour,

rectangular – three chambers in a row – but in the next one the chambers were arranged in a triangle, making the pump more compact.

The first one to go out into the field was taken to Tanzania in January 2009 by the MIT D-Lab team of which Rebecca A. Smith, a Mechanical Engineering student, was a member. They built and tested the pump at the Global Alliance for Africa Vijana Centre (GAAVC), a vocational training school for orphaned and vulnerable children. On her return to Boston, Rebecca wrote: "… we had one prototype eventually working very well during our time there, and we were able to use local materials and pour the concrete for a second pump before leaving. The working water pump was really awesome, and I love it." Knowing that Jock needed details, she amplified. The first pump leaked a lot and some of the concrete pieces started to crack. When the team broke up the base and one of the top pieces, they saw that the cement contained some "large rocks." They had trouble finding parts locally: in the nearby town, the bolts were

---

in 1864) and that itself sank immediately afterwards. http://www.imbd.com. Accessed on 23/1/ 2010. (Additional information from Jock.) During the making of the movie, one of the problems was constructing the hand-operated water pump that controlled the submarine's balance, sinking, and floating. Jock, whose work in devising special effects was well known in film-making circles, was asked whether he could build a replica of the pump. Working from copies of the original drawings – Civil War buffs would want it to be accurate – he constructed the prop and sold it to the film company. It was this that got him thinking about simple water pumps. The rocker pump is an improved version of the one on the CSS Hunley.

expensive and the "PVC-like tubing ... was thinner and more brittle than typical PVC." However, the next pump, made with locally bought metal angle pieces, angle iron, and tubing, as well as less expensive bolts, worked very well. "We took it down to the stream with all the hose to see how far it could pump, and it went the length of the hose easily. ... We completed as much testing as was possible in the time .... The longest [hose] that we used was approximately 25 ft. [8 metres] long, and the highest height we were able to test at was approximately 12 ft. [4 metres]. Several people, of different weights, sizes, etc. were able to fill a five-gallon [23-litre] bucket in less than a minute." Later that year she was back in Tanzania with molds for the then-current version, and made several more pumps.

By the time we went to Malawi in May 2009, Jock had developed the triangular model and made other modifications, so he now had a design that he himself would test under the actual conditions of a Malawian farm.

Although, as I wrote in Chapter Five, the pump roused great interest in Lilongwe, much remained to be done. Back in Wilmington, Jock redesigned it so that it could be operated by a person of lighter weight: Jock aimed at someone weighing about 140 pounds [65 kg], a more-or-less typical weight in developing countries. The operator's weight affected how much suction and pressure the pump would have, and how it would be used. He had learned that, on small plots of land and with a fairly low-pressure system like this, farmers could use three types of irrigation: the tiny irrigation ditches which we had seen, drip irrigation using a perforated hose lying on the ground, and spot-watering with a hand-held hose. Spot-watering was the preferred method. That required a fair bit of pressure, so he had to take into account the amount of pressure that could be produced by particular elements of pump design, hose diameter, and the weight of the operator.

On 13 June 2009 he reported:

> Our [rocker] pump got tested today, with a 150-lb [68 kilo] operator, and with very little effort the pump was sucking water up 20' [6 metres] and pushing water up 40' [12 metres]. Volume is about 5 gallons per minute [23 litres], reducing slightly with a large height difference. This means that livestock wells can be easy water sources for agriculture, and pumping water up from deep stream beds is also possible. In Malawi, the materials cost for the pump is estimated at $30 with another $30 for the long [outflow] hose. This could be a game changer for dry-season agriculture for the poorest farmers. That's because the real issues of food shortages are mostly water issues, and there is no way that shallow wells and foot power can destroy the aquifers the way that the big deep-well projects in India have done.

* * *

When he returned to Lilongwe in August of 2009 he took the new molds and again built pumps to test. In an e-mail he reported that he was still finding some "little design glitches. ... That aside, it's looking good. The very first one with all its problems (cracked cylinder head, etc.) is still [in use] in Bryan Payne's village."

He demonstrated the pump and talked about it. During a meeting with a representative of the aid organization Heifer International, he learned that it could give the Malawian dairy industry a big boost. "A dairy cow in Malawi drinks an average of 50 gallons

[230 litres] of water a day, and ... water pumping is the biggest stumbling block for dairy start-up." Heifer International, he was told, operates in 30 countries in Africa, and the pump is needed in all of them.

* * *

Back home again, he continued developing the pump. To reduce its weight, he experimented with plastic instead of cement. In Africa (as everywhere else) there are mountains of plastic which could be (and to a limited extent are being) recycled. It was hoped that Coca Cola – aware that empty soft-drink bottles are a major component of that mountain, and being also a major user of water – might be interested in partnering with FBP to use recycled plastic to make the water pumps. Though this partnership didn't happen, Jock still visualized pumps made entirely or partly of plastic. Having learned to work with vacuform plastic, he experimented with plastic cylinder heads on a concrete base. This plastic-topped pump was 25 pounds [11kg] lighter than the all-concrete model and did, at one time, look promising.

Then he created one that was made completely of plastic. Brian Connors, receiving photos of it, wrote back: "I really like how this looks." His ruminations give insight into how a device like this fits into an African village as well as into 21st-century marketing and distribution systems:

1. Easy to carry, esp. by people with HIV/AIDS, and women and children;
2. *Looks good*, which has to play a part in the marketing;
3. Easily printable with a logo or message – an HIV message, or the name of the NGO sponsoring the project;

4. Very few parts to replace or repair. The inner works mostly, and not the main part;

5. NOT made of heavy cement that can break if someone trips and falls, or if it falls off a bike;

6. Easy to put on a bike or shoulder for carrying to the field;

7. A cement pump might be left in the field more, which reduces its security – it can be stolen or broken by a competitor.

The platform could be made of expanded metal to keep wet and muddy feet from slipping off, and to reduce replacement costs. That part could be made here.

Also, a couple of holes could be placed in the bottom lip for staking down, to keep it steady, when using.

He asked for more pumps – there was no mini-factory available yet, so they were made in Wilmington and shipped – which he wanted to demonstrate at conferences.

On 28 September 2009, Jock wrote an e-mail titled "Acre in a box":

Today I am sending, to Malawi, a plastic, foot-powered water pump, 20 feet of collapse-resistant water suction hose, and 170 feet of distribution hose, all packed into one 18" x 18" x 24" carton. Add some packets of NCSU [N.C. State University]-approved seeds and you just might have an agricultural revolution on your hands. This will be enough hose and seed to turn an acre of land, normally idle during the dry season, into a big circle of food, food which can be harvested when prices are good and nutritious food is scarce.[4]

---

4   To avoid cluttering up the passage itself with metric equivalents: "... 6 metres of collapse-resistant water suction hose, and 52 metres of distribution hose, all packed into one box of 45 x 45 x 61 cm...."

By December 2009 there was a significant innovation. In the beginning Jock had embedded PVC tubing in the base as the concrete was being poured, but in this new development the channels are created by embedding rubber hose in the concrete while it's being poured and then, when it's dry, pulling the hose out (a process made easy by the fact that rubber hose, when pulled lengthwise, becomes slightly thinner).

By the end of that process, then, there were all-concrete, all-plastic, and half-and-half rocker pumps. However, at the time of writing only the all-concrete ones are being made because the plastic parts can't be manufactured in Africa.

* * *

In January-February 2010, in Malawi once again, Jock vigorously promoted the pump. Comparing it with the jatropha sheller, whose continuing failure to take off was probably caused by the fact that there was not yet a large enough jatropha crop, he comments: "The [rocker] pump, however, seems to be arriving right on time." Meetings with the Clinton Foundation and Heifer International created much excitement and early orders for testing. Alliance One, the tobacco-buying firm, "want 50 to test out for crop diversification by their farmers." Tested in a village where a Peace Corps Volunteer was located, the pump with a 200′ [61-metre] hose watered a corn field "at a rate which we calculated would amount to 2 acres [just under 1 hectare] in a day."

Jock later asked Dr. Greg MacDonald, Associate Professor at the University of Florida and one of the expert advisors for the peanut-growing project in

Guyana, to do some calculations for him. "At the end of 200' of ½" garden hose, we were getting enough flow to spot-water the 200' radius. Can someone do the math for me and figure out how many kilos of peanuts that would add up to?" Greg replied: "Rough calculations – area of a 200' radius circle is 125,600 square feet, which is 2.88 acres. Based on irrigated yields of 3,000 lbs per acre you could make 8,650 lbs or a little over 4000 kilos. Not bad at all...."[5]

In the early months of 2011 the pump came under the eye of MIT's D-Lab for further development. This was because Ron Ngwira, at Alliance One, had reported that the pumps made by C to C were mostly of very poor quality (though the BBC team had talked to a farmer whose pump worked very well).[6]

An expert assessment

Michael Brugger, the CNFA volunteer (already mentioned) who went to Malawi in April 2010 to provide technical advice to C to C, gives follow-up information. His report is based on meetings with 17 individuals and organizations. He considers issues of cost: could the pump be manufactured in regional centres to reduce transportation? Would farmers be able to get government or NGO funding, or pay by installments? He considers promotion by means of radio, pamphlets,

---

5 Metric equivalents: "At the end of 61 metres of ordinary garden hose, we were getting enough flow to spot-water the 61-metre radius." The area covered would be 1 hectare which produce 4,000 kg of nuts.

6 The pump that worked well seems not to have been part of the defective lot that went to Alliance One, but no other details are available.

and demonstrations at agriculture field days, and analyzes how the information should be designed so as to be useful to different kinds of groups: NGOs and other organizations working with farmers, companies that buy farm produce, agricultural research centres and extension workers, and the farmers themselves. He suggests other uses: "The pump can be used to aerate fish ponds by pumping water from the pond and spraying it into the air and into the pond," he writes, and "There may be a good market for the pump in the processing industry as well, especially for use when the electricity is off [a common occurrence in Malawi]. Look at how the pump would work with other liquids. Also, look at if a similar pump could be made so that it could be used for products consumed by people. Sanitation and ease of cleaning are concerns."

Besides these recommendations, which would be of use to C to C and anyone else interested in building, promoting, and using the pump, others were directed at Full Belly. The pump that Brugger was assessing was the all-concrete one, and he observed (what Jock and his colleagues already knew) that it was too heavy for one person to carry. Could it be made lighter? Brugger asked if capacity could be increased. He wrote about the need for a manual on operation and repair, and suggested that the kits should contain all the tools needed to build the machines because there are few tools in African villages. He reported that there were large numbers of farmers who would be able to use it.

By May 2010, mini-factories were being turned out for the all-concrete pump. Pete Klingenberger made the fiberglass molds from which Accu-form Polymers in Warsaw, N.C., made the ABS plastic molds that went into the boxes – making them free, as a donation to Full Belly.

Ten pumps went to Zimbabwe in a container being sent by U.S.-African Children's Fellowship, which sends used schoolbooks to that country, but all that is known is that the pumps were distributed.

Guyana

Two of the mini-factories went to Guyana. As we've seen, drought there had severely affected the 2009 peanut crop. Jerry LaGra at S-SOS tested the all-plastic pump and reported that the farmers liked it in principle but that its light weight made it unstable on uneven soil. Moreover, they wanted to be able to pump water into a 15-foot-high [4.5-metre] storage tank and then use drip irrigation. They had been unable to get more than 3.5 gallons [16 litres] per minute.

In his next e-mail he reported that the pump was in the shop being repaired because "some of the welded spots have not held up during operation. Jeffery tells me you need to train your students a little better in welding." He was looking forward to receiving the molds and instructions; the pumps would be made in the same shop – Jeffery Sankar's – that was successfully making the pedal-operated peanut sheller.

Other water technology

In earlier chapters I mentioned a well-drilling device, a deep-well pump, and windmills. At the time of writing, these are no longer current projects. Instead, Jock is working on a solar-powered pump, and first tests show it to be extremely promising. I'll deal with this in the next chapter. One of its chief virtues is that it is portable – the pump is on a trailer and can be moved from one field or livestock pasture to another – which gives it an advantage over a fixed well with stationary pumping equipment.

The solar pump was preceded by the gravity-powered water pump. Jock had been thinking for some time about using the current of a small stream to drive a pump – a system that would not require big dams, water wheels, and all the large-scale technology that humans have invented over the centuries to harness the power of moving water. He had in fact been asked about such a pump when, at the Purpose Prize ceremony in December 2008, he met Nasrine Gross, the founder of The Roqia Center for Women's Rights, Studies, and Education in Afghanistan, and its American partner organization, Kabultec. [7] Nasrine described a typical irrigation problem in Afghanistan: there are streams near the cultivated fields but they're in deep gullies, and moving the water to the fields in buckets is back-breaking work.

Then, in the early months of 2010, came the first request from Foothills Connect in western North Carolina (mentioned in the previous chapter), where the problem is very similar.

To meet this need, Jock developed the gravity water pump. It lies in the stream and uses a fall of as little as 20 inches [50 cm] to pump water uphill into a livestock-

---

7 The names come from http://www.kabultec.org. Accessed on 3/10/2010

watering trough, or into a water tank from which it can be used for irrigation. Its development is such an integral part of the work being done in North Carolina that it will be dealt with in the next chapter.

TEN

Bringing It Home

The idea that all of the industrialized world is equally "developed" is, of course, a myth. So is the idea that all of it will – or can – continue to "progress" on its present course. The Full Belly Project is aware of the realities behind both of these myths. Serious poverty, and the drought caused by climate change, are to be found in the industrialized world and – specifically for this story – in the Appalachia area of western North Carolina, which has lost its textile industry and is now dealing with some third-world social and climatic conditions. Although the tools that Jock invented for the developing world don't necessarily fit North Carolina farms, the idea of appropriate technology definitely does. It also suits the times – in North Carolina and far beyond – with the increased interest in local food and the trend towards small farms. So Jock is translating concepts and approaches developed for the "poor" world into tools for farmers in industrialized countries.

Interest in small-scale farming is growing.[1] Bill McKibben, in *Eaarth* (2010), writes: "The number of farms has actually been increasing in many parts of the United States in the last few years, and all the growth is coming in just this style of agriculture. ... Nationally, 300,000 new farms sprung up this decade."[2] This is of course linked to concern about industrial farming's heavy dependence on petroleum. "Modern industrial agriculture has been described as a method of using soil to turn petroleum and gas into food. We use natural gas to make fertilizer. We use oil to fuel farm machinery and power irrigation pumps, as a feedstock for pesticides and herbicides, in the maintenance of animal operations, in crop storage and drying, and for transportation of farm inputs and outputs. Agriculture ... is the single largest consumer of petroleum products as compared to other industries. By comparison, the U.S. military, in all of its operations, uses less than half that amount."[3]

The trends towards slow food, local food, fresh food, and organic food all favour small farms. McKibben explains that these farms, each growing a variety of crops, will be better able to deal with climate change;

---

1 "USDA [US Department of Agriculture] wants to foster the viability and growth of small and mid-size farms and ranches, and we want to create new opportunities for farmers and ranchers by promoting locally produced foods." http://www.usda.dov/wps/portal/usda/knowyourfarmer. Accessed on 9/6/2011.

2 McKibben, Bill, *Eaarth*, 174.

3 Richard Heinberg, *Peak Everything*. (Gabriola Island, BC: New Society Publishers, 2007), 48. John Steinbeck's *The Grapes of Wrath* gives a vivid and tragic picture of the beginnings of industrialized agriculture.

this kind of agriculture can also restore depleted soils and in fact produce more food than is done by industrial agriculture.[4] "In North America, center of the mechanized megafarm, the U.S. Department of Agriculture reports that according to the latest census smaller farms produce far more food per acre, whether you measure that output in tons, calories, or dollars."[5]

These farms require small machinery, and the times we live in dictate that this machinery should use little or none of the world's disappearing oil and increasingly expensive electricity – in other words, appropriate technology. There are differences: in the industrialized world, muscle power is mostly replaced by water, sun, and wind, and the devices don't need to be designed so that they can be made from kits. But the principles of appropriate technology apply, including the emphasis on adding value at the level of the producer and the local community rather than providing profit for big corporations.

Foothills Connect

In 2009 – as mentioned earlier – Jock was approached by Tim Will, founder and at that time Executive Director of Foothills Connect, an organization set up

---

4   Jock told me that a field to be harvested by hand can be planted twice as densely – and therefore produce twice as much food – as one planted for mechanical harvesting. While this is only anecdotal information, it indicates that there is a significant difference.
   On a small-farm scale, depleted topsoil can be restored in a few years with compost, green manure, specially-designed crop rotation, and other non-chemical means.
5   McKibben, *Eaarth*, 168.

in Rutherford County, N.C., to help people in the Appalachia region of the state who had lost their jobs when the tobacco industry declined and when NAFTA and the resulting globalization caused the textile industry to move to developing countries.[6] Many of the unemployed workers were still living on the small farms that had been in their families for generations; this land was a resource, but they had to find ways of making a living from it in a time when subsidized industrial agriculture was pricing locally-produced, small-farm food out of the market.[7]

Foothills Connect was set up to "encourage, develop and support entrepreneurship." Its Farmers Fresh Market Initiative connects local farmers with the nearby city of Charlotte, providing the farmers with a market and supplying restaurant chefs, health-food stores, and individual consumers with fresh local produce. It makes farmers into entrepreneurs whose specialty is growing food, and it helps to make small farms work by increasing the farmers' income fourfold: if by chance they were able to get their produce into a big-box store they would keep less than 20% of the retail price whereas through Foothills Connect they keep 80%.

And Foothills Connect also "instruct[s] aspiring farmers in sustainable, small scale agriculture methodologies to create jobs through farming."[8] In an

---

6 Information about the effect of globalization comes from http://www.foothillsconnect.com/history.html. Accessed on 19/4/2010.

7 Because of the region's hilly terrain, industrial agriculture had never taken hold there.

8 http://www.foothillsconnect.com. Accessed on 19/4/2010.

e-mail, Tim Will wrote: "Each one of these farms will be a new entrepreneurial business just like the way this country was built."

Central to the success of Foothills Connect is Tim's use of the internet to sell, buy, and ship produce, and to educate farmers. In Jock's words, "he has taken the best of amazon.com and Fedex and put them together to benefit small farmers."

* * *

But small farms, as I said, need small equipment. Industrial-sized machines are expensive to own or rent, and in any case there's no room for them to manoeuvre on a small farm. Moreover, in most cases each machine does only one kind of job; farmers in the region remember with nostalgia the small tractors their fathers and grandfathers had, which could be equipped with attachments for ploughing, harrowing, planting, mowing, and other tasks. "Developing and manufacturing low-cost technology is crucial to sustaining the return to farming in Rutherford County."[9] It was this need that led Tim Will to contact Jock.

Jock admits that, at first, he didn't see how his devices could be relevant to North American agriculture. However, in December 2009 he actually met Tim: Jock, as the winner of a 2008 Purpose Prize, was one of the people presenting the 2009 prizes, and that list included Tim.

From there, progress was rapid. It began with the peanut sheller but quickly moved on to the need for a no-

9 Larry Dale, "Project may help farmers", *The Daily Courier*, July 21, 2010, Vol. 42, No. 173.

electricity, no-petroleum water pump. Also of interest was the corn cracker, dealt with in an earlier chapter, which Jock had invented to process corn for livestock feed. (Think of the advantage for a small farmer of growing his own corn and cracking it himself to feed his own livestock – and think of the benefit to the consumer of having this economy passed on in lower costs for food.) These are all problems of food, water, and energy, and Rutherford County is representative of many areas of the industrialized world where these problems exist.

Once Jock expanded his vision to include Rutherford County as well as the developing world, he became enthusiastic. Tim told him that what was needed was the recreating of traditional, small-scale ways of doing things, and this is very close to Jock's heart.

Rutherford County

In April 2010 Jock and his friend Josh Heinberg went to Rutherford County for a day-long series of events. First of all, they made a presentation to students at a high school. Then, at an organic farm and garden-supply store, Jock demonstrated the sheller, the corn cracker, the rocker pump, the corn stripper, and a hand-cranked corn thresher made in Guatamala. At 2:30 he was at a farm demonstrating the rocker pump again. At the end of the afternoon he was back at the school, this time to give a talk to the general public "on sustainable agriculture and the future of the small farmer."

Among the people he met were Duncan and Mary Edwards, and Duncan's parents Henry and Edith. Both couples, after careers in cities, had moved to Rutherford County; Henry inherited the farm which had been in his family since 1770 and where both he and Duncan had grown up, and Duncan bought the one next to it. Duncan, a geologist, had worked in the oil industry. The Edwards' farming experience – both of current conditions and of how it had been when the two men were young – provided information on the issues and conditions in the region. The gravity water pump which was to be Jock's first project in this new phase of FBP's work would be tested in a small stream on Henry's farm, and Duncan would become the site manager.

Being in Rutherford County was as informative to Jock as his talks and demonstrations were to people there. Four days after the trip he sent his hosts an e-mail outlining some of his ideas.

Many of the people need to have small, portable machinery available for 1 or 2 days a year. Like the people who shell walnuts or pecans. The people who crimp oats, crack corn, extrude soy, whatever. My thought is ...

Imagine the steam rug cleaner .... You only need it every year or two, for a day. So you rent it. You'd be a fool to buy it. Imagine that our garden-center guy and a dozen like him in the foothills [have] these machines ready to slide into the back of a pick-up truck or hook on to a trailer hitch. The customer takes it home, runs his product through it and returns it .... That means he can profit from small-scale growing. He never needs to do repairs or keep spare parts.

Imagine a soy harvester the size of a ride-on lawn mower. Or one that slides into the back of a pick-up with the cutter bar sticking out the side. Forget the big harvest contractors that charge you so much just to show up [that] you need ten acres to break even. Do the same for spelt and bulgar. Machines that off-load into hoppers that slide into the back of pick-up trucks, rather than those big trailer hoppers that weigh ten tons when they're full. In Asia, they have a lot of small-scale mechanized stuff for small-scale rice farmers.

Now imagine that the small metal-working shops that used to support the textile industry are making all these machines and selling them, not just in your area but in surrounding states. Job creation for farmers and manufacturers that lost their jobs to China. With current metal-cutting technologies you don't need high volume to make it practical like you did when metal was stamped out. You shove one sheet of steel in and the computer cuts all the different parts for one final product, with 'dart' patterns so that everything welds together just right. That way it's efficient to make one machine one day, and a completely different one the next.

It's interesting to see a cluster of ideas, resources, opportunities – and needs – converging and meshing so well. As indicated, the implications do indeed go beyond the region: according to a grant application to the Z. Smith Reynolds Foundation which Jock wrote, "there is every indication that Rutherford County will become a center for teaching sustainable agriculture. Foothills Connect will be central to that, and ... [FBP]'s machinery will be featured." The production of new small farm machines can begin now in North Carolina and spread with the spread of small farms that is already happening.

Also in that grant application, Jock writes: "Small-scale farm machinery already exists in America. The Amish never adopted the monocrop mechanized model. Farm museums and the patent record might offer ideas." However, this was not simply a regression to the past: Jock would combine historical elements with modern materials and production techniques. Inventing machines like this requires what E. F. Schumacher in *Small is Beautiful* calls the flair to "make things simple again"[10], using high-tech developments but moving beyond them.

Water-pumping in Rutherford County

Besides small machinery, Rutherford County needed water pumps. In North Carolina and elsewhere, cattle are being put in pastures again, and they need water. There are often streams nearby, but farmers are under pressure from several federal and state governments and departments "to improve surface water quality by fencing animals out of streams." When animals walk in streams to drink they not only defecate and urinate but they break down the banks, which causes erosion. "Where animals would formerly [drink] directly in the stream, fences [now] prevent access and animals get water from alternate sources, typically a new well drilled on the upland." Not only is drilling a well costly (an average of $10,000 per installation[11]) but, as Tim Will explained to reporter Larry Dale: "... farmers have been using electric or gasoline pumps to bring water from the fenced-off streams to watering troughs for their animals. That can be expensive."[12]

Water is also needed to irrigate crops. Conditions are becoming drier. From 2005 to 2010, average rainfall in Rutherford County was 44.3 inches [112.5 cm],

---

10 Page 126.
11 Grant application to North Carolina Rural Economic Development Center, Inc. I received it in an attachment to an e-mail of 17 December 2010. This information is given in the Project Summary.
12 Larry Dale, "Project may help farmers."

significantly lower than the long-term average of 50 to 56 inches [127 to 142 cm].[13] Duncan Edwards, who provided me with these figures, wrote to me: "As a youngster growing up here, I recall irrigation only when new grass seed was put out. Garden vegetables needed water only to start growing at the time of transplant, not during the remainder of the season. ... Farmers must now ... water crops thru the dry period that we must expect each year." On 30 June 2010 he wrote to Jock: "Our last good rains were 1/3 inch on June 6, and 1/2 inch on June 11. [each about 1 cm] ... This means that with practically no rain for 3 weeks while the summer twins [heat and humidity] are in the 90s [96°F = 36°C], some crops, such as my Dad's sweet corn [and] my garden potatoes, have failed without irrigation. I haul 2 buckets of water at a time to the blueberry plants from the creek." Two weeks later he's still carrying buckets: "I must irrigate [the blueberry plants] every other day, meaning that I use 5-gallon [23-litre] buckets to move one-half ton of water from the stream up to the berry bushes. Not real efficient...." Jock's wry comment on this was that the only difference between Duncan and a farmer in the developing world is that Duncan has two buckets instead of one.[14]

13 Information from Duncan Edwards, giving information from his own rain gauge and data that he obtained from the weather office.

14 Larry Dale, the local reporter already mentioned, also did some research for me and found, among other things, the following report, dated 13 January 2009: "RUTHERFORDTON - Meteorologists say the drought in Western North Carolina is the worst in a century despite recent rains that have caused flash flooding and boosted water levels in rivers and streams. North Carolina's

As Duncan's report of carrying buckets indicates, a creek runs close to his blueberries. "There's a lot of people who have streams running through their property with a big dry field next to them."[15] "Most streams in the county ... run through a valley, but most farmland is terraced on the sides of hills or is on the top of a hill, so farmers need to find an inexpensive way to move the water to the crops."[16]

To meet the need for livestock-watering and crop-irrigation, Jock invented the gravity water pump already mentioned in the previous chapter. [17] In the streambed lies a trough which has a dividing partition midway between the two ends. Some of the water from the stream is channeled into a pipe whose outfall is located precisely over the partition; the water pours into whichever half of the trough is emptier and therefore uppermost. When that half is full, that end of the trough tips down and empties back into the stream while the water from the pipe fills the other half. As it rocks, the trough drives a piston pump located underneath it, which lifts water from the stream to wherever it's needed. The weight of water falling 20 inches [50 cm] is enough to drive the pump, which runs constantly, without petroleum or

mountain region, which includes parts of Rutherford County, is entering its third year of serious drought."

15 Jock, quoted by Larry Dale, "Project may help farmers." This is the same situation as the one described by Nasrine Gross in Afghanistan (see Chapter Nine). When Jock was starting to have good success with the gravity pumps, he contacted her to report that he would soon have a pump that she could use there.

16 Tim Will, quoted by Larry Dale in "Project may help farmers."

17 Jock had heard that a device like this had existed in pioneer times but had never seen one and knew no details.

electricity. The channeling of water into the pipe is done by means of a small upstream dam made of concrete modules; one module incorporates the opening of the pipe, and the others are shaped so that the rest of the stream's water slides over them.

The gravity-powered water pump, with Duncan Edwards.
Picture credit: Jock Brandis

When the North Carolina Rural Economic Development Center was considering an application for funding to develop the pump, they asked Jock in what ways this one differed from others on the market. Jock explained:

> What makes this design different is the ability to harness what is really a very small amount of available kinetic potential energy from a short-distance water drop. History is full of devices that harness the power of water wanting to go downhill. Obviously, that's what Hoover Dam is. And the water wheels that have been around for untold centuries. A late-comer is the ram pump, but it only operates with any efficiency if you can get water to

drop more than 10 feet [3 metres]. Those kinds of drops in agricultural areas are not very common. It would take an expensive dam/delivery sluice to get a ten-foot drop in any of the dozen streams on our test-site farm. And 10 feet is the bare minimum for operation. To say nothing of the fairly high flow rate required. ...

What our pump can do is harness *any* flow rate at a 20-inch [50 cm] drop. So if the flow is cut to a quarter of the normal volume it will still deliver a quarter of the normal water to the same height. ...

The other aim was to create a design that would use moving parts that are available at a big-box hardware store.

Not only is a small "drop" sufficient, but the pump can be operated by a tiny stream. The test site is a small creek called Sweet Shrub Branch, located on Henry Edwards' farm. Duncan told me that its normal width is 2-3 feet [just under 1 metre] – "you can step across it at most places" – and that the typical flow is 50-60 gallons [250 litres] per minute. Of that amount, 80-90% is temporarily "captured" to operate the pump but is then immediately returned to the stream; the pump extracts only about 5% of the water in the stream (so that there is very little impact on downstream water use and ecology), but that miniscule amount will, in 24 hours, fill a 1,000-gallon [4,500-litre] tank, which is enough to water 27 head of cattle or provide irrigation for a crop. The current in that tiny stream is enough to lift the water 25 feet [7 ½ metres], and to move it to the tank which is 700 feet [212 metres] from the stream. When used for livestock watering, the outflow hose from the pump passes through the fence (the one that keeps the livestock out of the stream) and fills a water trough.

There are lots of these tiny streams in Appalachia, and there's lots of hilly land in other parts of the industrialized world with small streams flowing through it and farmers who are trying to deal with the effects of drought.

* * *

In a memorandum of 18 April 2011, Duncan wrote: "This project began one year ago when Jock was standing barefoot in the stream with a group of interested and curious observers who saw a wooden box bounce back-and-forth as water was poured from a plastic bucket. At the time, I thought, 'I can't believe I'm seeing *this*.' And now that we've tested 8 pumps [prototypes], my thought is 'I can't *believe* I'm seeing this.' Those words are the same, but the emphasis is very different because the pump now provides usable quantities of water to a site where irrigation is required to grow a crop. Without irrigation, crops of the past several years have failed completely." Duncan told me that drought is now so common that farmers don't even plant crops in areas where no irrigation is available.

The development of the gravity pump took time; it's a more complex piece of equipment than the earlier inventions, and – as always – Jock is learning as he goes along. As Duncan indicates, there have been a number of prototypes. Duncan, the site manager, sends Jock detailed (mostly daily) reports on how they work, and Jock goes to Rutherford County every few weeks with improved prototypes or parts. In the summer of 2011 there were three pumps working on the Sweet Shrub Branch, filling a water tank that is at the uphill end of the field on which Henry Edwards is again (now that irrigation is available) planting sweet corn. On 12 April 2011 Duncan wrote to Jock:

> Henry planted one-third acre corn yesterday. While he was on his final rows, I picked up your garden hose with the water coming out of it [from the tank]. He laughed because he couldn't believe it, but he couldn't wait to water his corn. April 11, 2011, will be the date in the history books … as the first irrigation of agricultural crop with water from the gravity pump. I know he was having fun, because he said to tell you that with your water, the corn had already sprouted [and] was growing so fast that we had to grab the mature ear as the stalk zoomed straight up past us.[18]

* * *

The project of developing the pump has involved Foothills Connect, which is the equivalent of the "partner on the ground" that FBP always lines up for its work in third-world countries. Funding of $126,000 was provided by the North Carolina Rural Development Center, and that grant includes the cost of setting up a small factory to manufacture the pumps.

* * *

---

18 Henry Edwards (Duncan wrote to me) uses no-till agriculture for his corn, which means that the land is not ploughed or deeply disked, so that the soil is not turned. Thus there's a build-up of organic matter over the years. It's a long-term commitment to improve the soil, reduce the run-off of water, and reduce erosion; the corn patch has been used for some 30 years, since Henry ended his dairy operation in the 1970s. The corn is planted with a 1960s tractor with a planter implement attached – a perfect example of the smaller and more versatile machinery that is needed on smaller farms.

Meanwhile Jock was branching out. In the first place, though water emerged from the tank with enough pressure for drip or trench irrigation or for hand-held hoses, there was not enough for sprinklers. So he devised a solar-powered pump which would draw water from the tank and then push it on with enough pressure for sprinkling. And he realized instantly that a solar pump could be used to pump *directly* from a stream, a well, or a pond, and that meant that it would be ideal for use in flat country where there are no streams, or where streams are so slow that they don't even have the 20-inch drop required for the gravity pump.

In the preamble to an application for a grant to develop solar pumps, he wrote that agriculture is an area where solar power has real possibilities. Solar power is expensive for residential use because of the need to raise the voltage from 12 volts to 120 and also to store the energy. But with a solar-powered water pump for irrigation or livestock neither of those is necessary. The power doesn't have to be stored because if the pump fills a tank for eight hours a day that's fine – it can simply shut down at night. And it can do this with 12-volt current. It would mean that pumping could be done far away from the electrical grid and without the need for a gasoline-powered motor. So the basic solar unit would be much cheaper than a comparable unit designed for a house. Because it could be eligible for subsidies to promote small-scale farming, it would be affordable for many farmers.

"Essentially," he wrote in an e-mail, commenting on all the water technology on which he is working, "we want to have no location where we can't provide a solution so farmers can get water."

Jock did not wait for the grant. In May 2011 two of his shop volunteers set up a solar pump and, together with Jock, installed it on the Edwards farm. Jock reported: "165 watts of 12v. DC was able to pump 5 gal/min [22 litres] from a stream and through a commercial Rainbird irrigation head, covering a circle 75 feet [23 metres] in diameter. Henry Edwards, who has experience of irrigating that same field in the past, estimated that he could move the [sprinkler] head 4 times in one day and, assuming no rain in the interval, would have to return to that spot in 8 days. That means that this solar unit ... will water approximately 3 acres [just over 1 hectare]."[19]

Jock explained to me that the solar pump would enable farmers to cultivate highly fertile bottom-land – flood-plain land that's (by definition) close to streams which can provide water but have too little "fall" to operate the gravity pump. And the pump doesn't necessarily have to be attached to a sprinkler; Henry Edwards is going to use it with trench irrigation. I asked Jock about the water table and learned that it's very high in that area, as little as three feet [1 metre] below the surface. It would be easy to have a shallow hole (not a well) dug by the kind of machine that digs utilities trenches, and five gallons per minute is well within the capacity for such holes.

But that first test was only the start: much more extensive R&D had to be done, and grant money was

---

19 Preamble to Solar Irrigation Grant Application, attached to e-mail of 31 May 2011.

needed. The preamble to the grant application explains. First of all, existing solar-power systems are designed for roof tops and not for ground-level installation on farms, so "ground-level anchorage which is wind-resistant" has to be developed. And he puts forward the idea of "a solar trailer, which the farmer can move from one spot to another, to irrigate or fill livestock troughs. A 4' x 8' PV [photovoltaic] array can move 300 gallons [1,400 litres] per hour at a pressure equal to that of any utility-powered pump."

The solar trailer that Jock built consists of a solar array and pump fitted on a trailer that is

> light and small enough so the farmer can move it around the farm with a golf cart or ATV. (We towed it down the highway to the farm at 65 mph [regular highway speed].) Simply aim the panels at the sun and drop the single aiming handle into the locking ring. Then flip the switch and the pump starts. There is an optional immersed pump that can be lowered down the well if the water is lower than 20ft [6 metres]. [There is also an electrical cord so that trailer can stand in the sun but the pump can get close to the water.] ... There is full flow even on moderately cloudy days. In Appalachia, where farmers have a lot of small fields widely separated on good patches of "bottom land" next to streams, it means that [the farmer] can cover his whole farm with one portable water source. It pumps about 2500 gallons of water [11,300 litres] per day. ... This will really open up a lot of land too far from electrical utilities. And let's guess at the price of a gallon of diesel in 5 years. The 60 psi means a water lift of about 110 feet [30 metres]. One of these units is now moving water up about that far to large storage tanks 900 feet [275 metres] away.

These statistics were produced by testing in Rutherford County and also on the flat land of eastern North Carolina.

Jock took the solar-pump trailer to the farm of Edward Stephens in Bladen County.[20] Edward had taken part in creating Down East Connect, an organization which Josh Heinberg has set up in emulation of Foothills Connect. At the time of writing Edward has about seven cows and twenty hogs. "The area we use as a pasture is not near electrical service so we have a tank on a trailer [filled from a well]. In a summer week we use about 500 gallons [2,300 litres]. Jock's pump will provide about 3 gallons a minute[21], more than enough to keep the stock happy. With some additional equipment it could be used to supply drip irrigation tape for row-crop produce." Edward's overall assessment: "The pump worked well. I was disappointed when they took it back to Wilmington."

In June 2011 Jock and three FBP colleagues met with the top executives at Southern Energy Management. This is "a North Carolina-based sustainable energy company serving the Southeast with energy efficiency and solar power for home owners, residential and commercial builders, companies, non-profits, and government

---

20 Edward Stephens is the fifth generation of his family to live on the same farm. He studied Agronomy at NCSU and, while there, "met professors that had the same world view as Jock – find a solution that is long-term and local. I recognized that trait in the Full Belly Project and gave an open invitation for testing of stuff in general, and it ended up being a solar-powered water pump." E-mail of 5 July 2011. He sells meat through Down East Connect.

21 Three gallons = 41 litres. Duncan reports that the pump moves 5 gallons[22 litres] per minute, and that is the number that Jock has given me, so presumably Edward is giving an approximate figure.

clients."[22] Like Mali Biocarburant, the guideline is "people, planet, and profit."

Solar-pump trailer, with Henry Edwards. This is the cornfield from which he had had no crop for three years because of drought. The grey object on the back of the trailer is a trough which can be set on the ground and filled when the pump is being used to water livestock.

Photo credit: Tim Will.

Jock hoped to enlist SEM in providing expert advice in the area of components and "to confirm or correct our design steps and comment on our results." He hoped that this consulting could be regarded as "an in-kind contribution" – in other words, a donation to FBP's coffer. He also hoped to be able to buy components through SEM and benefit from their volume discount. SEM agreed to all this …

22 http://www.southern-energy.com. Accessed 8/7/2011.

Then they surprised us all. Although in my preamble I made the assumption that we were getting into an area where they had no interest, they said that their mission was to make solar available to everyone. They really liked our idea, and they would like right of first refusal to manufacture our design and make it available through our rural networks. That was pretty flattering, given that we have been in solar for all of 6 weeks now. We agreed.

* * *

In July 2011 the water technology was officially unveiled at an Open House where about 60 farmers and government agricultural experts saw the devices in operation. Jock wrote a short account of the event:

The day of the Open House on Henry's farm was a hot and dry 95F [35C]. It was the sort of day when the tree leaves are sagging before noon.

Visitors went first to the high corn field and saw two old recycled oil tanks holding 2000 gallons. All pumps fed water into those tanks, and all irrigation water was drawn out of them. They were filled by the gravity pump night and day, and by the solar pump during the day. [Visitors were told that] for people who couldn't get tanks we would be testing a large "water corral", a steel-mesh frame lined by a plastic bladder. Near the tanks was a solar pump that could sprinkle three acres of crops on the highest fields.

Then the visitors saw a water-wheel-pump prototype, and the gravity pump filling a livestock trough. Moving to lower land, they saw drip irrigation for small trees and berry bushes and a two-gallon-per-minute electric pump that could clip onto a truck or tractor battery for drip irrigation or free-range chickens. Finally, on the lowest land, there was a fixed solar pump feeding the "water grid" that connected everything, and a solar trailer doing sprinkling and furrow irrigation in a rich bottom land.

As part of the Open House, the guides explained the government subsidy programs available to farmers who are interested in obtaining this equipment.

The response was very positive. The big question was, "When can farmers start buying this machinery?"

* * *

Since the beginning of the work in North Carolina, FBP had been thinking about the "Full Belly" name. It had been invented for use in the developing world, but its implications in North America were very different and rather undesirable. North Carolina is one of the worst states in the U.S. for obesity. So FBP came up with a trade name to be used for all the technology made and marketed in North Carolina: it will bear the logo $E=NC^2$. But the inventions are still under the umbrella of the Full Belly Project.

And elsewhere in North America …

In the summer of 2010, David Brydon in Texas began using the "classic" nut sheller to process pecans. He describes himself as a "want-to-be-agrarian homesteader", aiming for "a multi-generational farm that provides most of [our] own food and hopefully extra to share and sell." He found out about the sheller, ordered a mini-factory, and built the sheller himself. He wrote to me: "It was very easy to build with the instructions and parts they sent me. It does a fast and very good job cracking the pecans with little breakage of the halves." In a different e-mail he wrote: "Another mainstay of our diet is organic peanuts. We buy them in bulk. The thought of trying to process them ourselves was daunting …. But this year we planted a small experimental bed of peanuts and ... with the sheller I am confident we can process our own peanuts in an acceptable amount of time too."

And, from a completely different area, comes this: Terry Sharpe, a wildlife biologist and forester, belongs to a continental group which is reseeding the wildflower migratory pathways for butterflies, destroyed by herbicides and insecticides. This involves collecting seed pods and shelling them. In his search for seed hullers he found out about the Full Belly sheller. He went to the Wilmington shop with a plastic bag of seeds of wild white indigo. The problem was "to figure out a way to get the tiny seeds out of the tiny pods. So we [Terry and the people at the FBP shop] messed around with one of the 'midi' peanut shellers and it worked pretty well. We decided that doing the trick we do with coffee, where we cover the concrete rotor with rubber, would make it even better."[23] Terry was loaned a sheller and wrote to me: "Now I need to talk them into selling it to me so I can use it each year."

In Iroquois, Ontario, the nut sheller is being used to shell hazelnuts: Jim Usalcas obtained a mini-factory and made a sheller, keeping Jock informed about the process and asking a few questions.

At the same time – but independently – the Ontario Science Centre in Toronto became interested. Julie Jones, Science Researcher in the Science Content and Design Department at the Ontario Science Centre, wrote to me:

The Universal Nut Sheller was selected to be part of a traveling exhibition about innovation, created by the

23 "The Full Belly Newsletter", Fall 2010.

Ontario Science Centre. The choice to include it was an easy one. The area of the exhibition as a whole is focused on providing opportunities for participants to discover their innovative skills. The exhibit the nut sheller is featured in was created to tell stories of innovation driven by our basic needs of food, water and shelter. It is a place of inspiration within the exhibition. When searching for these types of stories Jock Brandis and the Universal Nut Sheller was referenced in many places and it was the story of Brandis gallantly offering to send a nut sheller to his friends, then realizing he would have to develop one to keep his promise, which added a very human side to this innovation story. This award-winning innovation needed to be part of the exhibition. An email to Full Belly Project proved to be fruitful as Jock quickly connected us with Jim Usalcas, a local food producer and farmer. Usalcas kindly made us our Universal Nut Sheller which is now traveling as part of the exhibition which starting in 2012 will be touring North America.

When I asked Jim Usalcas for his side of the story, I received a narrative which I'm quoting at length because it's a vivid example of the "difficult miracles" that make up the Full Belly story. He titled his narrative "The action of words and the journey of [the] Universal Nut Sheller *or* How the Universal Nut Sheller found a home at [the] Ontario Science Centre."

I never heard of Jock Brandis or Full Belly project on the morning that I sent an e-mail to an organization that had something called a Universal Nut Sheller. I came across the Full Belly website by way of Google, searching for "nut sheller". We have a few hazelnut bushes and I was looking for a way to shell the nuts for personal oil use. I don't write to organizations, this was my first. I am not a wealthy man, far from it, so it was purely selfish motive, the thinking being I will ask about the sheller and the cost, the worst that can happen would be that I could not afford the sheller forms [molds]. It was a start of a chain of incalculable events and a question of trust and the meaning of words.

Jock replied almost immediately and said that the best thing would be to phone him. I did not know that Jock would be travelling to Canada the next day.

What if Jock did not reply?
What if I did not pick up the phone and call that day, at that moment in time?
What if it was the day after Jock travelled to Canada?
What if Jock was not willing to schlep the sheller in his car and ship it once he arrived in Canada?
How does one calculate this chain of events?

This was just a start. Before phoning I did some research on Full Belly Project and Jock. I don't like wasting people's time by asking questions that could easily be answered by a little research. In our phone conversation we came to an agreement. I would get the forms [free] if I could do a report on whether the UNS worked on hazelnuts and how well it did its job.

What if I did not honour our agreement? After all I had the forms and Jock had my word and nothing else. I submitted my report, it was rather short and simple. The UNS worked well for my needs. Due to my inexperience the first cast of cement and sand broke as I attempted to remove the sheller from the forms. What if I gave up? I did not. The second casting came out much better, not perfect, better. I was now an experienced Full Belly mold filler and assembler. The castings that went to Ontario Science Centre were as they say almost perfect.

A few weeks after I submitted my report on UNS I received an e-mail from Julie Jones at the Ontario Science Centre. She wanted to know whether I would make a nut sheller for OSC. I felt that I owed Jock a little bit more than just a report and I was pretty sure no one else in Ontario (and perhaps Canada) had one. So I agreed.

What was Julie's interest in UNS?
What if Julie did not e-mail?
Why should I reply to her? After all I fulfilled our agreement. Easy out.
Spring around here is busy, 2011 even more than usual. What if I had waited for summer to build my first UNS instead of in middle of Canadian winter?

Without Julie this whole chain of events is null and void.
  These are just some of the actors and variables in this journey or chain of events. [The fact that] they represent the tip of an iceberg of actors and variables puts this on the edge of probability and into the realm of amazing. If all the actors and variables were uncovered it would put this into an area that I have no name for and no one on the planet would believe it.
  Without Jock and his word to another human being there is no story. This is who we are. This is what we do.[24]

One of the threads running through this book is the importance of human connections: it's a story about people as well as technology. Jim Usalcas is one of the people who make up the Full Belly wheel. Through him the sheller will come to the attention of whoever sees the Science Centre's travelling exhibition, and it is anybody's guess what that might lead to.

---

24 When I asked Jim to clarify what he meant in the last couple of sentences he replied: "'We' meaning, those who try and struggle with being human. It's not enough just to think, but to make an effort to *do*. Just about anyone can cast and assemble the UNS, but not too many can design something like the UNS and give it away for anyone to use. And not every person follows up on their word to another human. This is what makes Jock and the UNS unique. This is what I mean by a word. It's not about a proxy for something like cat, house, or food. It is something one person says to another and there is no question or promise required."

ELEVEN

Aflatoxin Again

In December 2010, news came which shook the Full Belly Project to its foundations. Dr. Rick Brandenburg of N.C. State University, whom we've met already, returned from one of his periodic trips to Malawi and sent Jock an e-mail.

Here is the bottom line on peanut production in Malawi. The levels of aflatoxin are very, very high in the crop grown there. Recent surveys by ICRISAT [the International Crops Research Institute for the Semi-Arid Tropics] have found levels as high as 3,800 ppb (EU tolerance levels are 4 ppb). Surveys by food scientists at the University of Malawi have found peanut butter on the shelves of stores measuring >200 ppb. RAB Processors Ltd. has expressed great concern over the aflatoxin contamination and NASFAM [The National Smallholder Farmers Association of Malawi] has reported whole shipments of peanuts being rejected in Europe (with catastrophic socioeconomic effects on villages in Malawi). The UNC [University of North Carolina] Project focusing on health issues in Malawi has uncovered "sky high" incidences of esophageal cancer and breast cancer in young women in many of the peanut producing areas. The health effects also include immune system suppression and liver disease.
There is a significant interest among the various institutions and agencies both in Malawi and North

Carolina to put together a strong multi-disciplinary team to effectively address the significant aflatoxin problem in Malawi. This project would combine the sciences of agriculture, engineering and health care. UNC has committed to assembling a working group in January to begin putting together a proposal with NC State and other agencies for funding from agencies such as the National Institute of Health. The joining of the forces of these disciplines for global health issues is a unique configuration, but a necessary one if we are to address this serious issue. Harvest, shelling and storage are major components in this effort, and the efforts of the Full Belly Project to improve shelling and develop a tool to help sort [out] aflatoxin-contaminated peanuts would be a quick and effective step in the right direction to move this effort forward while the university inertia slowly gets shifted and moved in this direction. I fully encourage and would welcome Full Belly participating in helping develop and promote a shelling/UV system to help us address this serious health situation in Malawi.

This was the first quick bad news. In his more detailed report Rick pointed out that aflatoxin contamination is extremely serious for the RUTFs (or RTFs – Ready to Use/Ready to Eat Therapeutic Foods) that are so effective in treating malnourished children. One of the groups he met with in Malawi was Valid Nutrition, which produces an RTF. Rick wrote: "Cost and availability of RTF products ... are increased due to aflatoxin contamination and cost of purchasing peanut from other countries in order to meet international standards for RTF with respect to aflatoxin contamination." He reported that the WHO (World Health Organization), the FAO (Food and Agriculture Organization), and other organizations have set the research into and the solution of the problem as priorities.

Besides getting sick from eating contaminated nuts and paste, it now turns out that people in peanut-producing countries who shell nuts by hand absorb the toxin through the skin of their fingers. The sheller is a help because it reduces handling, and we've seen that it can be set to screen out most of the aflatoxin-contaminated nuts, but this is not 100% reliable.

Aflatoxin also affects cassava and grains including rice and corn (maize).[1] (We saw in an earlier chapter how dependent Africans are on corn.) Besides the health effects that Rick mentions, exposure to aflatoxin is associated with "growth faltering, particularly stunting" in children[2] and in farm animals. In livestock fed on aflatoxin-contaminated feed, "marked effects on growth are well recognized. In fact the adverse effects on growth of poultry, swine, and other species are a primary concern, with ... [a] link between aflatoxin consumption, the lower efficiency of food use, and reduced feed intake. ... However, until recently the literature on human exposure to aflatoxins has been silent on this point"[3] – a silence, the author points out,

---

1   The information comes from an article titled "HIV and hepatocellular and esophageal carcinomas related to consumption of mycotoxin-prone foods in Sub-Saharan Africa." The article is © by the American Society for Nutrition. The information I give comes from the Abstract. http://www.ajcn.org/content/early/2010/05/19/acjn.2009.28761.short. Accessed on 10/1/2011.

2   Wild, Christopher Paul, "Aflatoxin exposure in developing countries: The critical interface of agriculture and health." In Food and Nutrition Bulletin, vol. 28, no. 2 (supplement) © 2007, The United Nations University. Page S372.

3   Page S373.

resulting from the fact that livestock is the concern of agricultural experts while human diseases are in the field of medical experts, and that the two don't often meet. "The existing separation between health and agriculture was reinforced by largely separate funding streams, scientific conferences, journals, learned societies, and so forth, which did not naturally enhance cross-disciplinary working."[4] The multi-disciplinary team referred to by Rick Brandenburg would cross this gap[5] and would, furthermore, include FBP's engineering expertise: Jock would be the person who figured out how to identify the toxic food quickly and economically, and preferably at the village level.

Learning about aflatoxin screening

Jock had known about aflatoxin ever since he started to think about peanut processing but, like everyone else, had been unaware of the magnitude of the problem. When he and Jay Tervo first met with Dr. Tim Williams at the University of Georgia in Griffin in 2002, Dr. Williams "spent a lot of time talking about aflatoxin. ... At that time he described it as the biggest underlying cause of death from malaria, cancer, etc."

4 Page S373
5 The University of North Carolina is well-placed to engage in this work because it has a medical and research facility in Malawi. This is a health "research, care and training program" established in Lilongwe in 1999. It works in partnership with the Malawi Ministry of Health and is based on the campus of Kamuzu Central Hospital. Its mission is "to identify innovative, culturally acceptable, and affordable methods to improve the health of the people of Malawi, through research, health systems strengthening, prevention, training, and care." http:// www.med.unc.edu/infdis/malawi. Accessed 10/1/2011.

It came into Jock's awareness again when, during his visits to Haiti, he visited Meds and Food for Kids, which also produces an RUTF. He watched five workers visually sorting more than a ton of peanuts per day – doing the best they could but not doing it very effectively.

Then, in the summer of 2010, another piece of information went into the mix. Jock wrote to me:

> I visited a local farmer (he lived in Rocky Point, N.C.) whose family had grown peanuts for more than a century. I went to get some free sun-dried (not roasted) nuts.[6] These are country folk and you can't just do the big city "grab the peanuts and run" thing. I had to "set a spell" and have some sweet ice tea, and he mentioned aflatoxin, which surprised me. He described selling peanuts with his father. They would load up the wagon with bags, and hitch the mule. Then it was off to the peanut mill. But the mill was only allowed to buy on days when the USDA [U.S. Department of Agriculture] man was there with his "black light box." Wagons pulled up to the mill and each bag would be unloaded. An assistant would shove his hand deep into the bag and come out with a handful of nuts. They would be put into the box which would be closed. The USDA man would turn on the light and look inside from under a black cloth, like the very old camera operators. If the nuts glowed under the black light, they were contaminated. That's because the protein in the aspergillus fungus that produces aflatoxin converts UV light to visible light. The old farmer says he got a

6   Sun-dried nuts are hard to find in the U.S., where all commercial peanuts are roasted. (Incidentally, one thing I wondered about in connection with the consumption of peanuts in the developing world is whether peanut allergies are as common there as they are in industrialized countries. An anecdotal piece of information I came across is that it is roasting that creates whatever it is that causes allergies and that that's why such allergies are almost or entirely unknown in countries where peanuts are sun-dried.)

chance to look in once when he was a kid. "The bad nuts shone like stars in the sky," he said. They don't do it anymore, he explained, because better harvesting and storing techniques have solved the problem, and probably because the mass production and huge acreages planted these days tend not to fit the old mule-drawn methods of an earlier time.

The old farmer's story got Jock excited about the idea of a small device for screening nuts. He contacted his "PhD friends" at the University of Florida, the University of Georgia, and N.C. State. "'Can we do this in Africa?' I asked. The response was that the old guy might have overstated the effectiveness of the procedure. Yes, UV light might have been used, but it was probably discontinued for a good reason. Essentially, the response was tepid."

Implications for FBP

Then, in December of that year, came Rick Brandenburg's report. His findings have grim implications for FBP. The peanut sheller is one of the focal points of the organization's work and, as Jock wrote to Tim Will on the day after receiving Rick's bad news, "the fact that we are, right now, making the sale of what is clearly a toxic food more efficient would seem to suggest a moral imperative to address the problem." This was "a very serious problem which had taken everyone, even the experts, by surprise." Elsewhere he writes: "Aflatoxin is now a priority in Malawi, even greater than the food/water security focus of a few years ago. No point creating food security if the food is toxic."

Testing for aflatoxin exists, of course,[7] but it's expensive and slow.[8] Jock and Rick agreed that what was needed was a way "to sort out the contaminated nuts at buying stations, the places where RAB and Plumpy'nut buy their product." They visualized "a portable solar-powered UV screening device, about the size and weight of a cooler" – in fact, something rather like the one that the old farmer in Rocky Point had described.

Jock got to work immediately. The first thing he needed was information about the precise UV frequency that would pick out nuts contaminated with this particular fungus. He contacted Louis DeAngelis, who had offered FBP his services and who "knew computers." Jock told him what he already knew and then explained what he hoped that Louis would be able to find for him.

Aflatoxin is a serious problem in a lot of foods that Full Belly machines process, especially peanuts. At an industrial level they use UV light to identify and discard contaminated peanuts. We have been asked to make a very simple device that can be used in Africa in the places where peanuts are bought by volume buyers. Contaminated peanuts shine brightly under UV light if the aflatoxin fungus is present.

7   See footnote #5 in the Introduction.
8   An article in New Internationalist reports that there is a new and far less expensive test available now. "By cutting the cost of testing crops from $25 to $1 per sample, the kit has started to re-open doors to export. This simple kit can even be used by the remote rural farms to monitor grains and nuts." [Alina Paul, "Peanut farmers back in business," in New Internationalist, 442, May 2011, p. 11.) Jock's information is that this test cannot actually be done in the field; it has to be done in a lab by trained technicians and is therefore not quick, though it is indeed less expensive.

There are several simple approaches. A dark box with UV lights and separate solar panels: shallow trays of nuts are pushed through and picked over. A box with a top which is a UV filter so that the sunlight becomes pure UV when entering the box. Same series of shallow trays move through. A "welder's helmet" with UV filter instead of a welder's glass. You just stand in the sun and look at the nuts. This all depends on this question: when you see the bright object in UV light with the naked eye, is that because the fungus re-radiates the light at a different frequency? Or does it just reflect it at the same frequency? That is really a very basic question to which way we go.

He told Louis "that the UV spectrum was very wide, and there was a good chance that the protein in the aspergellis would only give off visible light under a narrow spectrum range. Could [you] find that wavelength?"

"Sixteen hours later," Jock told me, "[Louis] sent me an obscure English report from the 1950's that identified 360 nano-meters as the best wavelength."

Jock built prototypes of several different devices like those that he had outlined to Louis. By the second week in January he had constructed a box with a UV light on top and with an operator standing on each side to sort, while a third person put the nuts onto trays with a central hole into which the contaminated nuts could be dropped. Though at that moment he had no contaminated nuts for testing, he was interested in assessing the device's general practicability. Knowing that on average 5% of any unsorted batch of nuts was contaminated, he bought peanuts and painted 5% of them with fluorescent paint. The two shop volunteers who did the testing were able to sort nuts at the rate of a ton in a 10-hour work session. This at least showed that the idea of the box and the trays worked. The device would be powered by a solar panel: during the day this would charge the battery for the UV lamps so that in the evening – the best time for this work in an African village – the day's harvest could be sorted.

Other designs he tried included an ordinary flashlight adapted so that it gave the right frequency of UV light, and a large table on which stood objects like desk lamps but equipped with UV lights. He also considered the little mushroom-like objects, placed alongside a garden path, which are charged by sunlight during the day and emit UV light at night. Operators of any of the devices would be supplied with protective goggles. To deal with the problem that aflatoxin penetrates the skin of people doing the sorting (as well as those shelling by hand) he suggested the finger guards used by bank staff to count bills, or latex gloves, or just wrapping some masking tape around the fingers that touch the nuts.

At the time of writing, the device being used is a hand-held light which can be shone over nuts spread out on a surface in a dark room.

Testing the devices

In order to test the various prototypes, contaminated nuts had to be mixed with good ones and put through the scanners. Jock requested aflatoxin-infected nuts from N.C. State and the University of Georgia, but neither sent him any, and Jock knew that contaminated nuts from – for instance – Haiti would not get through customs. So, rather than bringing the nuts to the scanners, he sent the scanners to the nuts. To MFK in

Haiti he shipped a package including "several kinds of UV, just to see what worked. Also included were LED lights." MFK now has a sophisticated lab where testing is done for aflatoxin, but Jock was told that it took three weeks to get results and the batch from which the sample had been taken might – in Jock's words – by then already have been eaten.

Results from the Haiti testing showed that one of the prototypes worked quite well. Eyleen Chou wrote to Jock that "some preliminary tests" with one of the devices had eliminated enough of the contaminated nuts so that in what remained the aflatoxin was 11 ppb. Jock told me, however, that the test had been done under less than ideal conditions – by daylight, with curtains drawn to screen out most but not all of the natural light – so the results, while remarkably good, were achieved by test procedures that were not rigorous enough.

In June 2011 Jim Nesbit took another device to the University of Georgia in Griffin to demonstrate it to Dr. Tim Williams. Thirty pounds of peanuts were spread on a table, the room lights were turned off and the UV light was turned on. Ten nuts glowed in the dark. Dr. Williams apologized for not having more "bad" nuts, but the test showed that the UV light worked.

* * *

Rick Brandenburg had, meanwhile, been looking for funding for the multi-disciplinary team and its work. USAID was interested in providing grant money. Jock reported to the FBP Board on a phone call he had had with Rick:

The grant looks for a 'system' approach for reducing
aflatoxin at the village level, using locally controlled
sustainable technologies. Aflatoxin can be dealt with [by
using] increased irrigation just before harvest (our pump),
mechanized shelling soon after harvest (our sheller), and
teaching about the dangers and sorting out the toxic nuts
to get a safe level (our different types of UV scanners).
The grant also needs to address the even bigger aflatoxin
source in people's diets, corn. Our scanning technology
works well with corn before it is removed from the cob.
The other key to the corn problem is harvesting in a timely
manner and storing after removing the husk. Again, the
UV flashlight is an essential teaching tool on this issue.

For this round of testing, serious prototypes would
have to be built. Updated ones would be sent to Haiti
for more rigorous testing, and Rick Brandenburg
would test them in three locations: at N.C. State's own
campus, in Ghana, and in Malawi. Jock himself would
test the equipment during a trip to the Philippines in
September 2011.

* * *

Among the organizations most involved in and concerned
about this situation is RAB Processors Ltd., a company
that buys produce from Malawian farmers, processes it
as required, and distributes it throughout Malawi and
overseas. Rick Brandenburg had met with them when
he was in Malawi in December 2010. RAB "works with
international markets that are now closed to Malawian
nut farmers because of the aflatoxin occurrence." RAB
and Full Belly had already had contact: when the FBP
team was in Malawi in May 2009, Jeff Rose and Jim
Nesbit had talked to them. Now RAB – which processes

substantial quantities of peanut products – was, like everyone else, in a hurry to see the invention of a small, inexpensive screening device, so that they could once more export Malawian peanuts.

* * *

As this book goes to press, Jock is just back from the Philippines, but he was unable to test the scanning equipment because the peanut crop was just being harvested and no nuts had been out of the ground long enough to have developed aflatoxin. "The protocol we planned to do with sorting and testing couldn't happen despite several agricultural departments looking for a 'bad' product."

So this is another chapter that ends in mid-air – the best possible illustration of how the Full Belly Project's work proceeds.

Conclusion

This story is unfinished because the Full Belly Project's work continues, and also because the story is part of two large global issues which are themselves ongoing: the urgent need to help the poor, hungry, and disadvantaged people in the world, and the equally pressing need for all of us to adjust to climate change and the declining supply of fossil fuels.

Jock once compared the Full Belly Project and its work to "a little furry mammal running around between the feet of dinosaurs." In the arena dominated by "big aid", FBP is indeed small-scale, and in the one dominated by "big agriculture" it is creating devices to make small farms vital and profitable. Appropriate technology itself is a "little furry mammal" in a world where bigness and growth have long been regarded with unquestioning faith. The fact that bigness of many kinds is becoming unsustainable makes it essential that we rethink how we provide ourselves with food and water, and how we use energy resources.

The story is both global and intensely local, reminding us that we are one planet. The globalization of trade that has been enriching China impoverished the textile workers of North Carolina. The high levels of carbon dioxide in the atmosphere, which affect the whole planet, are the result of decisions that each of us makes every day: whether to keep the car's engine idling while waiting for our child to emerge from the school, whether to buy the vegetables at the farmers' market or the big box store, whether to take a heavy-carbon-footprint holiday trip or an environmentally friendly one.

And it links present-day worlds which at first glance appear very different: the Full Belly Project's work in North Carolina shows that the appropriate technology invented for the developing world could, before long, help people in the industrialized world to survive.

Just as the story integrates big and small, there and here, it links past and future, drawing on remnants and memories of a way of life that was not yet dominated by fossil fuels and by "big." Jock actively researches past technologies, knowing that devices used in pioneer times could be revived and adapted to help small farmers in the 21st century.[1]

---

1   Other people are also going to the past to envision a simpler (and more sustainable) future. George Marshall writes in *New Internationalist*: "The early 1970s marked the first time in Britain when people's basic needs were largely met. Yes, there were still pockets of absolute poverty, but by and large, people were housed, fed, clothed, and in work. They had weekends off, annual holidays and spare cash for entertainment and leisure. It was not a time of great plenty – but of ample sufficiency. ... With this in mind I have been re-examining my own memories of 1972, supplemented by the statistical evidence. I want to know how it felt to live with lower consumption and lower expectations. What lessons can we learn, and can we move forward in a way that is

This backtracking doesn't mean abandoning everything that modern technology has made possible: Full Belly ships its mini-factories by courier or by air, and molds are made of plastic. The backtracking involves looking at the technology that was available a century or two ago – much of it the precursor of what we have now – and considering what can be rethought and used again. And looking not just at the technology but also scrutinizing the *thinking*, the *attitudes*, the *expectations*.

* * *

When I asked Jock for a few words to put in the conclusion, he came up with this:

> As the big Open House on the Edwards' farm [in July 2011] was winding down and the temperature was approaching 95F [35C], I was standing with Henry Edwards looking at his sweet corn. Henry told me that when he began farming that very same land with his Dad they did it all with two mules and a horse and manpower.
> I got to thinking about Henry's life on that farm. The sheds and the weeds told the story of his move to industrial agriculture. Six tractors and lots of attachments, most of them abandoned. John Deere and International Harvester were happy to get him hooked, but when he failed to follow them into the brave new world of giant monocrops, he got left behind. His diesel engines started to rust. The weeds grew around his four-gang plow. And when the climate started to change and less rain fell, the only thing that the big guys could offer him was high-tech irrigation equipment heavily dependent on petroleum and electricity.
> And then came the "flatland liberals", as we FBP folks jokingly called ourselves when we arrived in the

intelligently informed by our own recent past?" [George Marshall, "Back to the future" in *New Internationalist*, NI 438, December 2010, p. 26.]

mountains. We showed up with a wooden box that tipped back and forth when a bucket of water was poured into it. This gadget, we told Henry, was going to get him a thousand gallons of water a day [4,500 litres] way up on that hill. No electricity meters, empty fuel tanks, fan belts, or radiator hoses.

Not for a minute did he believe it.

Now it was a year later and he was getting much more water than that.

So Henry and I were standing on that hill and I was thinking about him being 87 years old.

"Henry," I said, "I've been thinking about you and your mules, and how you don't need six big diesel cylinders if you don't want to fluff up the whole field but just want to plant it. When you worked with mules, did you fluff up the field?"

"I can see you never plowed a field with a mule," he observed, meaning that fluffing up is a useless – and topsoil-damaging – luxury made possible by big tractors and cheap fossil fuel.

"How's this, Henry," I said. "Next year we're going to get you back where you were when you were a kid. No fossil fuel, no grid electricity. And ... OK ... no mules either. You're going to be the first guy with a solar-powered electric tractor. So this November, set some time aside."

Not for a minute does he believe it.

* * *

The story began with the woman in Woroni and her peanuts, and ends – for now – with Henry Edwards, who is a link with the past and, in spite of (or because of) his age, points the way towards the future. It's a story of seeing needs as opportunities, and it could be a parable for the coming years, when there will be plenty of needs and also some opportunities for people who can think differently about solutions.

List of Inventions

This is the list as it exists at the time of going to press (September 2011). Not all devices are ready for public use, and some have been discontinued; I have made the list as comprehensive as possible so as to be useful for general reference. See Index for passages in the book where the devices are dealt with.

Shellers:
- Classic (the "Universal Nut Sheller", UNS)
- Mini
- Midi
- "Granola"
- Pedal-powered sheller
- Electrically-operated sheller
- Walnut sheller
- Brazil-nut sheller

Peanut thresher
Oil press (for peanuts and soy)
Peanut planter
Pedal platform with attachments
Aflatoxin scanners
Corn cracker

Cocoa-pod opener
Cotton gin
Jatropha factory-in-a-container
Jatropha hand-picking device
Water technology:

- Rocker pump
- Well-drilling device, and the bailing tube that goes with it. DISCONTINUED
- Deep-well pump. DISCONTINUED
- Gravity pump
- Hand-washing station
- Windmills ("wind-waver") DISCONTINUED
- Solar pump trailer

Wheelchair

Note on Sources

I have documented only the published sources; readers are welcome to contact me for further information about or from those that are unpublished. In the e-mails, I silently corrected spelling typos but kept some of the idiosyncratic punctuation and other signs of the headlong style of writing – which is, after all, part of the story.

The footnotes indicate which published (print and internet) sources I have quoted directly.

Additional notes, and suggestions for further reading

Books

The stream of books coming out on peak oil, climate change, and the challenges to the world's food supply help to provide the context for the Full Belly Project's work. A library or internet search of these subjects will provide a wealth of titles.

In addition to the books mentioned in the footnotes is one on which I drew indirectly: Gwenyfar, *The Promise of Peanuts*: A real-life fairy tale, photography by Maaike Brender à Brandis (2006, © Gwenyfar, Trafford

Publishing, Victoria, B.C.). This is the story, written for children, of the invention of the peanut sheller.

Electronic resources:

Because the Full Belly Project's work is ongoing – is, indeed, galloping ahead as drought and other changing conditions make its inventions rapidly more relevant and needed – the best way to find out what is happening now is to go to its website: www.thefullbellyproject.org

On YouTube there are a number of videos about the Full Belly Project, including instructional and informational ones: just enter "Full Belly Project." There is a Full Belly page on Facebook.

My website – www.mariannebrandis.ca – will allow you to contact me.

Acknowledgements

This book could not have been written without the help of many people, most of whom I've never met and some of whom are not even aware that they contributed. Most are mentioned in the text, and I thank all of them.

There are some people to whom I'd like to extend special gratitude and appreciation.

William Brender à Brandis, Gerard Brender à Brandis, Madzy Boonacker, and the late Madzy Brender à Brandis – in the form of the writings that she left behind her – contributed to the large picture and the details of Jock's early life. Bill and Gerard, and other family members, have also been unfailingly supportive and encouraging.

People in and close to the Full Belly Project have provided essential information. The invention of the peanut sheller and the early days of the Full Belly Project were greatly illuminated for me by Jay Tervo, who not only forwarded hundreds of early e-mails to me but also lent me the CDs on which he had recorded the narrative of his and Rex Miller's trip to Uganda. In addition, he provided his perspective on events and developments. When I was in Wilmington I had useful talks with him and with Diana Rohler, John Fogg, and a number of volunteers; during the trip to Malawi I talked with Jeff

Rose and Jim Nesbit. The latter has also been helpful in answering e-mails. Daniel Ling has provided important help. Colin Pawlowski and Tom Ellsworth contributed their illuminating narratives.

Martin Harbury gave me permission to use the film *Peanuts*; because it was not, at that time, licensed for sale in Canada, Bullfrog had to obtain his special permission for me to receive a copy.

I thank Brian Connors for his help in answering questions when he was stationed in Malawi, and both Brian and Mike Connors for their hospitality when I was an always-welcome in-and-out guest at their house in Lilongwe.

Titus Galema provided important help regarding the project in Honduras and also supplied me with general information on jatropha cultivation, and Jerry La Gra kept me informed about the work in Guyana.

Keah and Bryan Payne provided insights into Malawian life accumulated during their several years of service there.

I especially thank Sarah Pedersen and David Campbell for their invaluable e-mails and their inexhaustible patience in answering my questions, and David for his photos.

I greatly appreciated Danielle Wiegel's information about life in "her" village in southern Malawi, which enlarged my understanding of what I myself had seen and what I read in books and on the internet. She told me about the book by Dick Wittenberg, which has been a wonderful resource.

Dr. Rick Brandenburg and Natalie Hampton at North Carolina State University provided information about the use of the UNS in Ghana and other projects where their work and Jock's connected.

The chapter on the work in Rutherford County, North Carolina, would have been impossible to write had I not had the help of Duncan Edwards, who supported the project and answered e-mails in careful and fascinating detail. Larry Dale sent me the newspaper articles which he wrote about Full Belly's work in the area and did additional research into weather patterns. Edward Stephens in Bladen County contributed information about the testing of the solar pump.

Other helpful people in North America included Jim Usalcas, Julie Jones, David Brydon, and Terry Sharpe.

Joanna Glass, Rick Hopper, and Bruce Cogill suggested publishers whom I might approach. However, my decision to self-publish enabled me to get the book into readers' hands more quickly than would have been possible had I used other channels.

Sheila Russell has been an extremely sensitive, helpful, and supportive editor.

As always, I accept full responsibility for mistakes – hoping that the reader will understand that this is an ongoing project and that the picture is changing constantly.

Jock Brandis is almost the co-author of this book but did not want to be named as such. I thank him not only for his enormous contribution to its creation but also for his inspiration. His example of inexhaustible energy and optimism – both in his own work and in regard to this book – helped me to overcome obstacles and persist in my desire to tell the story of the Full Belly Project.

Index

Jock, the Full Belly Project, and the peanut sheller (UNS) are mentioned on nearly every page. This index lists only the main points.

mechanical harvesting: 131ff
two strains of: 87
uses and benefits of: 86f, 88,
90, 94, 95, 134
Jatropha-factory-in-a-container:
145
Jatropha sheller/husker/
dehusker: 88, 93, 144
See also: Mali Biocarburant,
CEVER school, Gota Verde
Jones, Julie: 297f
Jordan, Dr. David (N.C. State): 85

Kabultec: See: Roquia Center for
Women's Rights, Studies,
and Education
Kamkwamba, William: 150
Kenya: 73
Klingenberger, Pete: 44, 46, 207,
271
Knowles, Alastair: 83
Knutson, Gayle: 125

La Gra, Jerry: See: S-SOS
Lahens, Gerthy: See: Women's
Peanut Butter Maker Co-op
(Haiti)
Litwin, Josh: 99
Livestock watering in pastures:
283, 285, 295
Lueng, Ming: 206
Lulu: See: shea
LuluWorks: 74
Lumu, Tony: 51, 64ff, 223

Maize: See: corn
Makutu, Lameck, Jr.: 159
See also: C to C

Makutu, Lameck, Sr.: 159
See also: C to C
Malawi: 17, 50, 77, 147ff, 233f
Acceleration of Innovation in:
244ff, 251
aflatoxin in: 301f
agriculture: 147, 170, 172
Chilombo (village): 81
community centre: 179
corn (maize): 152f
cotton: 148
deforestation: 149
dependency on bicycles: 166f
dependency on chemical
fertilizer: 148
drought and irrigation: 150,
170ff, 185f, 265ff
jatropha in Malawi: 94, 156,
165f, 269
marketing village produce:
175f
rocker water pump in: 265ff
sanitation problems: 174
setting up village industries:
176ff, 182
soil degradation: 148, 151
the peanut sheller in a
Malawian village: 165
tobacco: 148, 172
Mali: 13, 23, 41, 47, 125, 233
cotton in: 25
fatalism: 231
jatropha in: 91ff
peanuts in: 99
Mali Biocarburant: 91ff, 101,
131, 219f
shop for making jatropha
huskers: 94
Manary, Dr. Mark: See: Project
Peanut Butter